Drawing
/for Graphic
Design

First published in the United States of America
by Rockport Publishers
A member of Quayside Publishing Group
100 Cummings Center
Suite 406-L
Beverly, Massachusetts 01915-6101
Telephone: (978) 282-9590
Fax: (978) 283-2742
www.rockpub.com
Visit RockPaperInk.com to share your opinions,
creations, and passion for design.

ISBN: 978-1-59253-781-5

Digital edition published in 2012
eISBN: 978-1-61058-411-1

Library of Congress
Cataloging-in-Publication Data
Samara, Timothy.
 Drawing for graphic design : understanding
conceptual principles and practical techniques
to create unique, effective design solutions /
Timothy Samara.
     pages cm
 Summary: "Here is a complete, comprehensive
drawing reference for design students and
professionals alike who want to implement
drawing as a professional tool. In Drawing for
Graphic Design, Timothy Samara empowers
readers to add drawing to their design vocabu-
lary, featuring case studies of commercial projects from start to finish along with a showcase
of real-world projects that integrate drawing
as an intrinsic part of their visual communication. Filled with original author drawings and
sketches, it's a must-have reference that will
benefit designers of all levels"-- Provided by
publisher.
 ISBN 978-1-59253-781-5 (pbk.)
 1. Graphic arts--Handbooks, manuals, etc.
2. Commercial art--Handbooks, manuals, etc.
I. Title.
 NC997.S235 2012
 741.6--dc23

2012007626

Cover and book design, book photography, and
illustrations by Timothy Samara.

Printed in China

Drawing

Understanding
conceptual
principles and
practical
techniques to
create unique,
effective
design solutions

/ for Graphic Design

Timothy Samara

Rockport Publishers
100 Cummings Center, Suite 406L
Beverly, MA 01915

rockpub.com • rockpaperink.com

Co/nt-ent(s)-

*A directory of
designers who
contributed
their work to
this book
appears under
the inside
back cover flap.*

Foreword

Thoughts On Drawing: In Design Culture, Education, and Practice

A woodcut self-portrait (top) and a gestural figure sketch (bottom), both drawn by the author while a high school student in upstate New York.

Dating as far back as 35,000 B.C.E., the first drawn images were discovered on the walls of caves in the Ardeche Valley and Lascaux, in France, and in Altamira, Spain. From that time forward, humanity has given visual form to ideas with marks inscribed on a surface—first, with the hand itself and, eventually, an array of tools invented specifically for that purpose. This profoundly human of activities has helped record family histories, day-to-day experiences, and the edicts of tribal and imperial leaders alike; provided instruction for hunting and building shelter; marked the passage of time, the seasons, and the movement of the stars; visualized the spirit world and that of the imagination; offered experiences for contemplation, delight, and persuasion; and constructed written language. Drawing has been a part of human communication from the beginnings of civilization and informed every aspect of humanity's visual life.

Drawing is a fundamental part of who I am. From a very early age, encouraged by my family (all artists of one kind or another), drawing became the activity I enjoyed most. When I decided to pursue an education in graphic design, I was fortunate to find a program in which drawing was a core focus; it helped build a foundation for conceptualiziation that still guides every project I do. As I gained professional experience, however, I came to realize that this was in marked contrast to many of my colleagues, who never picked up a pencil if they could avoid it; indeed, most had never had design-based drawing classes in school. And, when I began teaching some years ago—seeing my students consistently turn to photographic solutions for their projects—it became clear that drawing was systemically absent from the discipline of graphic design. Understanding how the profession evolved has provided some insight into the matter.

Until the end of the nineteenth century and the invention of photography, all imagery was hand drawn. Simultaneously with the rise of the graphic design profession, refinements to the graphic process and experimental drawing approaches afforded these visual communicators of the Industrial Revolution strategies to support the new, manufacturing-driven marketplace. During design's early phase, practitioners came from the ranks of fine arts printmakers and painters; and even as photography evolved into a prevalent form of expression, the primacy of the fine artist–cum–designer remained. As recently as the 1970s, it was a given that graphic designers could draw. Following changes in aesthetics that encouraged neutrality and a visually clean, journalistic approach—ultimately championed by the International Style design movement of the 1950s—photography became the medium of choice for visualizing concepts. The technological progression of subsequent decades subsumed photography into the cut-and-paste efficiency—and remarkable inventive capabilities—offered by the computer. One was no longer required to draw to be a virtuoso practitioner.

In one sense, this paradigm shift has been extremely beneficial. It has democratized a once-insular profession and opened it to a far greater diversity of visual voices. At the same time, however, a speeding up of the design process and a fascination with the glossy, glamorous, sensuous, slick, and luxurious—have all

The author's hand-generated explorations for a visual identity (top) and the final mark, implemented in color on a business card (bottom). Completed while Senior Art Director at Pettistudio (now Pettis Design): Valerie Pettis, Creative Director *United States*

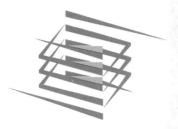

A nonpictorial identity symbol drawn by the author for an IT consulting firm.

catapulted the photograph into a position of even greater importance. It's easy to acquire, it's shiny and seductive, and it gets the job done quickly: all useful qualities in a practical sense.

What is greatly diminished, it seems, is specificity: A photograph is a photograph; the more successful ones carry the mark of a particular photographer's vision, but in many cases any photograph of a product or a concept may be easily swapped for another with little loss of effect. The ubiquity of photographically-driven design solutions has homogenized design in direct contradiction of one of a graphic designer's preeminent goals (and that of visual branding especially): to differentiate and, in so doing, to clarify and imprint understanding. Of equal concern is the loss of a design's humanizing potential: individuality, powerfully compelling and uniquely constructed visualization, a viewer's joy and awe in engaging with an invented image, the unparalleled visceral connection it creates between designer, client, and audience.

Given the denigration of drawing in general practice, it comes as no surprise that its role in education has also diminished. Beyond the typical foundation-year academic drawing course, most graphic design programs in the U.S. (and likely elsewhere, with some exceptions) do not include drawing in their curriculums.Many programs, and their nostalgic or frustrated older instructors, pay lip service to its value, but few and far between are those that actively build drawing into the conceptual and form-making skill-sets of their students (never mind simply sketching layouts). Clearly, education must keep pace with technological developments and the transformation of aesthetics they invariably bring. This necessity, however, need not result in the extinction of equally valuable methodologies.

Two-page spreads from a private school's recruiting brochure, featuring hand-drawn translations; also designed by the author

Painted gouache studies / Andrew Iskowitz *Unites States*

Since 2005, I have happily seen a slow but decisive reappearance of drawing in mainstream communication; consider the recent proliferation of showcase publications devoted to illustration, designers' sketchbooks, and hand-made imagery. My estimation of this aesthetic pendulum-swing: a general backlash against the slickness of digital and photographic surface; a culture-wide yearning for more intimate, personal quality in day-to-day interaction; and an industry-specific search for strategies to meet those conditions through the unique experiences drawn imagery can deliver. While the will is there, the expertise, as yet, seems lacking. I find much recent drawing awkward or amateurish in its quality. By no means is this to say that there's one way to draw, or that it must be accomplished with Renaissance virtuosity to be strong and compelling. Drawing can be many things and regardless of native talent or the academic naiveté with which it is created, can exhibit a compelling, forceful presence in designed communication.

The process of drawing is a powerful tool on many levels. It is an activity of invention, rather than appropriation, and so encourages originality. The gestural quality of sketched concepts, even if destined to become layouts only of type and photographs, imparts a vitality that a designer can look to as a goal to achieve in the final work. Most importantly, drawing fuses disparate skills on which designers rely: perception, cognition, and mechanics; verbal and visual narrative creation; analysis and intuition.

Drawing descriptively from observation attunes a designer's facility for analyzing form and structure in the real world. Underpinning and supporting that facility, drawing nonpictorially (using abstract form alone) hones the designer's perception of empirical structure—the ability to deconstruct and, hence, reconstruct or recast that form for reinvention. Drawing nonpictorially liberates the designer from the requirements of pictorial reproduction and so builds not only conceptual and interpretive skills, but furthers understanding and confidence in composition that will have significant impact on layout and formal command of other media, including photography. Drawing strengthens a designer's eye.

Leaf translation / Luis Rego, San Diego State University *United States*

Collage drawing with leaf / Taewan An, UArts *United States*

Mixed media collage / STIM Visual Communication *United States*

Nonpictorial marking study / Eva Surany, UArts *United States*

And let us not forget typography, no less a drawing than any other kind. From the minutae of stroke and stylistic detail formation among the individual letterforms of a logotype to the composition of voluminous columns of text, type is an abstract line drawing. A rare experience for most design students these days, the construction of original type forms demands a degree of observational and formal sensitivity that is seldom necessary in for the most strictly naturalistic replication of empirical reality. Drawing typefaces and letter-based logos and sketching layouts both further train the eye and, even more importantly, offer opportunities for originality and experimentation. The design of titling, mastheads, and logos need not be confined by a designer's limited typeface library—it may be completely custom, articulated to be the most appropriate it can be for its specific communicative function. Drawing and sketching type helps break down the often insurmountable barrier between verbal and visual, which prevents designers from deploying type in seamless totality with pictorial matter.

Beyond these important aspects of skill development, drawing is quintessentially a means of telling stories. It may convey a product's quality through a beautifully sensitive rendering; it may evoke the poetic and intangible through abstract marks that signify memories and impressions; it may illuminate the issues of our time with visceral images that provoke and disturb, or entertain and inspire; it may offer us insight into the grand, elemental complexities of the cosmos, hinting at new thresholds of understanding to be crossed. Graphic design is now, after all, the great cultural connector of our time. It binds our fragmented constituencies, narrates our rituals, both spiritual and commodified, and creates the visual and experiential lifescape through which we travel together. For all of our fascinating, networked, and elegant technological modernity, drawing tells the stories that connect us at the deepest level to our own humanity, to our history and, ultimately, to the future.

Timothy Samara
January 2012

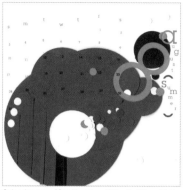

Calendar page / Soo Yeon Lee, School of Visual Arts
United States

Calendar page / Yoon Deok Jang, School of Visual Arts
United States

Nonpictorial narrative study / Eric Bruno, School of Visual Arts *United States*

Mixed media type drawing / Kirk Bray, Tyler School of Art: Temple University *United States*

Typographic logo / Jin Kwang Kim, School of Visual Arts *United States*

Hand-drawn letterforms / Timothy Samara, UArts
United States

Poster / Kelly Chew, Parsons [The New School for Design]
United States

Poster / Paone Design Associates *United States*

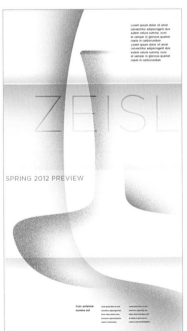

Brochure / STIM Visual Communication *United States*

PISCEAN
AQUATIC
INSTITUTE

Visual Identity / Michelle Huey, SUNY Purchase
United States

Poster / Christopher Beesley, School of Visual Arts
United States

Poster / Scott Laserow / *United States*

MATHS
DREAMED UNI – 0 to 100,001
VERSE.
—

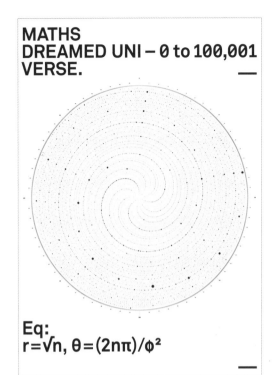

Eq:
$r = \sqrt{n}, \; \theta = (2n\pi)/\phi^2$

—

Poster / The Luxury of Protest *United Kingdom*

Drawing
/ for Graphic
Design

Foreword

**Thoughts
On Drawing:
In Design
Culture,
Education,
and
Practice**

Editorial type treatment / Alex Trochut *Spain*

Dis/cov-ery.

This section introduces fundamental notions about drawing, illustrating varied functions in communication and explaining those universal principles upon which designers rely to deliver the most dynamic optical, narrative experiences.

A drawn image is a constructed inter-pretation of a subject or an idea; in that sense drawings are, intrinsically, designed images. Their varied subject matter—whether depicting observed reality, stylizing or reducing that reality to iconic simplicity, or presenting nonpictorial forms to evoke intangible concepts—is an invented experience. As such, the power that drawing affords a designer is the opportunity to influence every aspect of an image in the way most appropriate for a particular project. In drawing, the designer has the authority to selectively edit what is shown for greater focus and specificity of its message; to organize the subject's elements in the composition that best integrates it with other images and typography in a layout; to enhance or neutralize aspects of that subject; to deliver a unique expression through choice of medium and approach that differentiates the communication for greater impact and memorability; and ultimately, to powerfully influence the message's interpretation.

While for many designers, confronting a blank page or screen with type and photographs on hand comes easily, doing so without such ready-mades is unnerving. The need for complete invention, using skills that never were developed or that have lain dormant since foundation classes in school, seems like an insurmountable obstacle and so is often avoided. Even when the need, skill, and desire may be there, the designer is often stupefied by his or sense of having to dust off unexercised skills and get them "up to speed," which usually sounds like a burden of time they simply don't have. And, of course, many designers are of the belief that because they've never tried to draw, or weren't successful in the past, it's a skill they have to give up.

Overcoming these obstacles depends first on becoming familiar with the many kinds of drawing that are possible, and so recognizing that powerful image-making need not entail da Vinci-esque realism—it may be something altogether different. Given that freedom, it becomes a ques-tion of knowing how to explore other approaches and what visual qualities will make them successful.

Territories of Drawing in Graphic Design

Drawing occurs in a mind-boggling number of ways in graphic design, exploited during every stage of ideation and planning, as well in creating finished works. For many, illustration comes immediately to mind, and then possibly the notion of sketching.

Sketching /A/ informs all drawing processes, sometimes an end in itself—quickly roughing out layout ideas, for instance—but also as an evolutionary process that emerges into a final work, a searching mechanism through which a designer experiments with and gradually refines the form of an image. The sketch process may be evident within the final image's form as original marks and erasures or obliterations, showing the means by which the designer arrived at a stage of resolution. But just as often, this process is hidden, implicitly revealed by the final form's apparent "cleanliness" and "rightness"—the sense that it has crystallized into a sleek, ultimate state—as is the case with logos and type forms.

Given that sketching is, more or less, a universal component of design drawing, one may yet distinguish various territories of presentation and function in design drawing for the sake of discussion /B/.

All drawings—all images, for that matter—fall within a spectrum of representation between literal and abstract. At the macro level, drawing roams between these two major territories: the presentation of an image's subject (what it shows, or its content) either corresponds to observable, physical experience (pictorial); or it is made up of graphic forms that don't appear to have a source in physical reality (nonpictorial) or it may lie somewhere in between. Both major territories contain sub-territories, specific "geographies" of difference; and their boundaries are fluid and mutable: The aspects of a drawn image are likely to cross from one territory to another, or combine characteristics from several in unlimited permutation, depending on the designer's goal and the drawing's function within communication or the design process.

A Typical designer's sketchbook /
Ken Carbone, Carbone Smolan Agency
United States

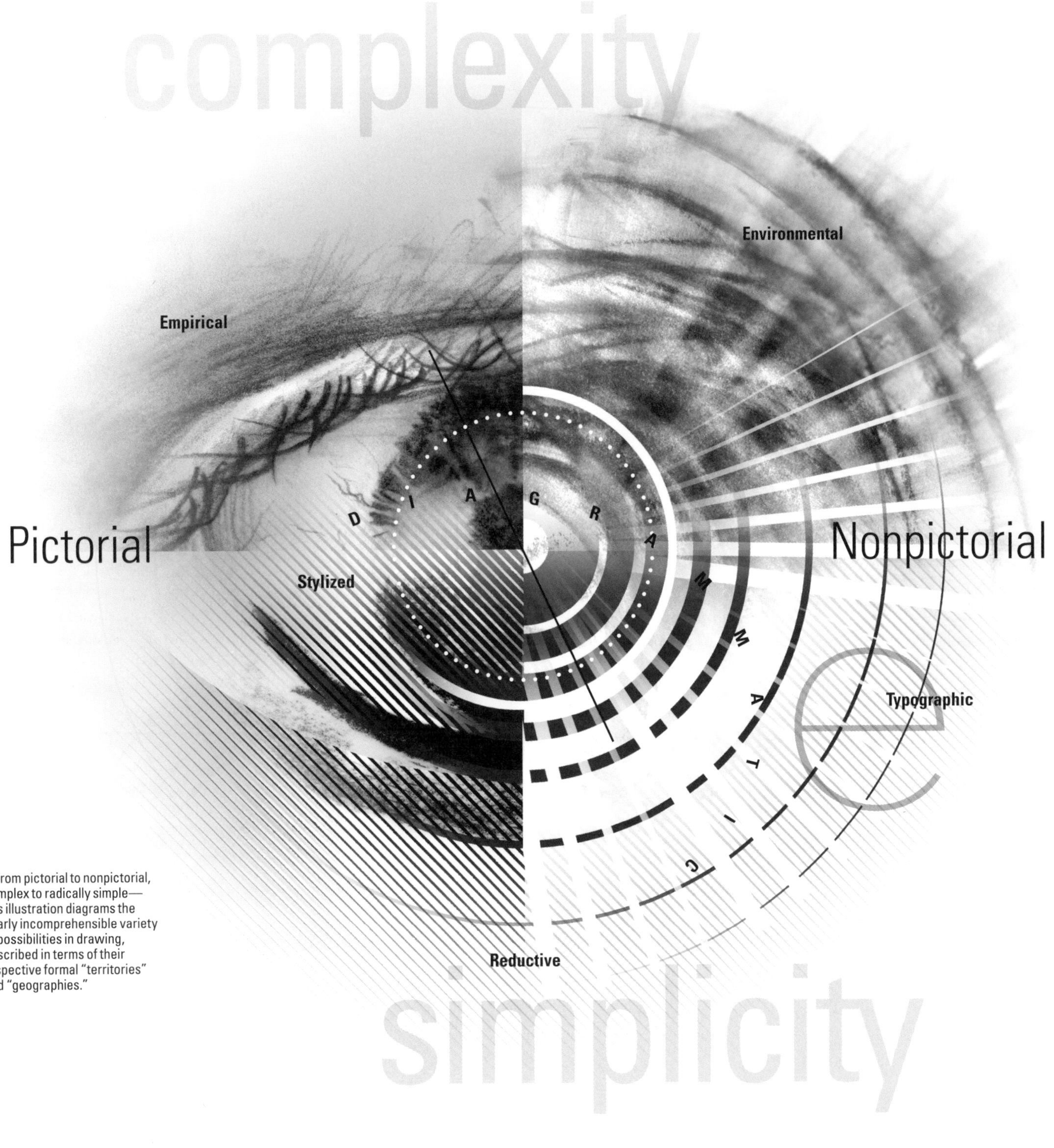

complexity

Environmental

Drawing
/ for Graphic
Design

Discovery

**Territories
of Drawing
in Graphic
Design**

Empirical

Pictorial

Nonpictorial

Stylized

DIAGRAMMATIC

Typographic

B From pictorial to nonpictorial,
complex to radically simple—
this illustration diagrams the
nearly incomprehensible variety
of possibilities in drawing,
described in terms of their
respective formal "territories"
and "geographies."

Reductive

simplicity

A Pictorial naturalism / Jin Sook Bae, School of
Visual Arts *United States*

A2/SW/HK ♂
Artis Conceptualensis Biequipus

VII

Scott Williams y Henrik Kubel formaron A2/SW/HK
en el Royal College of Art en 1999 mientras
estudiaban comunicación y diseño. El estudio
utiliza un enfoque conceptual en diseño impreso,
audiovisual y espacial. A Williams le preocupa
especialmente el pensamiento lateral aplicado
al diseño, mientras Kubel dibuja una tipografía
específica a medida para cada nuevo proyecto.
La lista de clientes del estudio incluye: D&AD,
Penguin Books New York, International Society of
Typographic Designers, British Council, V&A
Museum, Phaidon, Royal Mail, Tate Modern y
Vogue UK. Recientemente han realizado el diseño
de la exposición del prestigioso Premio Turner
para la Tate Britain.

Scott Williams and Henrik Kubel formed A2/SW/HK
at the Royal College of Art in 1999 whilst studying communication art and design. The studio
uses a conceptual approach to problem solving
in design for print, screen and the environment.
Williams is concerned with lateral approaches
to design whilst Kubel draws bespoke type for
all their projects. Their lengthy client list
includes: Penguin Books New York, International
Society of Typographic Designers, D&AD, British
Council, V&A Museum, Phaidon, Royal Mail, Tate
Modern and Vogue UK. They recently designed the
annual Turner Prize exhibition at Tate Britain.

www.a2swhk.co.uk

B Pictorial naturalism / Studio Astrid Stavro
Spain

YOSHIMOTO BANANA

TUGUMI

THRUSH

C Reductive graphic translation / STIM Visual
Communication *United States*

D Stylized icon / Büro Uebele Visuelle Kommunication *Germany*

Pictorial images show such recognizable subjects as objects, figures, and landscapes.

Within this territory, a drawn image may inhabit differing geographies of mediation, or degrees of complex naturalism versus stylization or simplification. One such geography might be called empirical—reproducing the characteristics of objects and scenes as they are observed in space /**A, B**/. The primary purpose of such drawing is as an alternative to photographic depiction, whether because photographs are unavailable or because the concept and message of the communication demands a particular form and visualization.

Images of subjects in which a designer noticeably exaggerates elements, edits out information, or imposes a stylistic conceit (while retaining a generally naturalistic presentation), inhabit a sub-territory of stylization /**C–G**/. This kind of drawing exploits the recognizability of the concrete to ensure accessibility, but offers greater opportunity for metaphor, targeted and focused narrative interpretation, or conceptual evocation /**E**/. As a bonus, the stylistic qualities that are exaggerated or imposed will likely integrate more fluidly on a visual or formal level with other material, such as typography or nonpictorial symbols.

As a pictorial drawing's subject is dramatically simplified, and its forms abstracted to essentials—as in a graphic translation /**C**/ or icon /**D, F**/—it migrates to yet another sub-territory that one might call reductive. The even more stylized quality of drawings inhabiting this geography radically augments both specificity of message and metaphorical power; its distilled simplicity creates a bold optical presence that facilitates perceptual immediacy and deep imprinting, making them especially useful for logos /**G**/ and critical informational messages. In such drawings, empirical form and purely abstract visual qualities assume a simultaneous, even equivalent, presence, delivering a visceral and vital tension between the concrete and the conceptual.

Naturalistic
Representational
non-Rep

G Stylized icon / Steff Geissbuhler, C+G Partners LLC *United States*

E Stylized icon / Mehdi Saeedi Studio *Iran*

F Stylized icon / Topos Graphics *United States*

The subject of nonpictorial images is graphic forms—marks or shapes—that aren't literally observable, what is often referred to as abstract or nonrepresentational.

They do, in fact, represent ideas (and, very often, physical experiences /**A**/); defining this territory as nonpictorial may be more accurate. Drawing of a nonpictorial nature is profoundly unique, enabling a designer to create a completely custom experience for a client's audience.

A Nonpictorial visualization of swimming / So Won Lee, UArts *United States*

Images in this territory also occupy distinct geographies. The first might be categorized as environmental or expansive fields of marks and shapes which, similar to empirical, pictorial drawings, also establish a sense of complex, articulated space governing objects or figures /**B, C**/. Such drawings are often used as an alternative to pictorial depiction outright where high-level conceptual messages are concerned (intangibles such as music /**B**/, poetry, and emotions). They are also useful in creating metaphorical and visual bridges between other compositional elements. In this role, they may not only communicate ideas but also help visually unify communications within a series or program /**C**/, as in corporate identity or branding applications.

B An environmental, or expansive field, nonpictorial drawing used in the design of music album covers / Dextro *Austria*

VALERIE'S BASKETS

Home		Products	Custom	Shop
About		Kitchen	Gallery	Cart
Materials		Bed & Bath	Ordering	Checkout
Classes		Utility	Pricing	
		Decorative		

C An environmental nonpictorial language creates visual connections between brand language and pictorial images to unify applications / STIM Visual Communication *United States*

D Reductive nonpictorial drawing /
STIM Visual Communication *United States*

VESSEL

F Reductive nonpictorial
pattern / Julian Norton, SUNY
Purchase *United States*

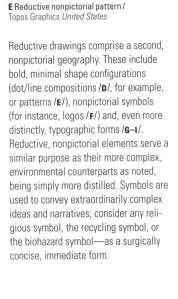

E Reductive nonpictorial pattern /
Topos Graphics *United States*

H Stylized typographic drawing / Slang *Germany*

Drawing
/ for Graphic
Design

Discovery

**Territories
of Drawing
in Graphic
Design**

Of this reductive geography, typographic drawings—and all typography is, indeed, nonpictorial drawing—bear greater inquiry. A letterform is a configuration of line, mass, and space /**G**/; words and paragraphs are visualizations of spoken language. Typeface styles are simply manipulations of these forms' visual attributes. And all, of course, serve the same purpose, to visually express sequences of verbal information. It's difficult, often counterintuitive, for designers to conceive of type as an image—one of the reasons why it's commonly the most difficult component of design to master. To consider type a drawing, governed by the same qualities as are any other kinds of image /**H**/, liberates it from its purely verbal function and allows a designer to impart it with similar vitality... and to use it more dramatically in layouts /**I**/.

Reductive drawings comprise a second, nonpictorial geography. These include bold, minimal shape configurations (dot/line compositions /**D**/, for example, or patterns /**E**/), nonpictorial symbols (for instance, logos /**F**/) and, even more distinctly, typographic forms /**G–I**/. Reductive, nonpictorial elements serve a similar purpose as their more complex, environmental counterparts as noted, being simply more distilled. Symbols are used to convey extraordinarily complex ideas and narratives; consider any religious symbol, the recycling symbol, or the biohazard symbol—as a surgically concise, immediate form.

G Gestural letterform drawing /
Massimo Pallelo, ABC Atelier *Italy*

SAISON 2003 1000 PLACES POUR LES JEUNES

LVMH

I Reductive drawing with typography / Rudi Meyer *France*

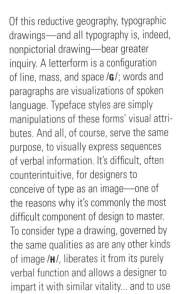

One particular geography [we'll call it diagrammatic] spans both pictorial and nonpictorial territories: maps, charts and diagrams [or *infographics*], schematics, and layout compositions.

B A mash-up of type styles and graphical forms deliver pop-cultural contradictions / Strange Attractors *The Netherlands*

Drawings in this territory juxtapose subjects as fragments within a unified space that may be clustered or an open field, integrating pictorial /**A**/ and nonpictorial /**B**/ components from any geography and, oftentimes, in combination. Pictorial subjects may be taken from a variety of source contexts and intermingled /**C**/; space and time may be mapped, empirically or not /**D**/; steps in a complicated process may be simplified, data exploded, deconstructed, and reordered to clarify understanding /**E, F**/; and a layout sketch /**G**/ is a plan for how numerous design elements will engage each other within a non-empirical space—the page or screen format.

A Reductive pictorial and typographic forms in a deconstructed, diagrammatic space / Flúor *Portugal*

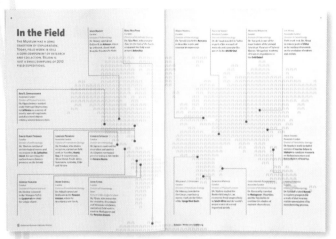

E Editorial layout of typography and diagrammatic imagery / Hinterland Studio *United States*

C Iconic, pictorial elements arranged in a diagrammatic configuration /
Scott Laserow *United States*

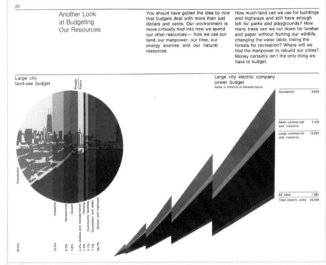

F Informational diagrams in a page detail from a brochure: a combination of pictorial and
nonpictorial elements (left) and symbolic, nonpictorial elements (right) / Steff Geissbuhler,
C+G Partners LLC *United States*

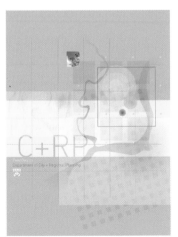

D Map elements and intersecting planes of
texture deconstruct the environment /
Paone Design Associates *United States*

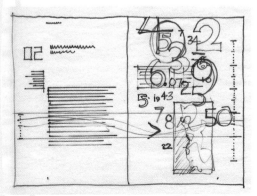

G Pencil layout sketch for a brochure's page spread / Gee+Chung Design
United States

Universal Principles of a Strong Drawing

No matter the medium, style, or purpose, every successful drawing embodies the resolution and integration of fundamental qualities—universal principles that must be evident regardless of which territory that drawing inhabits /**A**/.

It's worth noting again that capturing an accurately real depiction is not one of the characteristics assigned here to "successful" drawings. Too often, realism is equated with success. Remember that a drawing is always an abstraction to some degree: It distills essence and reconstructs it with specific intent. If the intent, in a given context, is to accurately reproduce observed forms in space, this may be another criteria upon which to judge a drawing's success. However, a decision in favor of pictorial realism is narrative, solely dependent on the nature of the communication; only then should success also be evaluated on this basis.

Unified Form Language
A specific combination of marks, shapes, and gesture

Positive/Negative Vitality
Dynamic rhythm and interplay between forms and spaces

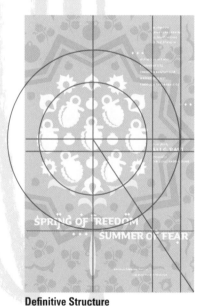

Definitive Structure
A sturdy set of recognizable relationships among form axes and contours

Perceptual Space
The creation of engaging, illusory dimensionality

Linear : Planar
Geometric : Organic
Angular : Curvilinear
Large : Small
Restful : Energetic
Uniform : Varied
Simple : Complex
Delicate : Bold
Cubic : Elliptical
Deep : Compressed
Field : Singularity
Dark : Light
Volumetric : Schematic
Regular : Irregular
Repeating : Distinct
Ordered : Disordered
Dense : Open
Orthogonal : Diagonal
Soft : Sharp
Opaque : Transparent
Concrete : Abstract
Single : Multiple
Fluid : Staccato

Most important to understand is that all the universal principles are informed by one overarching aspect: the notion of contrast. Creating states of differing presence or quality—states that contrast with each other—is inherent in avoiding visual monotony. Contrast established among aspects of one principal will usually affect aspects of the others. While the term "contrast" applies to specific relationships, it also applies to the quality of difference in relationships among forms and spaces interacting within a format together. The confluence of varied states of contrast is referred to as tension. For example: A composition with strong contrast between round and sharp, angular forms in one area, opposed by another area where all the forms are similarly angular, exhibits tension in angularity. A composition that contrasts areas of dense, active line rhythms with areas that are generally more open and regular might be characterized as creating tension in rhythm.

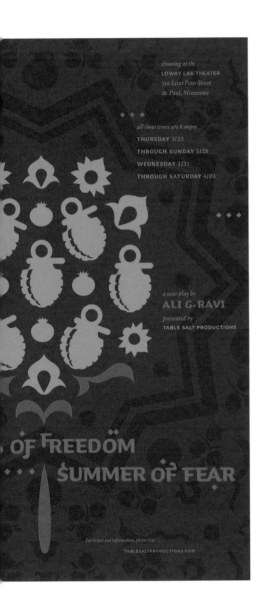

A This poster exhibits all the universal principles to be achieved in a successful drawing / STIM Visual Communication *United States*

First Principle

Every successful drawing expresses a specific, unified form language.

Universal
Principles
of a Strong
Drawing

Drawing entails complete invention from the ground up. Through a process of trial and error, designers discover what kinds of graphic shapes may work to articulate a given subject, as well as how they might act together. They invent a palette of form elements (a syntax), each having its own purpose and quality, along with the behaviors in which those parts engage (a grammar)—a language of form that, in a visual way, corresponds closely to the analogy of spoken language. Form elements are like sounds, or even words; they contain basic identifying information much the same way that verbs, adjectives, or nouns do. And, as with speech, these "words" are combined in patterns specific to that language; they behave in a particular way in French, for example, that is different from German or Japanese. In drawing, designers build form languages unique to each drawing.

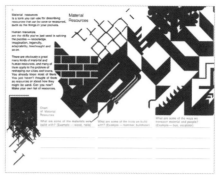

A Planar and linear geometric syntax / Steff Geissbuhler *United States*

B Dot- and grid-basd geometric syntax / The Luxury of Protest *United Kingdom*

C Organic, linear syntax; geometric structure / Catherine Harvey *United States*

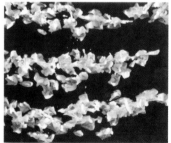

D Organic form syntax arranged gesturally / STIM Visual Communication *United States*

E Organic syntax / Eva Surany, UArts *United States*

Possibilities for defining a form language are, of course, endless. It may be fundamentally defined by purely geometric syntax /**A, B**/; alternatively, it may be defined by organic syntax /**C–E**/. It goes almost without saying that syntax of either kind may be hybridized in any combination. The syntax may be very rough /**C, E**/or highly refined and sharply articulated /**D, F**/, whether geometric or organic. While the medium used will contribute to the language /**E**/, the basic geometric or organic nature of the form syntax will typically remain identifiable.

F Dot-based geometric syntax, organically arranged / Shinnoske, Inc. *Japan*

I Gestural and textural syntax derived from the mark-making tool in a nonpictorial drawing / Christine Zelinsky *United States*

Drawing
/ for Graphic
Design

Discovery

**Universal
Principles**
First Principle:
Unified Form
Language

Any form language may be appropriate for any context. Sharply refined syntax may be just as useful in environmental, nonpictorial images /**F, G**/as similarly refined geometric syntax is in pictorial images /**H**/; extremely gestural, tool-based syntax, as that which results from dense graphite or charcoal and erasing, may be equally useful for generating complex nonpictorial narratives /**I**/ and expressing empirical form /**J**/.

G Hard-edged, linear and planar organic syntax

H Geometric syntax (ovals, circles, and dots)
G + H AdamsMorioka, Inc. *United States*

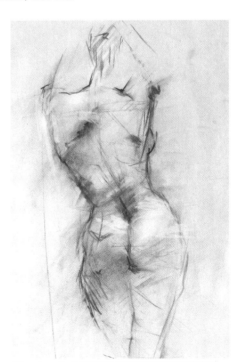

J Organic, gestural syntax in volumetric pictorial depiction / Paone Design Associates *United States*

Fundamental Syntax: The Mark

The syntax of a form language derives from the mark: the physical evidence of a tool, such as a piece of charcoal, striking a sheet of paper and leaving a trace. While the discussion here, admittedly, will be somewhat biased toward conventional drawing, let it be noted that marks made digitally—whether by vector pen or filter operation—are still marks. For that matter, forms made with media other than a hand-held stylus, such as a pencil, chalk, or brush (for example: ripped or cut pieces of paper, twigs, and so on) are also marks. The fundamental conception of the mark is that of an atomic element, a positive form introduced into a space as the universal building block of all form languages. It may have specific qualities depending on the tool or method used to make it but, nonetheless, there are only two basic kinds of mark: line and mass.

A line is a tracking mark. It describes direction and movement from its point of origin (the *attack*) to its ending point (the *terminus*). The movement in a line appears to travel along its body, or *stroke.*

Line

Although a line's point of attack may be evident, viewers usually perceive movement in both directions along the stroke. Lines may be heavy /**A, B**/ or delicate /**C**/, continuous or broken, sharp or rough, angled or curvilinear. Each quality that a given line embodies affects its identity and, therefore, its syntax in a form language. But its identity remains that of a line so long as its length is appreciably greater than its thickness.

A Rough, massive lines structure a composition and establish movement / Tina Mukherjee, UArts *United States*

Lines serve a number of functions in drawing. They most typically articulate form, describing its contours (as in the figur drawing /**B**/) and establishing its structure and movement or directionality within a format /**C**/; lines also may be used together, forming a texture, to create shapes /**D**/. Lines may help enclose or separate groups of forms or information /**E**/; they may also create explicit visual connections between spaces or components in a layout /**F**/. On a purely visual level, they offer sharp, detailed contrast to the massive presence of planar shapes /**G**/.

B Lines enclosing spaces and describing pictorial form / Fang Chen *United States*

C An elegant, linear logo brands a line of hair-care products / Design Tôge *Japan*

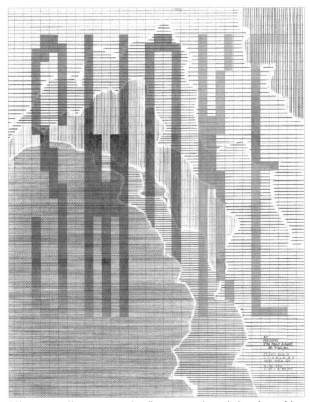

D Lines, arranged in patterns, may describe masses or planes; the letterforms of the titling element are also lines/ Alejandro Posada (Cuartopiso) and Pablo Gómez Uribe *United States*

E Lines used to describe form, as well as to enclose space and separate elements in a hierarchy / Mookai Communications *Canada*

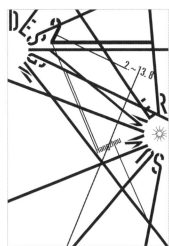

F The extended strokes of characters become a connective structural network / heSign International GmbH *Germany*

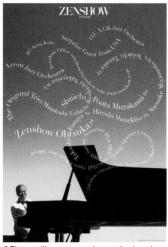

G The curvilinear text setting emphasizes the type's linearity; it contrasts the piano's planar mass and itself becomes a kind of image / Shinnoske, Inc. *Japan*

Drawing
/ for Graphic
Design

Discovery

**Universal
Principles**
First Principle:
Unified Form
Language

Lines create the essential language of typographic drawing; letters, such as the logos at right /**H, I**/, are groups of lines, and groups of words or sentences are described, quite intuitively, as lines of text. The larger or bolder a typographic element becomes—even at tremendous scale—the more mass becomes apparent, but it never really loses its fundamental linear quality /**I**/, even as the counterspaces themselves become lines. A sequence of typographic elements, ultimately, resolves itself as a line or group of lines /**J**/.

H Two lines form the structure of a letter / Hinterland *United States*

I The sharp, triangular counterspaces become lines / STIM Visual Communication *United States*

J Individual sentences of text are lines; paragraphs or columns of text are also lines/ Irina Lee, School of Visual Arts *United States*

Mass

A mass is a focal mark; it first defines a kind of visual weight and a specific location in space. Upon further appreciation, a mass defines a particular form identity, or shape, as well as proportion.

Within a given space, a mass will act as a dot (if relatively small); as it increases in scale and its outer contour becomes appreciable, it takes on the quality of a tangible object or plane /**A**/.

B Simple arrangements of masses describing a pictorial subject; masses contrast lines / Un Mundo Féliz *Spain*

C Masses may exhibit lighting effects or the appearance of volume / Max Fisher, UArts *United States*

A Scale change affects a mass's identity: small dots become circular planes / Bo Rim Kim, School of Visual Arts *United States*

D Individual masses describe geography; clustered, they create an iconic form, also a mass / Slang *Germany*

E A large, circular mass is created from a field of small textural elements. / Masa Watanabe Design Institute *Japan*

Masses may be geometric and angular, and regular in their contours /**B**/; they also may be organic and irregular /**C,D**/; and sometimes they may be both. Masses may be solid and flat in appearance, as well as volumetric /**C**/ or textural, exhibiting shading in light and dark or being built up from an accumulation of smaller, more detailed dot-masses and even lines /**E**/.

As with lines, masses may be used to accomplish a number of different goals in a drawing. They may themselves be used to describe the shape and structure of pictorial forms /**F**/ or create nonpictorial shapes that act as environments /**E, I**/; they are also often used to support the structural framework of a drawing that is linear, in essence "filling in" or "adding weight" to areas or shapes already described by line elements /**G, H**/.

Drawing
/ for Graphic
Design

Discovery

Universal
Principles
First Principle:
Unified Form
Language

F Masses are often used themselves to create forms / STIM Visual Communication *United States*

G Masses are often used to fill forms described by lines, adding weight and contrast / TAXI Canada Ltd. *Canada*

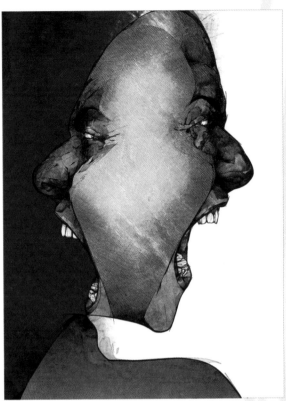

H Masses may appear as positive forms, negative forms, or both / KAKO *Brazil*

I Marks (both masses and lines) may be made subtractively by erasing and covering / STIM Visual Communication *United States*

Masses are most often positive form elements, but negative spaces may also be appreciated as masses or shapes themselves (see page 50); sometimes, as in the illustration of overlapped faces /**H**/, a mass may appear to be both: note how the white area appears first as a negative space (the background into which the dark face intrudes), but then transitions into an apparently solid form, the chin and mouth of the light face against a dark-value space. It follows then that masses (as well as lines) may be made subtractively, as well as additively, by obliterating—by erasing, smudging or wiping, or covering with opaque elements that appear to be part of the surrounding space /**I**/. The act of subtracting from pre-existing marks may result in yet a new kind of mark that also becomes part of the form language's syntax.

A This nonpictorial drawing shows a variety of gestures: waving, staggered, aggressively angular, curvilinear and meandering, fluid and staccato / Christine Hiebert *United States*

Behaviorial Grammar: The Gesture

The mark expresses a specific movement called its gesture, and it's this quality of drawing that gives it life. Gesture translates into energy and behavior. It may be passive and delicate or bold and aggressive; it articulates directionality, rhythm, punctuation, and fluidity through repetition, variation, and pattern—clustering, dispersing, rising or falling, circulating, and so on /**A, B**/. As marks accumulate, this gestural rhythm becomes an identifiable, fundamental part of the drawing's form language. Further the specific nature of the gestural rhythm will contribute to the drawing's narrative (see pp. 80–81) influencing the viewer's emotional response to the message /**C**/.

C Dramatically swooping downward and upward gestures impart a sensation of movement / Flúor *Portugal*

B A singular, continuous, looping and arcing gesture / LoSiento *Spain*

In conventional drawing, gesture results from the body's movement. If one is working digitally using a tablet, this authentic rhythm is translated directly; creating gesture with the tools in a software application may be challenging, given the limitations of movement imposed by a mouse, the spatial disconnect created by the screen interface, and the mechanical nature of point-based vector drawing. However, drawing software usually offers brush forms that mimic the irregularity of conventional mark-making, and working digitally also allows a designer analytical control that is nearly impossible when working conventionally by adjusting the points and line segments of a vector shape, or by distorting and skewing.

D Pushing and pulling curvilinear gestural motion ensures dynamism in a reductive symbol / STIM Visual Communication *United States*

Maintaining gestural rhythm in reductive drawings /**D, E**/ is critical for their liveli ness. Symbols, logos, diagrams, and letterforms rarely exhibit surface activity beyond that of their actual form compo- nents. What must be discernable is a culmination of many evolutionary gestures so that they appear to pulse, to push and pull against each other.

E The wavelike, lateral gesture of the line patterns is restated by the type's back and forth movement, but contrasted by its vertical gesture / Rudi Meyer *France*

Refined letterforms /**F**/ express gesture derived from their source in writing /**G**/; the evidence is their shading, or thick-and-thin contrast, as well as in their width proportion and the "speed" at which strokes modulate from thick to thin. Selecting a particular typeface for a project often depends on how tight or open it feels, how far the strokes rise and fall from the baseline, and how this movement repeats itself from character to character /**H, I**/.

F Gesture is immediately evident in oldstyle (left) and script forms (middle), but may also be appreci- ated in more controlled forms (right).

G The fluid, bold, slashing gesture in this calli- graphic logo establishes a dynamic, confident feeling / PCD Estudio de Diseño *Argentina*

H An irregular, up-and-down gesture across the line of type imparts a casual, playful, quirky quality / Javirroyo *Spain*

I Feelings to be evoked in text depend on a given typeface's gestural cadence—the rhythm created by the alternation between the letters' strokes and counterspaces. Compressed faces usually impart a sharp, anxious, or energetic tone (top), while open or extended faces express a tone that is restful, or seems drawn out over time (bottom).

Attuning the Form Language

In a pictorial drawing, marks stand in for similarly shaped elements in the subject (the object or scene being observed). In a nonpictorial image, the marks themselves are the subject, and refer to ideas or feelings by association. Reductive images are marks edited to a minimum: a paring down to essentials for immediacy of recognition and bold imprinting on a viewer's conscious mind.

One of the decisions a designer must make is the degree to which the form language will mediate, or interpetively alter, the presentation of the subject; whether the fact of mark and gesture will be explicit or downplayed. In many instances a designer finds it desirable to minimize the presence of mark and gesture /**A, C**/ in favor of a "clean" presentation: An imposed imperceptibility of gestural rhythm imparts evidentiary credibility and analytical detachment— a perception of "realism" or objectivity— whereas works in which the drawing process is visible /**B**/ usually carry subjective or emotive qualities; this is true of both pictorial and nonpictorial images, especially those which are reductive /**C**/.

A Downplaying the form language typically results in an image that is more "believable" as real / STIM Visual Communication *United States*

B Although as "real," evidence of the drawing process makes it recognizable as an invention / STIM Visual Communication *United States*

C Reductive images convey objectivity or neutrality / STIM Visual Communication *United States*

The degree to which the drawing process is evident or obscured adds a level of interpretation or narrative to the image, affecting perception of the subject (see pages 70–87). Drawings in which the presence of mark and gesture is perceptible often inhabit the geography of stylization, but even in images intended as naturalistic articulations of empirical form, this presence actively generates some interpretation that may differ depending on the form language; note the change in understanding between the two studies of boulders /**D, E**/.

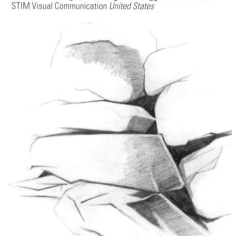

D In this study of stones, heavy planar forms convey a sensation of weight; their roughness suggests the surface / STIM Visual Communication *United States*

E In an alternate study, mass is dominated by line, focusing on the organic, yet structural, interconnection of edges / STIM Visual Communication *United States*

If the designer decides that the form language will be a visible component of a pictorial image, that form language takes on a dual role. First, it presents itself as an explicit syntax independent of the pictorial elements; and second, it becomes a vehicle for viewers to recognize the pictorial subjects. The shapes of marks may be considered for how they refer to observed elements in an object; short, tufted marks, for example, may texturally represent leaves or trees themselves—as they are—rather than as secondary components used to to construct a naturalistic illusion of flowers or leaves /**F**/. In following this route, the designer can attune the form language by choosing specific identities of marks and gestures that closely correspond to details, textures, shapes, and structures in the observed source /**G**/; in essence, referring or alluding to them in shorthand.

Images that engage the form language on a dual level merge pictorial and nonpictorial— their marks have a life of their own while still serving a depictive function. In this duality lies the image's evocative power.

G Sharp, delicate lines describe the crisp edges of the tea bag; textured masses suggest the qualities of its paper and contents / Ratipriya Suresh, UArts *United States*

F Although no pictorial representation of trees is visible, the leaf- and branchlike qualities of this syntax is undeniable/ Eva Surany, UArts *United States*

Drawings that walk this path between the two major territories often capture the imagination most dramatically and help create meaningful connections between a subject and its depiction /**H**/; they also liberate the designer from the perceived necessity—and often static, slavish dullness—of mere reproduction. Evidence of the hand, even in highly reductive symbols /**I**/ or typographic forms (where the only such reference may be in the small-scale ragged edge of a contour) affords the opportunity to introduce a sense of vitality and invention in an otherwise austere experience.

H The roundness and irregularities of the line language, together with their translucent washes, convey both the container and its contents / Ming Shao, UArts *United States*

I Rough, irregular contours impart a sense of history / Studio Apeloig *France*

A Red and green are complementary. /
Yuri Surkov *Russia*

B Analogous hues of similar intensity and value /
STIM Visual Communication *United States*

C Green, violet, and orange are split complements, or triadic. / STIM Visual Communication
United States

The
Visual Logic
of Color

A designer must also define a syntax
for color as part of the drawing's form
language or, more simply: a specific,
recognizable palette whose components
are defined by their respective hues
(identity), saturation (relative intensity),
temperatures (perceived coolness or
warmth), and values (relative lightness or
darkness). Relationships among the color
syntax components express its grammar.

**Color relationships are described
by the relative positions of hues on
the color wheel, a descriptive color
model developed in the 1800s.**

Complementary hues appear opposite
each other on the color wheel /**A**/ while
adjacent hues are characterized as
analogous /**B**/; this term may also refer
to close-in relationships of value, temperature, or saturation. Split complements,
or triads, appear at 120° intervals /**c**/.

It's always important to remember that
a color's identity is relative—the perception of its hue, saturation, value, and
temperature will change depending on
the identity of adjacent colors /**D**/.

Creating clear color logic usually means
limiting both the number of hues and
the number of different kinds of relationship in which they participate: The more
specific the palette, the bolder its imprint.
Logic may be expressed by a palette of
generally two analogous hues, perhaps,
varied in saturation and value /**E**/; a
similar strategy can be seen in the logo
for a youth conference to its right /**G**/.

This specificity is no less desirable in
empirical, pictorial drawings than in stylized ones. A quick perusal of even the
most naturalistic representations—the
editorial illustration of a bird, for instance
/**F**/—will immediately reveal a clearly
limited palette. Visible here is another
color relationship, extension: the volume
of one color required to optically balance
the volume of another; most often, large
volumes of cool colors require only a
tiny volume of a warm color to achieve a
sense of this balance.

D Although the line element appears to change
color, it is, in fact, the same color throughout .
STIM Visual Communication *United States*

E Warm, analogous hues of differing intensities, or saturation / STIM Visual Communication *United States*

OLIVIERO TOSCANI ♂
Photoadvertis Restlesso Creato-Colorus

II

F An overall, rigidly limited palette is counterbalanced by a vivid accent color—and just enough. / Studio Astrid Stavro *Spain*

6° CONGRESSO
MUNDIAL DA
JUVENTUDE

RIO DE JANEIRO
BRASIL 2012

G This logo also exploits a limited palette of three hues. / Felipe Taborda Design *Brazil*

Limiting the palette and relationships of extension can be approached from a systematic standpoint as a way of clarifying a drawing's color logic. Working with only one hue that is expressed in two opposing extremes of attribute could be an option /H/. Changing only a single identifying attribute while keeping the others analogous will create the simplest, most integrated logic; alternately varying the extension, or amount of each hue within the limited palette from component to component of a communication— for instance, among a series of web pages or spreads in a brochure—provides opportunities both for refreshing the viewer's experience and for establishing a clearly unified color logic in the system. Both these latter strategies can be seen in the two web pages at right /I/.

H An extremely limited palette (in this poster, two yellows—but one saturated and light in value, the other neutral and dark) offers tremendous contrast and an integrated color syntax. / Modern Dog Design Co. *United States*

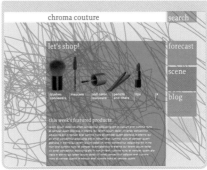

I Limited hues maintain consistent value and saturation; the extension of each in relation to the others, changes dramatically. / STIM Visual Communication *United States*

Second Principle

Successful drawings exhibit definitive structure that unites form and composition.

Universal Principles of a Strong Drawing

As marks accumulate and disperse, they give rise to shapes that construct a drawing's subject. Every successful drawing defines a sturdy skeleton of visual interconnections that allows viewers to understand what those shapes are and how to interpret them as a totality within perceptual space. This totality is structure. It's easiest here to invoke the analogy of architecture, such as a physical building; a drawing has a framework that holds it together. And, also like a building, that framework is made up of parts; it may be readily apparent, or difficult to perceive, because of what happens around, or on top of, that framework.

In a pictorial drawing, marks create structure to allow the identification of objects, or forms, in varying degrees of naturalism or stylization. Perception of a naturalistically rendered, or empirical, pictorial image's structure /**A**/ can be challenging because its complex detail and gloss of realism interferes with analysis; the structure is "buried" in its illusory naturalism. The structures of reductive, pictorial images and nonpictorial images /**B**/ are easily recognizable because the viewer isn't consumed by interpreting the "real;" structure is explicitly revealed.

A A structure of intersecting diagonals and planes helps the viewer interpet a naturalistic, pictorial scene. / Sean Ryan *United States*

B A similar angular structure as seen in **A,** above, is explicitly visible in this composition of nonpictorial forms. / Dextro *Austria*

Fundamental Geometry: Contour, Axis, and Plane

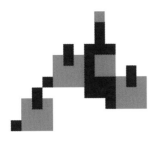

C An extreme reduction to geometric planes creates the structure and the expression of this image of a wine bottle and apples. / Ten Do Ten *Japan*

And therein lies the first step in being able to structure a drawing: seeing the simple shapes that underpin the complexity of images and the forms that compose them. At its most basic level, every pictorial subject can be described by geometry /**C–F**/; their parts are either rectilinear, curvilinear, or triangular. The fact of this geometric structure is called out as the basis for the iconic interpretation of wine bottles and apples above /**C**/ but in the other images on this page /**D**/, the geometric nature of their respective structures is no less intrinsic, although it may be downplayed, simply a vehicle for composition. Even the irregular, organic painting of the landscape /**E**/ is governed by geometric structure. Marks of different kinds may be used to describe this basic geometry. Lines can be used to trace it /**D, F**/ or masses used to fill it in as shapes /**C, E**/.

Lines and masses both first describe a form's object's outer boundary (its silhouette or profile) before articulating interior divisions with increasing complexity. In addition to its contours, a shape expresses an axis—or several axes— an imaginary line that bisects the form. Most shapes express two primary axes: horizontal and vertical. Objects or forms composed of several component shapes include a dominant axis or axis as a whole, as well as the sub-axes of each of its component shapes /**G**/. The sides, or facets, of forms and their components are characterized as planes. The drawing of a skull, at right /**H**/, has two primary axes (the horizontal dominating the vertical) but a number of less important axes suggested by the lighter-value shapes that describe the skull's planes, which were exaggerated to help understand the object's structure.

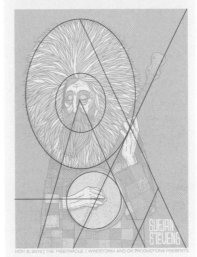

D Simple geometric structure / Jud Haynes *Canada*

E Organic syntax organized around the geometry of angles / Paone Design Associates *United States*

G A complex form expresses dominant axes that define its gestalt structure (solid lines) and secondary axes that create more intricate structural connections (dotted lines). / Mauro Melis *Italy*

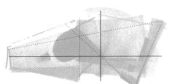

G Lines and planes contribute understanding of both contours and axes. / Eva Surany, UArts *United States*

Structure in Volumetric Form

A designer may establish a strictly planar structure, articulated only across horizontal and vertical axes; structure may also be established with a third axis to describe volume. Stylized pictorial images, as they approach greater reduction, tend to exhibit planar structure /**A**/; highly reduced icons, translations, and logos intrinsically exhibit this same two-dimensional structuring. In some cases, a sense of volumetric structure may be suggested by diminishing line weights or the density or scale of mass.

In empirically descriptive pictorial work, a subject's structure is typically conceived as developing outward from a cube /**B**/, allowing a designer to first articulate the simplest volumes and establish proportional relationships; to articulate curved forms, ellipses are constructed from the cube's plane surfaces; triangular structures result from connecting points at corners or along edges to other, similar points. Extending the axes of these volumetric structures helps find reference points for adjacent volumes, or components of the primary volume, including cylinders, cones, and other, increasingly complex polyhedrons /**C**/ that can be used to articulate the more elaborate structures. The same strategy informs even drawings of organic objects /**D**/, although the evidence may be removed to not distract from organicism.

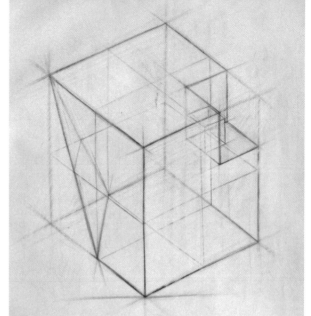

B A cubic volume divided by "cutting into" its planes /

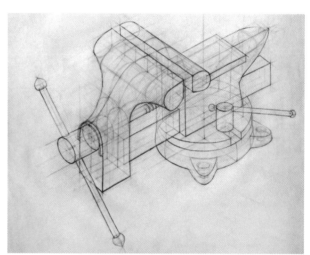

C The many divisions and elliptical forms in this vice are evolved from cubic, volumetric structure. /

A This poster's image plays with an optical conflict between the perception of flatness and dimensional planes. / Un Mundo Féliz *Spain*

open the door for every child in the world

D Looking closely at this drawing of flowers reveals an understructure of planar and diagonal axes. /

B–D Paone Design Associates
United States

Internal Typographic Structure

When working with letterforms, the designer is bound to honor an established set of archetypal structures /**E**/—the specific combinations of vertical, diagonal, horizontal, and curved strokes that permit recognition of the alphabet's characters. Deviation from the archetypes is, of course, possible (and the source for new character styles, of which there are currently more than 70,000), but the designer must be acutely aware of which structural elements in the archetype must remain adequately discernable to ensure legibility when experimenting.

Internal typographic structure is fundamentally a structure of horizontal and vertical axes /**F**/. While square proportion /**E**/ originally provided the basis for the ideal height/width ratio in the characters of the alphabet, over time the typical starting proportion for regular-width characters has narrrowed to roughly 80% of the height of the capitals. In italic forms /**G**/, a third axis defines the degree of slant; italics typically lean 12°–15° to the right off the vertical axis. While the slant widens the physical space that each character occupies, it doesn't affect the actual height/width ratio of the stroke formation itself.

Stroke weight is an intrinsic part of its structure /**F**/; the archetypal structure of a letter is considered a kind of invisible "spine" /**H**/, from which the weight organically "bleeds" or "grows" outward, pushing and reshaping the counterspaces around and within the letter. Strokes in a character set may be uniform in weight, or their weights may vary between thick and thin. In manipulating the shaping of strokes and altering or creating contrasts in weight, the designer must generally adhere to the distribution of weights historically defined by the alphabet's brush- and pen-drawn origins; these tools have imparted specific weight rhythms in the letters that are evident today /**I**/, even in contemporary, uniform-weight sans-serif faces. Changing these relationships may result in very interesting forms, but most often will result (at best) in an intangible awkwardness or (at worst) illegibility.

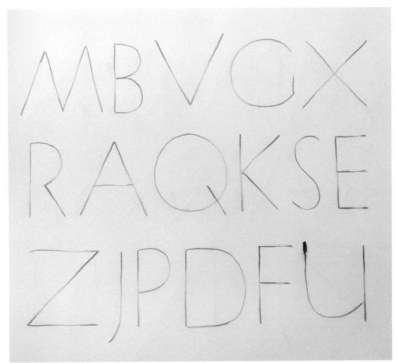

E A study of archetypal letter structure in roman proportion: square, half-square, circle, and semicircle / Mariel Perez, SUNY Purchase *United States*

E E E E E E

F Basic letter structure incorporates its width, as well as its weight, studied through hand-painted forms. / Shiho Osumi, SUNY Purchase *United States*

H E

G Italic forms include a third, diagonal axis in their structure. /

H Weight in letters grows outward from an internal "spine." /

I The distribution of thicks and thins—and the degree of this contrast—is historically driven, and also fundamental to typographic structure. /

Compositional Structure: Organizing Form in Space

The form structures in a drawing are only half the story. The other half is their organization: compositional structure that ties these components together in totality within the format space. And, as with component form structure, compositional structure may be achieved through geometry as an underlying strategy among all territories of drawing.

A viewer first appreciates compositional structure through the perception of the form objects' axes. At the macro level, even before the perception of contour intervenes, the axes create an underlying, gestural framework of interconnections across space /**A**/. These are the broad strokes: vertical, horizontal, or diagonal orientation, relative to the parallel axes established by the edges of the format; position high or low, left or right; axis lengths, and their corresponding relationships to each other, their parallelism or divergence and, ultimately, the rhythm of proportional breaks around the format.

The contours of forms are secondary axes that generally follow the primary ones, although they may deviate slightly. Planar or volumetric structural divisions within forms extend interior structure outward into surrounding compositional space and define increaisngly detailed structural connections within the framework.

A Primary axes are shown as solid lines; secondary axes are denoted by dotted lines. / Timothy Samara *United States*

The most basic compositional structures tend to be diagonal /**A,B**/ or orthogonal /**C**/, meaning defined by vertical/horizontal axes. Diagonal axis-based structure is incredibly dynamic because the axes aren't parallel with edges of a (typical) format. Orthogonal structure is most prevalent in typographic drawing and typographic layouts—in particular, in situations where there is an extensive volume of text /**D**/ that, for the sake of readability, is usually arranged as horizontal lines stacked in vertically-proportioned columns.

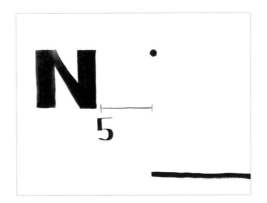

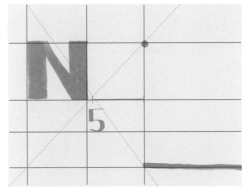

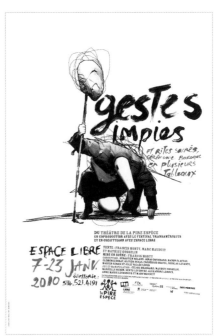

C Axes in typography are primarily orthogonal (solid lines), although diagonal axes (dotted lines) are also common. Note how the dot anchors a number of axes. / Yoon Deok Jang, School of Visual Arts *United States*

Orthogonal and diagonal structures may be freely combined, of course (it could be argued that an orthogonal structure implies diagonal axes by virtue of the implied connections between nodes, or junctures between vertical and horizontal axes). In such circumstances /**D**/, the designer is often likely to "hang" the diagonal structure from the orthogonal—simply because the orthogonal structure is perceived as more stable or grounding, helping to tame complexity if needed.

D A dominant structure (in this case, an orthogonal axis division [solid lines]) underpins, and helps organize a complex set of conflicting diagonal axes (dotted lines). / Laurent Pinabel *Canada*

B Diagonal axis-based structure tends to be extremely dynamic compared to orthogonal axis-based structure. / Timothy Samara *United States*

The Logic of Organization: Symmetry, Asymmetry, and Other Strategies

Compositional structure, defined by the directionality, interconnection, and positional relationships among axes and contours, may be organized first in consideration of two opposing kinds of logic: symmetry and asymmetry.

Symmetry is a structural logic in which forms respond positionally to a central axis of the format (horizontal, vertical, or diagonal); the forms might also be arranged in relation to each other's central axes. A composition may be structured very simply around a single axis /**A**/ or, for greater complexity, two or three axes /**B**/. The relationship of form structures to the format's axis is likewise open to variation; they may be mirrored, or positioned to reflect across the axis (bilateral symmetry), or they may invert in orientation across the axis (rotational symmetry).

Asymmetry, on the other hand, is a structural logic in which the relationships among the axes and contours of subject forms do not respond to a single axis /**C, D**/. In contrast to the condition established by symmetrical logic, this means, generally, that no set of spaces, nor the contours of any forms, will correspond with each other in a direct, one-to-one repetition /**D**/.

A Landscape and trees arranged symmetrically around a central, vertical axis / KAKO *Brazil*

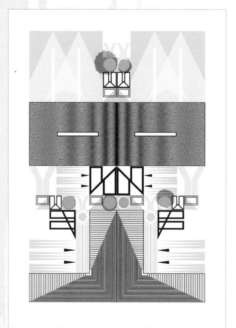

B While the symmetrical vertical axis is dominant, the image is also divided symmterically above/below the central horizontal axis. / Slang *Germany*

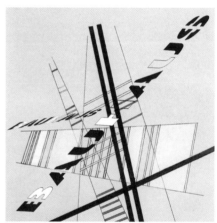

C An asymmetrical composition of type and line forms / Sung Jin Park, School of Visual Arts *United States*

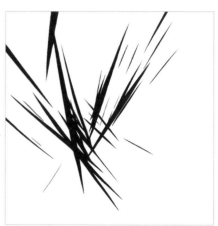

D The axes in this asymmetrical line drawing divide the format into triangular shapes that are all very different from one another. / Catherine Harvey *United States*

E The vertical and horizontal symmetry of the major axes is contrasted by the asymmetrical position of the headline. / Yuri Surkov *Russia*

Symmetry and asymmetry rarely integrate well with each other. Symmetry imposes a strict order on arrangement that usually creates formal disconnect among elements that violate it. Asymmetrical arrangements, in contrast, require continual differentiation in structure to achieve resolution. Another potential concern deriving from symmetry is its inherently static quality. That said, the challenge of combining symmetry and asymmetry, if met successfully by the designer **/E/**, rewards the viewer with unequivocal directness, accessibility, and emphatic movement.

Aligning

Staggering

Clustering

Stepping

Stacking

Mirroring

Chaining

Radial

Concentric

Spiraling

Waving

Orthogonal

Diagonal

Parallel

Rotational

Grid-Based

Proportional

Branching

Constellational

Networked

Nodal

Following either symmetrical or asymmetrical logic, numerous conditions may combine to define compositional structure /F/.

F This seemingly simple poster incorporates at least six kinds of structure, expressed at different scales— can you identify them? / Shaung Wan, School of Visual Arts *United States*

Part-to-Whole Structural Relationships

Whether complex and gestural or reductive and highly edited, the internal organization of any drawing's parts must correspond with each other and engage in a visual dialogue; to achieve this condition, a designer must enforce part-to-whole relationships throughout the work even among elements that contrast each other /**A**/.

First, each component part of a subject form must express a clear relationship with the others in that form. Second, each form must express a relationship with the other forms around it. Third, the group of forms must then be considered relative to the entirety of the drawing. The kind of relationship seen at one level is often restated—directly, at larger scale, perhaps or indirectly, through a rotation or in a different proportion. For example /**B**/: dots clustered in one area may be aligned in a pattern as part of a type treatment; a dominant S-curve that governs the whole drawing may be seen again at a smaller size, rotated at a different angle. A drawing's organizational structure is somewhat fractal in this way, becoming clearer and more interesting from the recurring part-to-whole relationships at each level.

B Similarities between structural axes and contours, as well as contrasts—at different sizes—create intricate part-to-whole relatonships. / Vladimir Dubko *China*

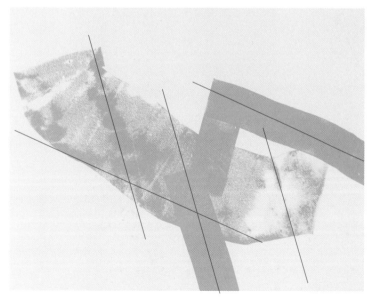

A Repetitions of two major diagonal axes create a kind of visual "call and response" between line elements of very different syntax. / Christine Hiebert *United States*

C The locations of small, positive details—for example, the right-hand terminus of the coffee cup's upper rim—helps complete our appreciation of the pot's volume, as does the curvature of the pot's handle as it encounters its invisible "edge." / Catherine Harvey *United States*

D Radically different form languages—even drawn elements and photographic ones—exhibit formal unity because they share a similar, curling structure, as well as restate important axes. / Laurent Pinabel *Canada*

Part-to-whole relationships often stand in for edited information /**C**/, working to complete understanding of the source subject's entire structure—an effect referred to as closure. This effect demonstrates the profound impact of clear part-to-whole relationships, creating a very complex experience that far exceeds the image's apparent simplicity.

In a diagrammatic pictorial image, where disparate subjects may be removed from their original contexts and juxtaposed or recombined—or where extremely different syntax /**D**/ or media share the same space—part-to-whole integration serves to conceptually (as well as visually) bind them. This, too, ensures a kind of closure.

Directing the eye through a composition, from the most emphatic entry point at the top of a visual hierarchy through successively less important focal points, is usually a result of part-to-whole relationships. In compositions of only a few major elements /**E**/ that are separated by considerable distance—and an apparent lack of strong axis connections—part-to-whole relationships do the heavy lifting of leading the viewer through the work.

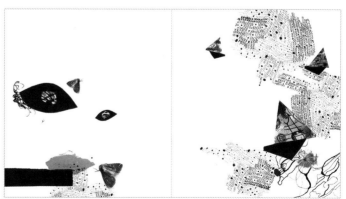

E Subtle part-to-whole relationships direct the eye from focal point onward. Compare the aggregate shape of the heavy elements at left and right-hand contour of negative space at right; also note color and form repetitions at decreasing scales. / Aylin Önel *Turkey*

Further, part-to-whole relationships may be intrinsically related to comprehension in such diagrammatic drawings as maps or info-graphics, whose structures are literally part of their meaning /**A**/. The challenge in this kind of drawing is structuring it to convey the requisite information and still yield a dynamic compositional structure. Despite the requisite of accurately informing the viewer about the subject being diagrammed, some leeway for interpretation may exist. Symbolic forms may offer the possibility of creating a relevant shape /**B**/ that will accurately express data, as can reductive translations of pictorial forms /**C**/.

The one caveat to this liberation lurks in structuring diagrams of a nonpictorial nature. The elements of a diagram showing a process, or a more conceptual mapping of an idea, may still be configured with a relatively abstract structure, but any diagram that intends to describe experiential relationships—distance, time, proportion—such as maps or timelines, depend on the drawing's structure corresponding to these relationships in a way that a viewer will be able to understand them and, so, remain useful as information.

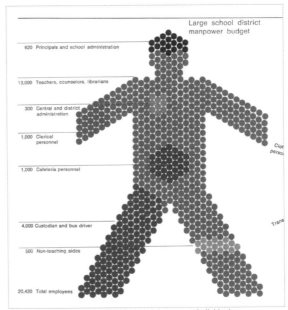

A Color changes among groups of gridded dots create individual organs within the figure. / Steff Geissbuhler, C+G Partners LLC *United States*

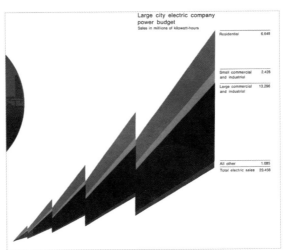

B This combination of jagged lines, representing electrical power, shows divisions that correspond to monetary allotments in a fiscal budget. / Steff Geissbuhler, C+G Partners LLC *United States*

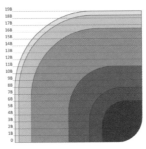
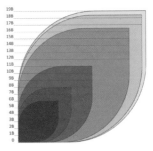

C Structuring the shapes that represent data relative to values creates clear relationships between their values, as well as shows growth as a kind of germinating seed or leaf / KAKO *Brazil*

Typography—driven by tension between masses and voids—derives fundamental cohesion and dynamism from part-to-whole structural relationships. Within a single letter, logotype /**D**/, or typeface style /**E**/, relationships of shape, joint and detail style, and proportional rhythm create unity among forms. In compositions of text /**F, G**/, these relationships define, most significantly, the structure of space. Spaces in typography become form elements that are more greatly varied in proportion and movement, counteracting the repetitive, linear form language and horizontal gesture emphasized by positive text forms. In strong typography, axes and spatial contours appear to act upon the type, rather than the reverse.

AFRIQUE CONTEM-PORAINE

D Corresponding diagonal axes, triangular structures, and their reorientation around a narrow vertical express part-to-whole relationships in this logotype, as does the alternation of color. / Studio Apeloig *France*

RGANmgfax

E Text typefaces exhibit part-to-whole relationships in the alternation of stroke and counterspace proportion, similarity of diagonals and curve radius among alternate characters and, more generally, in consistent weight, contrast and detail shapes. / Andrew Scheiderich, SUNY Purchase *United States*

F Repetition and reversal of diagonal axes, parity between diagonals and staggered sqaure text blocks, and alignments among edges and details creates a complex, multi-scale dialogue between shapes and shaped spaces. / Patricia Cué *United States*

G The vertical axes of symmetrical elements correspond with, or are brought into alignment with, axes and contours of asymmetrically-placed forms. / Type.Page [Park Woohyuk] *Korea*

Third Principle

Strong drawings exhibit dramatic positive/ negative vitality.

The articulation of structure works to establish a relationship between the elements that are created and the spaces within and around them. This relationship is that of positive and negative /**A**/, and it is quite possibly the most important of the universal principles with regard to the dynamism and energy of a drawing.

The "positive" aspect of this relationship is the "stuff" that is the subject: lines, masses, shapes, objects, textures, letters, and words. Space is considered "negative"—not in a bad way, but as the opposite of the positive. The negative is the "ground" in which positive becomes a "figure." The relationship between positive and negative, or figure and ground, is complementary and mutually dependent /**B**/; it's impossible to alter one and not the other.

A The blue elements are positive; the yellow areas are negative. /
Steff Geissbuhler, C+G Partners LLC *United States*

B Dynamic negative spaces—all in tense, rhythmic relation to the type they enclose—
would completely change if one type element changed position or proportion. / Irina Lee,
School of Visual Arts *United States*

C The corner forms appear both positive and negative—as does the central blue form.

D A narrow space appears as a thin, positive line.

C+D The appearance of positive becoming negative (and vice versa) is called figure/ground reversal. / STIM Visual Communication *United States*

E The narrow vertical counter-space in the initial O may also be perceived as a positive form on a green field, in addition to the negative C that "crosses through" the OM combination. / Pettis Design *United States*

F The icon of the cat's head appears as a positive form, despite being clearly connected to surrounding negative space. / Tactical Magic *United States*

G Figure/ground reversal allows perception of the face in the contour of the key's teeth. / Fang Chen *United States*

In some compositions, the figure/ground relationship can become quite complex, to the extent that what appears positive one minute appears negative the next— an effect called figure/ground reversal. It may occur for any number of reasons—for example, tightly cropping a large form /**C**/ may yield negative spaces that appear as positive; two heavy lines close together may produce the effect of a very narrow positive line /**D**/ on a negative field; or the intrusion of a small shape of exterior negative space, relative to the positive form, causes the negative space to take on the quality of a positive form /**E, F**/ while still allowing the eye to perceive the primary form as positive overall. Figure ground reversal presents a dramatic tool for concisely merging images on a practical /**F**/, as well as conceptual level /**G**/.

The two opposing states are absolutely explicit in reductive forms, of course, but sometimes less easily perceived in more complex images. When looking at a collage that presents multiple levels of foreground, middle ground, and back-ground, for example, it's very often the case that elements within each of these spatial zones will appear to alternate in identity between positive and negative.

The figures at the bottom of this poster appear to be in the foreground of the yellow shape—which acts as their nega-tive space—and yet the yellow shape itself is a positive form against the blue and beige background /**H**/.

H Foreground, middle-ground, and background elements or areas sometimes alternate in identity. / Atelier 480 *Canada*

A The single form creates new shapes of space. /

B As more forms appear, so too do new spaces—and the perception of more activity in general. /

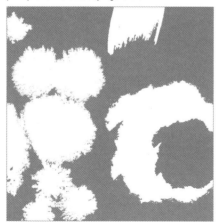

C Intricate alternation of positive and negative increases the perception of activity. /

A–C STIM Visual Communication *United States*

Activating The Negative

Space is defined the instant a form appears within it /**A**/, no matter how simple. Each element brought into the space adds complexity but also decreases the literal amount of space—even as it creates new kinds of space /**B**/, forcing it into distinct shapes that fit around the forms like the pieces of a puzzle. These spaces shouldn't be considered "empty" or "leftover;" they are integral to achieving flow and rhythm among positive forms.

The mutual interplay of positive and negative establishes the perception of varying degrees of energy, sometimes restive or static, at other times, dynamic or aggressive. The degree of activity might depend on how many forms are interacting in a given space, the size of the forms relative to the space, or how intricate the alternation /**c**/ between positive and negative appears to be.

The vitality of drawing to be captured through positive/negative interaction stems first from the negative spaces appearing active or involved with the positive elements throughout the compositional space.

One of the first aspects of a drawn image a designer can contemplate is the outer contour of its form. This is easy to consider in the context of a reductive singularity, such as a logo or icon /**D**/, where the positive element isn't confined within another shape. The spaces around the form become more active when the contour's movement tracks inward and outward with greater relative distance from the central mass; this effect is augmented when the proportions of each of the contour's sides is very different.

D Movement of a contour inward and outward in varying degrees activates space around such reductive forms as icons. / STIM Visual Communication *United States*

Focusing the majority of visual activity into one area of a composition—for example, by clustering—is an excellent way of creating emphasis, as well as a contrasting area for rest. But this strategy might also result in spaces that feel empty or isolated from this activity /**E**/. In all such cases, the space can be called "inert," or "inactive." An inert or inactive space will call attention to itself for this very reason: it doesn't communicate with the other spaces in the composition.

During the process of composing positive and negative interaction, portions of space might become disconnected from other portions. A section might be separated physically or blocked off /**F**/ by a larger element that crosses from one edge of the format to the other; or, it might be optically separated because of a set of forms aligning in such a way that the eye is discouraged from traveling past the alignment /**G**/and entering into the space beyond. Sometimes, the smallest element or detail, carefully positioned, will activate a space without destroying its openness and intrinsic contrast to positive form activity /**G, H**/.

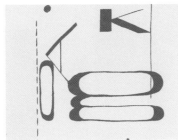

E Inactive negative space (top) becomes active with closer edge proximity. / Anna Kim, School of Visual Arts *United States*

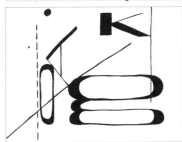

F The space at far left is cut off from the composition by the dotted line, but activated by breaking that boundary. / Younsin Cho, School of Visual Arts *United States*

G Another inactive space at right becomes active when a dot is introduced—without destroying its comparably restful quality. / Hyung Kyu Choi, School of Visual Arts *United States*

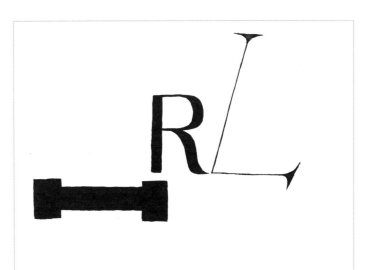

H The dramatic serif on the capital L's baseline stroke is all that's needed to activate the lower right-hand space. / Sayaka Sekine, School of Visual Arts *United States*

Interval and Dynamism/ Symmetry and Asymmetry

Fighting the tendency of two-dimensional form to feel static—in an awkward state of inertia—is always challenging. A static visual condition usually results when positive and negative elements appear optically equal; when positive forms have similar mass or presence, when spatial intervals are of similar shape and size, and when these spaces also appear about the same size as the positive forms. Positive and negative need not be physically the same shape to appear equal in presence, so it is necessary to evaluate the aggregate mass of each, independent of their specific shapes.

The simplest strategies for ensuring dynamic composition, then, focus on enforcing differences in the variables of proportion and interval—larger versus smaller; verticality versus horizontality; cluster and overlap versus tight proximity or generous spacing between elements; and linearity versus mass /**A**/.

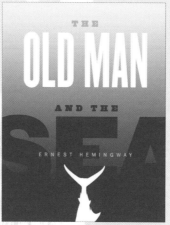

B Varying width, directional emphasis, and interval enhances symmetrical compositions. / STIM Visual Communication *United States*

Symmetrical arrangements inherently confront the designer with a potentially static condition because the spatial intervals and shapes surrounding the material that is organized around the symmetrical axis are the same. To counteract this problem (in a bilaterally summetrical, vertical format, for instance), a designer may look to: exaggerate lateral width, spacing, and vertical emphasis changes /**B**/ as well as differences in vertical intervals; unexpectedly interrupt a repetition of intervals /**C**/; or violate the symmetry by shifting an element out of its mirrored relationship with corresponding elements across the axis /**D**/.

C Overall regular intervals between type forms in a symmetrical layout are counteracted by unexpected weight distribution high and low. / Takuji Omori *Japan*

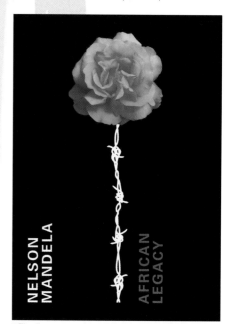

D The directness and strength of symmetrical presentation is made richer by introducing an asymmetrical component. / Milani Design *Italy*

A A symmetrical form gains from decisively different compressed, linear elements— both positive and negative—and expansive, curving, masses. / STIM Visual Communication *United States*

Even when participating in an asymmetrical structure, multiple forms situated around similar spatial intervals create static interaction. Altering the intervals between form elements /**E**/, or between elements and format edges /**F, G**/, creates a dynamic composition. The movement of the eye is enhanced as these intervals exhibit greater contrast with each other, becoming compressed or expanding with a directional thrust.

Drawing
/ for Graphic
Design

Discovery

**Universal
Principles**
Third Principle:
Positive/
Negative
Vitality

F The red elements help direct the eye from tighter inervals at bottom and right—inducing anxiety—to an open, simply defined large spatial interval at upper left. / Takuji Omori *Japan*

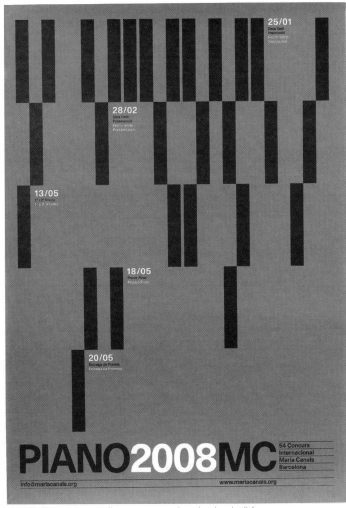

E Irregular intervals between line groups creates lateral push and pull. / Studio Astrid Stavro *Spain*

G The proximity of the format edge to any type element is always different around the type's contours. / Sung Jin Park, School of Visual Arts *United States*

Movement and Rhythm: The Interplay of Positive and Negative

Activating the negative components of a drawing and manipulating the proportions of both positive and negative areas creates visual rhythm: a kind of optical "pulsing" that results from the appearance of form and space compressing and expanding.

A Spaces between the water droplets open and compress in an undulating rhythm, supported by the back and forth movement of the title's ragged lines. / Yuri Surkov *Russia*

Varying the proximity of positive forms or, more simply, placing some closer together and others further apart, is chiefly what contributes to the perception of rhythm and movement. Irregular, or organically shaped, forms /**A**/ lend themselves more readily to achieving this dynamism; their contours already exhibit changes in both proportion and inward/outward directionality. Geometric forms, especially lines and rectilinear ones, typically need exaggerated interval and proportional differences to initiate the desired pulsing or shifting /**B**/, but once this occurs they can appear just as rhythmic as their organic counterparts.

The optical sensations of "squeezing," or compression, and "opening," or expansion, may first follow any one, or combinations of, such laterally-emphasized logic as: alternation, where positive negative proportions flip between compressed and open states in repetition, sometimes at differing overall scale /**C**/; progression, in which the interval differences between positive and negative components transition /**D**/ from one state to another (for example, from tight or compressed to open or expansive); or opposition, where one general area expresses a singular, specific rhythm in contrast to that expressed by another area /**E**/.

C Slow, as well as rapid, alternation between compressing and expanding

D Positive and negative in an evenly diminishing progression of alternation, and uneven

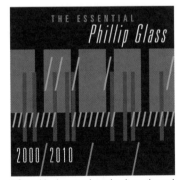

E Opposition between irregular alternation and consistent alternation

C–E STIM Visual Communication *United States*

B Constantly changing linear weights and spatial intervals create the perception of rising and falling. / Shinnoske, Inc. *Japan*

F Figure/ground reversal proportionally defined as a progression from deep proportion to shallow, bottom to top / Andrew Iskowitz *United States*

All three kinds of logic may also inform the interplay of positive and negative in perceptual space. Figure/ground reversal may create the same alternation, progression /**F**/, or opposition, not only laterally, but also with the appearance of moving "backward" from foreground to background. Value changes among elements in foreground, middle ground, and background may accomplish a similar effect.

Translations, icons, and symbols /**G–I**/ benefit tremendously from the rhythmic interaction of positive and negative—in fact, relying on it to avoid potentially dull or overly simplistic presentation that often seems cold and lifeless. Brand marks, in particular, require dynamic proportional and interval-based rhythm in their positive and negative components not only for visual interest, but also often to deliver emotional or conceptual messages. Extreme contrasts in spatial interval and negative shapes—some expansive and ovoid, others tight and almost linear—impart a dynamic push and pull that is almost alive, suggesting the creative impulse in a mark for an arts magazine /**G**/. Tightly controlled repetition of compressed and open positive negative forms of similar proportion creates a sense of stability in a logo for a home builder /**H**/, while intricate, squeezed transitions suggest precision and craftsmanship. A similar stability in a mark for a real estate developer results from the precise interaction of rectilinear forms around a symmetrical axis /**I**/ as a progression of negative intervals—tighter toward the bottom and open toward the top—create rhythm and movement as well as a sense of growth or expansion.

G A rich variety of negative spaces contributes to the optical "whiplash" of this logo. / Mehdi Saeedi Studio *Iran*

H Figure/ground reversal helps integrate pattern forms with a letter. / STIM Visual Communication *United States*

LARGAVISTA
COMPANIES

I Extremely simple line syntax and rigidly controlled gesture draw life from unexpected interval changes. / Hinterland *United States*

Typographic Rhythm

AGMR
AGMR
AGMRS
AGMRSKDHB
AGMRS
A G M R S
A G M R S

A Comparison of rhythmic variations perceived because of changes in positive/negative proportion and interval /

Typographic styles are, in essence, specific systems of positive/negative rhythm; along with the shaping of the strokes and structural proportion, it's the fundamental differentiating aspect among them. Comparing typefaces of differing weights and widths **/A/** reveals tremendous variation in positive/negative rhythm logic: thin strokes alternating with wide counters, thick strokes alternating with narrow counters, and every variation in between. In a single letter, the vitality of the form derives from this rhythm; in the expanded character set, the same positive/negative rhythm, expressed among a variety of structures, contributes to the stylistic unity in the face.

Positive/negative rhythm is important to achieve a lively typographic layout, but governed more rigidly by systematic approaches that support reading. Type in a layout must typically establish rhythmic consistency for purposes of encouraging a sense of continuity among the parts and enforcing clear informational hierarchy; this logic is often constrained within orthogonal, mathematical systems (such as a grid **/B, C/**) that enforce consistency in some aspects—for instance, the widths and height positions of text columns—while incorporating options for variation in compression and openness, achieved through positional spacing.

Five New York Fashion Designers

Sept 12, 2009

Lincoln Center 132 w 65th st

New York City's fashion designers

Alice Roi 2-3pm
Erica tanov 4-5pm
Pierre Garroudi 6-7pm
Eileen Fisher 8-9pm
Donna Karan 10-11

B Rhythmic consistency—similar column proportions in a grid—may be offset by selectively filling only specific columns. / Matthew Willett, School of Visual Arts *United States*

CUBISM AND ABSTRACT ART

COMPUTAÇÃO GRÁFICA

C Alternating wide and narrow spaces between text columns establishes rhythmic push and pull across the page spread. / Bizu Design *Brazil*

D The perception of time is affected by how type appears flat (and slow) in some areas and distorted (fast) in others. / Eun Young Kim, School of Visual Arts *United States*

E Active contouring and constant change in proportion and interval enhances this broadside's bold dynamism. / Christopher Beesley, School of Visual Arts *United States*

Typographic color—variation between densities and voids among type elements and surrounding spaces—depends on the mutual interplay of positive/negative proportion and optical weight, achieved through size (elements increasing in mass as they become larger) and weight (the use of light, medium, and bold faces). Weight contrast can dramatically exaggerate the push and pull of spatial change—for example, by lightening the weight of text so as to render it almost non-existent, while exaggerating the mass of extruded elements /**D**/, or forcing together extremely large and/or bold elements of different width proportion in response to deep inclusions of negative space /**E**/. Typographic color changes in a more subtle range may call attention to rhythmic interval changes without sacrificing a desired overall quietness /**F**/.

New Typographic Voice: An Exhibition

The Poetics of Form and Structure in the Twenty-First Century and Beyond

An investigation into recent developments in typographic design, presented in the context of pre-Industrial Revolution innovations—seeing the future of language in its past and present. Curated by Rick Poyner and Michael Ian Kaye.

Exhibition Opening Wednesday, November 21, 6:00pm

American Institute of Graphic Arts; National Gallery
164 Fifth Avenue (at 21st Street)
November 22–December 24

*Gallery hours are 10:00am to 5:00pm
Monday through Friday*

F A very classical, symmetrical text setting gains life from a close-in range of sizes, weight, and interval without losing its quiet elegance. / Na Yeon Kim, School of Visual Arts *United States*

Fourth Principle

Universal
Principles
of a Strong
Drawing

A strong drawing creates the perception of illusory dimensional space.

Artistic investigation for centuries has focused on fighting the physical flatness of the surface. The illusion of depth (and it's important to always remember that it is an illusion) plays a significant role in both pictorial and nonpictorial drawing—even among such reductive forms as icons and typography /**A**/. Perceiving depth engages viewers, draws them into the context of the communication, and encourages them to disengage with the outer world by helping to focus their attention. An image that defies its inherent, physical flatness seems worth deeper investigation.

B An extreme close-up with exaggerated details creates a deep, engaging space in this illustration. / KAKO *Brazil*

It's important to first understand perceptual space relative to compositional space—even though they share mutually affective attributes. The space of a composition is defined by its format, in whatever medium, and is clearly finite (although a screen interface enables navigation through spaces beyond the screen's confines). Spaces are created and manipulated by form elements within the format, responding in negative to their positive state.

Perceptual space, on the other hand, has to do with the sensation of dimensionality. This illusory experience of indefinable (possibly infinite) depth is a cognitive invention triggered by optical stimuli in the drawing—an "otherworld" that appears to exist simultaneously with the outer world, but only while looking at it through the "window" of the format.

Regardless of territory, there are two aspects that attend perceptual space: first, its spread, or extent; and second, its amplitude, or its relative perceived depth.

A The illusion of depth—achieved here through value and size contrasts—is important for typography as well as pictorial drawing. / Irina Lee, School of Visual Arts *United States*

The issue of spread is more closely tied to the compositional attributes of format. Perception of a space will either acknowledge it as a field /**B, C**/ or a singularity. The essence of a field is that, theoretically, its space extends outward beyond the edges of the format that captures it; it's an environment of scope, part of a continuum. The perceptual space of a singularity /**D**/ exists independently and is cognitively finite, a self-contained environment distinct from the space around it. This space is reflexive, meaning that its illusory depth continually refers inward, rather than outward.

D A logo is typical of a singularity—and of compressed amplitude. / AdamsMorioka,Inc. *United States*

The quality of amplitude is refreshingly tangible; the space either appears deep /**A–C**/ or compressed /**D, E**/. Space that is perceived as deep corresponds directly to our physical perception of space in the natural world, and so could be described as being more empirical.

Even highly reductive or planar material may encourage a perception of staggeringly deep space, most often as a result of extreme scale and value changes—especially in the case of typography, where line and limited color are dominant /**C**/. Progressions of value, which may be enhanced by color /**F**/ also suggest deep amplitude.

But drawn images may also present a compressed, or flattened space—a space that is more intellectual than experiential. Planar geometry, presented in an arrangement of static intervals and detached from each other /**G**/ most typically present a compressed amplitude. Still, organic form and language that are often quite varied in weight, mass, and linearity /**E**/, although most likely to contribute to perception of deep space, may sometimes exhibit a very compressed, confrontational depth as a result of extremely tight cropping and the anchoring of foreground elements to background elements.

E The compressed space of this gestural image exaggerates its confrontational presence. / Masa Watanabe Design Institute *Japan*

F A space of deep amplitude, achieved with overlayed paper / Max Fisher, UArts *United States*

G These graphic elements generally appear to float together in a shallow space. / TSTO *Finland*

C The space in this poster is perceived as a field—and deep in amplitude. / Niessen+deVries *The Netherlands*

Establishing Primary Perceptions of Space

Creating the perception of depth means replicating physiologically-perceived, optical relationships that the brain relies on to interpret the observed environment with the elements of a drawing's form language. While our eyes are not the best developed optical organs of those among all the planet's species, our highly evolved brains make up for it by being able to assimilate and order a vast complexity of incoming information (more so than any other species that we know of); supported by our facilities for analysis and reasoning, our brains help construct an intricate understanding of spatial reality. The intricacy of this process, however, allows us to accept discrepancies when they are presented and, therefore, to be easily fooled. A long time ago, people discovered how to make images (even simple ones) that fool the eye into believing it is looking at something else entirely.

A Larger forms appear closer, even in clearly stylized images. / Elly Row, School of Visual Arts *United States*

The most basic information the eyes and brain first compare is scale (relative size) of objects viewed in the environment.

The relative size of forms encountered in the perceptual field is usually the quickest determination the brain can easily make and then interpret; larger objects are interpreted as being closer and smaller objects as farther away /**A**/. Even when observing a landscape, where the scale of mountains or other large features is understood to be huge, the brain renders them smaller than any other object nearby /**B**/. Hence, the first strategy for introducing depth in an image is to enforce differences in size or mass. The image need not be naturalistic, or even pictorial, for that matter; reductive and nonpictorial drawings that present forms at different sizes will elicit the same interpretation of near and far.

B The bee, though empirically small, is extremely large in this drawing and so appears extremely close. / *KAKO Brazil*

C Forms tend to lighten in value as they recede. / Timothy Samara *United States*

D Forms of light value, however, can also be made to advance—similar to figure/ground reversal. / Timothy Samara *United States*

The second determination on which the brain relies to understand how space is configured is the relative lightness and darkness of elements, or their value.

Because this facility of the optical system evolved first, it's a more deeply ingrained aspect of perception and often trumps the interpretation of size relative to the position of objects in space. In the landscape, areas farther away tend to be awash with illumination and appear generally lighter in value /**C**/; ambient light reduces the darkness of shadows, and atmosphere contributes to overall lightening of objects seen in the distance. Areas or objects that are nearby usually retain the contrast of shadow against light, or themselves may be within the shadow of another object in close proximity, and so generally appear darker. Assigning different values to form elements in a composition will, as with scale changes, encourage a perception of different spatial depths.

The initially concrete spatial qualities established by scale and value may easily be thrown into question, even contradicted, by swapping their attributes—for example, giving foreground elements a light value /**D**/, or a small form an extremely dark value; overlapping a dark-value form with a light-value one /**E**/; or introducing transparency. Given this potential reciprocity between scale and value, the resolution of near/far logic depends on the relative contrast among those elements that are closer together in deep space being similar, and those that are intended to appear closer exhibiting a dramatic contrast in value with the former /**E**/. That is: If the image's background and all the forms that are to appear far away are overall dark in value, any forms that are dramatically much lighter will appear to advance; the opposite will be true if the situation is reversed /**F**/. No matter how large a form is, if it is closest in value to that of the surrounding negative space, viewers will perceive it as receding.

E The transition from foreground to background correlates with a progression from light to dark—except in the titling element. / Jewboy Corp. *Israel*

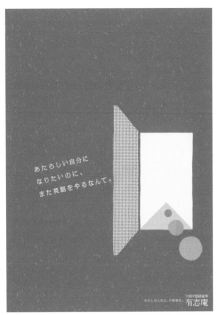

F The lightest-value element in this poster—the open door—ambiguously registers as an opening (a deep space) and as a flat plane; dark values occur in both foreground and background elements. / SIN [Yoshisada Nakahara] *Japan*

A One-point perspective; the horizon is located slightly higher than optical center. / Timothy Samara *United States*

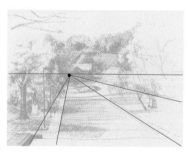

B Two-point perspective; the left-hand vanishing point is within the frame of the image, while the right-hand vanishing point is far outside the frame of the image. / Sean Ryan *United States*

C Progressive scale change in typography suggests dimensional depth. / Sung Jin Park, School of Visual Arts *United States*

Using Perspective

Another strategy for introducing spatial depth evokes the empirical observation of volume in space. Perspective is a system for describing volumetric structure that replicates an optical distortion (parallax), resulting from the eye's curvature and how the brain interprets it—as a narrowing of an object's edges towards each other as the object recedes in space.

A designer mimics this distortion by extrapolating imaginary lines from the foremost edges of an object to an imaginary point located on a horizon (which may be explicitly drawn or implied simply for reference). These lines establish a diminishing progression in the sizes of volumetric structures from near to far. Perspective may be created around a single vanishing point /**A, C**/, or two for greater complexity and nuance /**B**/. In either case, the position(s) of the vanishing point or points affects how extreme the angular convergence from foreground to horizon may be. As a vanishing point moves from the outer edges of an image's format toward its center—or, as two vanishing points come closer together along the horizon—the more extreme the convergence /**B**/, and therefore the greater the distortions of both objects and perceptual space.

D Light generally moves in one direction, illuminating one side of a volume and casting the other side in shadow. /

E Light distributes specific shadows and reflections. /

D+E Paone Design Associates *United States*

Achieving Depth through Shading

Introducing light and shadow to articulate form further enhances viewers' perception of depth. Clearly, light may be explored in a way that directly corresponds to its effects in a physical environment. It moves outward from a source in all directions, but typically a compositional space defines only a small portion of an environment—this means that, most often, light will appear to move in only one direction within an image /**D**/.

Light reflects, refracts, diffuses, and produces a number of effects on various surfaces; shadows also appear in different ways, too numerous and specific to enumerate. Most objects and figures will exhibit general effects of light /**E**/: highlight, cast shadow, form shadow, and reflected light.

Light may also be ambient or atmospheric, without a clearly defined source. The range of values in such a lighting situation will tend to be limited— the shadows won't be quite as dark, or the highlights quite as bright. A dim light source, as opposed to one of great intensity, will similarly diminish overall value contrast.

Light within nonpictorial images /**F**/ is less concerned with empirical aspects of describing form, and more about the luminosity within the visual environment. This luminosity is typically ambient; as the surface (most often white) is hidden by accumulating marks and revealed through erasure or obliteration, lighter areas swell and diminish, expand and focus sharply. A designer may also find it compelling to experiment with volumetric light effects /**G**/ and "cast shadows" to reference such observable effects to assimilate the abstract experience or to suggest narrative.

F A luminous quality in a nonpictorial image /
Ashley Simmons, UArts *United States*

G Volumetric light effects add visual interest and may suggest meaning. / TSTO *Finland*

Establishing Depth in Reduction

Perceptual depth is important for offsetting the intrinsic flatness of reductive images, although it's challenging to achieve, given these forms' inherent simplicity and, oftentimes, their purely positive/negative form language. Volumetric structure and even perspective /**A**/ may be used at times, reduced to a diagrammatic level; and exploiting an understanding of light and its action on objects is especially helpful for clarifying reduced form relationships and suggesting volume.

In reductive images, mass and weight play the most important role in creating depth, enhanced by changes in value if needed. Heavy linear or mass elements, as noted, will typically advance, while lighter or thinner ones recede. In a translation or icon /**B–E**/, modulating from heavy to light is a common strategy for expressing depth by describing a form's volume as affected by light, suggesting gradation from foreground to background. Overlapping forms, especially while reversing their conventional scale and value relationships, also helps distinguish foreground and background.

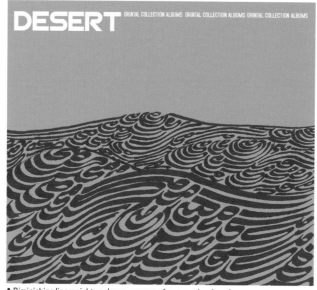

A Diminishing line weights enhance a sense of perspective; heavier elements advance toward the viewer. / Mehdi Saeedi Studio *Iran*

B Larger masses modulate into smaller ones as they articulate forms in this translation. Also describing some forms in negative (figure/ground reversal), creates a sensation of the subjects coming forward from a dark area into a light one. / Steff Geissbuhler, C+G Partners LLC *United States*

C Thinning and thickening lines suggests volumetric structure in reduction. /

D A buildup of density in specific areas creates the illusion of clusters in a foreground position. /

C+D STIM Visual Communication *United States*

E Two weights of line help dimensionalize these icons. / PCD Estudio de Diseño *Argentina*

Typographic
Color,
Typographic
Depth

JUAN**NAAB**®

At the extreme level of reduction in type forms, depth again becomes apparent through weight changes among strokes /**F**/ and the intervals between strokes and counters (the spaces between and around the letters' strokes). Illusory depth also is perceived through changes in proportion and suggested value /**G, H**/ that comes about through differentiation in the sizes, weights, leading, and line- or column-widths or depths—what is called "typographic color," an attribute of type that is very much like chromatic color, except that it depends solely on relationships of value and rhythm. Value in type may be manipulated by literally changing its color, whether in terms of gray tints or hue changes /**H**/; and by spacing it more loosely or more tightly /**I**/ to achieve the appearance of lightness and darkness.

Proportion (overall verticality or horizontality) also influences typographic space. Vertically shaped blocks of types, or columns, usually assert themselves more aggressively because vertical forms are perceived as more energetic—and so, with respect to text blocks that are wider than they are deep (or groupings of columns with horizontal emphasis), vertical columns will generally appear to occupy foreground space /**H**/. It's entirely possible to also use fundamental laws of perspective in organizing type within a page format or other space /**I, J**/, grouping smaller units in closer proximity to a "vanishing point" near a horizon to set them farther back, and larger or more expansive units outward from that point to "draw them forward" in space.

F Weight changes, and modulation of a circular enclosure, introduce depth. / PCD Estudio de Diseño *Argentina*

I Spacing changes and overlaps suggest planar perspective. / Sung Jin Park, School of Visual Arts *United States*

G Weight and size differences establish the illusion of depth. / Kevin Harris, School of Visual Arts *United States*

J Text blocks and columns stepped progressively in size and weight also suggest perspective. / STIM Visual Communication *United States*

H An effect of orientation—horizontal appearing to recede, vertical appearing to advance—is augmented by changes in tonal value. / Eun Young Kim, School of Visual Arts *United States*

Drawing / for Graphic Design

Discovery

Universal Principles
Fourth Principle: Perceptual Space

A The apparent spatial position of colors changes with hue: yellow advances; red is stationary; blue recedes. / Studio Astrid Stavro *Spain*

The Spatial Attributes of Color

Color dramatically affects perceptual space. Every strategy for introducing spatial depth in black-and-white changes, one way or the other, once color appears as a variable. Color exhibits a number of spatial properties. First, we perceive the three primary colors as existing at different depths in space /**A**/, a function of how our brains interpret the wavelengths of these colors. Red appears stationary at a middle distance and seems to sit on the surface of the picture plane, neither in front of nor behind it. Blue appears to recede behind the picture plane, while yellow appears to advance. Following this logic, cool colors appear to recede while warm colors advance.

Applying color to the elements of a drawing will immediately alter their apparent spatial locations /**B**/. The intrinsic relationships in a black-and-white composition might be exaggerated—applying warm (advancing) hues to foreground elements and cool (receding) hues to background elements—or made purposely ambiguous by reversing this logic. Distinctions in saturation and, especially in value /**C**/, also provide powerful potential for enhancing or contradicting apparent spatial relationships. Value works much the same way as previously discussed. Saturated colors generally advance and neutrals generally recede. That said, color relationships are mutually affective; altering one relationship will potentially change the behaviors of the others /**D**/.

B Color typically enhances the spatial qualities suggested by value and scale. / Jorge Alderete *Mexico*

C Value is arguably color's most powerful attribute with respect to illusory depth; compare the foreground separation of elements at left (greater value difference) with that to the right (less value difference). / Gee+Chung Design *United States*

D Altering the chromatic attributes of any one element in a composition will change its spatial relationship relative to other elements. / STIM Visual Communication *United States*

Relationships of hue, value, temperature, and saturation can quickly change not only the presence and apparent spatial depth of elements, but also the sequence in which they are perceived ("hierarchy"). A designer may first look to value to enhance an existing hierarchy, replacing black and gray tones with similar-value colors. Altering this logic may result in very interesting spatial complexity, but also may reverse the hierarchy. Within imagery this isn't necessarily a problem; in typography it may be catastrophic.

Although value greatly influences the sequence of perception, it is ultimately the totality of temperature, saturation, and value differences (or similarities) among form elements and background that the designer must consider. Form elements (or, forms and field) that closely share attributes will appear to join closely in space; the eye is likely to group such elements or proceed from one to the other more rapidly, meaning these elements will appear more hierarchically

E The element which is most different in its attributes will typically appear to advance because it calls attention to itself; in this case, although black shows greater value contrast with the background than do the saturated forms, black and the background are both also desaturated; the yellow-orange forms advance because they are different in two ways. / Mehdi Saeedi Studio *Iran*

F While the sky remains cool overall, helping establish its background position, variations in warm hues play with the spatial properties of red and yellow for interest; progressively darker values enforce this background to foreground ordering. / Sean Ryan *United States*

related. The greater the difference in each form's attributes (and the more attributes appearing to change), the greater their spatial separation /**E**/.

Establishing mutually supportive progressions in color attributes among forms—for instance, from cool and light value (in the background) to warm and dark (in the foreground)—tends to clarify and exaggerate their spatial ordering /**F**/. This strategy, which extrapolates the basic syntactic concept of limiting a palette (see page 35) is exceptionally helpful for ordering complex material.

Complicating the designer's task is composition: all the strategies discussed must also account for the relative scale and position of elements. As a form increases in size, its spatial presence will become more pronounced; the closer two forms are to each other, the more likely the viewer is to link them sequentially; both conditions will disturb whatever color logic the designer has imposed upon them. The challenge of integrating all these variables for a cohesive optical sequence can be appreciated in the examples to the right, in which students attempted to control color relationships so that a group of numbers would read in their proper sequence /**G, H**/. Both succeed using very different palettes, but similar strategies—the first being to create the greatest overall difference between the number 1 and all other material, and then to establish a progression in attributes among the remaining elements, adjusting for problems that arose because of size or position.

It is also easy to see that as the relative color attributes of type and background change, so do their apparent spatial relationships, along with legibility. Contrasts in hue and temperature help create clear separation, as does a strong contrast in value. As the value of a background's color comes closer to that of the type sitting on top of it, there is a loss of visual separation and, therefore, of legibility.

G A dramatic difference in temperature and value establishes a focal point; more subtle, analagous shifts in cool temperatures create a progression. / Yoojung Kang, School of Visual Arts *United States*

H A similar strategy as used in G pits the warmest and darkest element against a group in which value, relative to the background, slowly diminishes. Note the number 2 is lighter in value than the 3 to counteract the presence of its size. / Angela Pulice, School of Visual Arts *United States*

Message and Metaphor: Creating Narrative with Drawing

The ultimate purpose of a drawing is to communicate ideas and information. The very choice of drawing as a method of representation is loaded—an idea clearly dissimilar from that of choosing photography.

Form language and gesture, structure, positive/negative interplay, and spatial affect all contribute to interpretation. A designer may look to every geography of drawing, in both major territories; while a particular method will prove the most compelling for a given message, one may convey nearly any idea with any approach.

Pictorial drawings emphasize the content of their subject matter /**A–D**/, telling stories about that which they depict. Even if naturalistic, or nearly so /**A**/, they will communicate narratives that may be highly symbolic or metaphorical. This attribute is radically exaggerated as their representational qualities migrate toward stylization. Reductive iconography is consciously analytical, suggesting the symbolic, especially when subjects from disparate contexts are juxtaposed /**B**/; or when pictorial material appears to be influenced by nonpictorial or typographic messages /**C**/ or vice-versa /**D**/.

Nonpictorial drawings /**E–H**/ communicate with no less clarity or power (possibly more) given their inherently elemental language and their ability to tap into the vast emotional and associational reserves of the subconscious—drawing from individual memory /**E**/ as well as collective or communal graphic narratives that attend culture /**F, G**/ and socialization /**H**/.

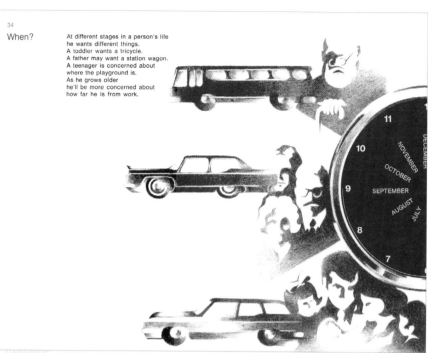

34

When?

At different stages in a person's life he wants different things. A toddler wants a tricycle. A father may want a station wagon. A teenager is concerned about where the playground is. As he grows older he'll be more concerned about how far he is from work.

A Relatively naturalistic pictorial images in this workbook page detail that discusses goals at various stages of life carry symbolic content. / Steff Geissbühler, C+G Partners LLC *United States*

B Pictorial icons, ranging from neutral to loaded with meaning individually, create interwoven narratives as a result of their grid-based juxtaposition. / Methane Studios *United States*

C A stark, graphically reduced female figure shows literal disfigurement in its face—and is metaphorically disfigured by the aggressive interruption of the headline. / Un Mundo Féliz *Spain*

D Symbolic elemental icons connote energy and freshness in branding a Japanese school for the study of Chinese. / SIN [Yoshisada Nakahara] *Japan*

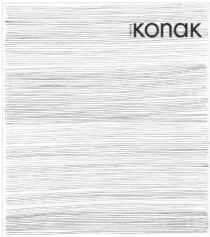

E The deceptively simple crayon drawing used to capture the theme "Childhood" for a magazine cover trades on universal memory. / Aylin Önel *Turkey*

F A dynamic collage of drawn type, symbols, and textures provide a kinetic, layered, urban, and branded context to resonate with members of snowboard culture. / {ths} Thomas Schostok Design *Germany*

G A scratched type treatment, reversed from black, conveys the materiality and luminosity of film, as well as the gritty quality of the genre—a shared cultural understanding. / Jee Song, School of Visual Arts *United States*

H Textural effects (glossy, metallic type forms against a corroded, industrial surface), create an urban context and suggest process; hand-scrawled notations convey the specific process of musical composition and creativity. / Studio Apeloig *France*

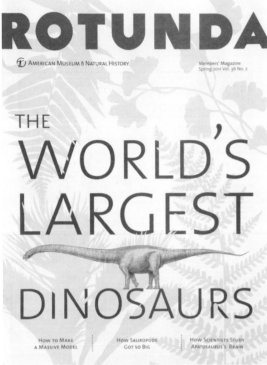

ROTUNDA
AMERICAN MUSEUM & NATURAL HISTORY
Members' Magazine
Spring 2011 Vol. 36 No. 2

THE WORLD'S LARGEST DINOSAURS

HOW TO MAKE A MASSIVE MODEL | HOW SAUROPODS GOT SO BIG | HOW SCIENTISTS STUDY APATOSAURUS'S BRAIN

A The naturalistic illustration of an unavailable subject makes it realistically present. At the same time, relevant historical context is suggested by the choice of vegetation, and the reversal of scale calls attention to the idea described by the headline. / Hinterland *United States*

B Audiences will usually project symbolic meaning (here, illumination as hope) on literalsubjects; the lightbulb here also captures the terrifying instability of the earthquake commemorated by this poster. / The Luxury of Protest *United Kingdom*

Subject Selection and Editing

Even though photographs are often highly mediated—their subject matter being extremely selective and manipulated—drawing affords the designer an even greater control over pictorial narrative.

The first strategy is the designer's choice of subject for representation: its content. It may be literal or illustrative (showing, denotatively, what accompanying text is discussing), even if the subject exists only in fantasy or fiction, or for which there is no physical source on hand—for example, subjects from early historical periods /**A**/. Or, the subject's content may be symbolic (even if depicted naturalistically) communicating ideas through connotation, simile, analogy, and association /**B**/.

Second is the designer's authority to edit. By recasting important elements and removing extraneous matter, the designer reinforces their importance, reduces distraction, and influences an audience's perception. Cropping, for example, may not only remove content, but dramatically change an image's relevance, as with a tightly framed portrait /**C**/, in which a face's confrontational quality suggests a narrative of psychological state over environmental context. Changing coloration, or imposing lighting or atmospheric effects /**D**/ on a naturalistic subject will immediately impart a mood that may be very different from that conveyed by the unaltered source.

C Tight cropping suggests involvement and, in the case of portraiture, a focus on the subject's state of mind. / STIM Visual Communication *United States*

D Atmospheric effects—in this case, introducing a soft haze and diminished contrast—can dramatically change mood. / Paone Design Associates *United States*

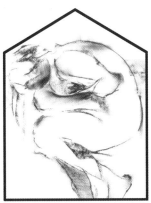

E The figure is governed, or influenced, by the enclosing frame; its posture may lead viewers to perceive this relationship as protective or threatening. / Clint Sorenson, UArts *United States*

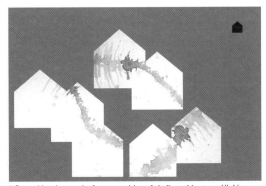

F Group identity results from repetition of similar subjects and linking by a gestural form; opposition results from visible difference. / Jennifer Betz, UArts *United States*

G Viewers construct complex narratives from minimally available information; the icon's lack of completion, however, is what allows a viewer to interpret the juxtaposition in numerous ways. / Kristen Isenberg, UArts *United States*

Extreme editing occurs in diagrammatic drawings that juxtapose subjects from different contexts. Each communicates its own identity before the viewer constructs new meaning from their interaction. Side-by-side juxtapositions typically create parity in meaning, especially if the two subjects are similar in size or shape. Juxtapositions in which a subject frames another /**E**/ suggest that one creates, causes, governs, or influences the other; the specific nature of each element's depiction informs the viewer's interpretation of any such relationship, and whether positive or negative.

Juxtaposing repetitions of one subject invites comparison. In the example at left /**F**/, the cluster of similarly treated subjects implies a shared condition, while the smaller, isolated subject opposes it.

Inserting an image into another situates the former within a chosen context and so alters both. Seeing the roofline of a house (identifiable, but incomplete) in a forest setting /**G**/ may suggest being at home with nature, or perhaps a narrative about pioneers building in unspoiled territory. As always, meaning perceived in a juxtaposition depends on how the

H The small icon, no longer grounded (and vulnerably transparent) is violently affected by its context. / Kay Gehshan, UArts *United States*

I Contrasting **H** above, this house is a strong shelter in the face of a similarly turbulent context. / Les Johnson, UArts *United States*

J Formal parity between judiciary columns and caskets hybridizes and conflates two cultural concepts and implies a causal relationship. / Pettis Design *United States*

components relate, not solely their subjects. Two images here /**H, I**/ juxtapose fundamentally similar subjects, but with radically different effect.

Yet another juxtapositional editing strategy, hybridization, conflates subjects' identities and individual meanings by merging shared forms or, sometimes, creating the perception of a new subject. Although the act of hybridization itself will imply some new understanding to be perceived, hybridizing subjects whose forms are not only similar, but whose respective content is already related /**J**/ will only be an asset with regard to delivering a compelling message.

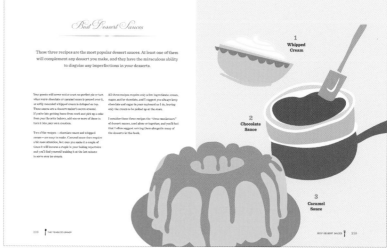

feel the future.

A In choosing a roughly brushed language and pronounced back and forth gesture, the designer conflates the client's product with the source of its power and the environment it protects. / STIM Visual Communication *United States*

VELVET PAINT & CO

B Simplification gives strength and authority, while an imposed texture alludes to product and brand metaphor. / Tess Wielozynski, SUNY Purchase *United States*

C An imposed line syntax introduces sensuality. / The Luxury of Protest *United Kingdom*

Stylization and Manipulation

The issue of the form language itself becomes increasingly prevalent as a designer leaves empiricsim behind in favor of stylization or reduction. The dominance of form language over naturalism is the very definition of stylization. A stylized image may refer very directly to the physical truths of its source subject— as it does in the brochure spread about wind power /**A**/ and the paint company logo /**B**/—but even those which respect these physical truths exhibit a dramatic degree of mediation.

Stylized images need not be distillations, of course. To impose a particular form language on a subject as an overlay or conceit—whether the form language is clearly intended to create a concrete, relational message in support of the drawing's subject, or is decorative— is entirely possible. Decorative stylization may, contrary to a Modernist view, contribute meaning through its form /**C**/.

D Stylization may lend a cultural, historical, or—in this case—nostalgic context, especially if the designer's approach to stylization evokes a commonly recognized period style. / AdamsMorioka, Inc. *United States*

Such conceits in the form language are connotative and, potentially, symbolic— they address a specific audience with the agreed-upon meanings of such styles established by their subculture, as with the nostalgic reference imparted by the images in the cookbook /**D**/. Decoration is itself a message, and the kind of decoration will, as with any form language, result in a particular interpretation.

E This frame from a nature program's promotional ad exploits stylization to help explain the program's content. / STIM Visual Communication *United States*

In a stylized or reductive pictorial drawing whose form language synergistically describes its subject's structure, the formal structure is pre-eminent. The way the designer manipulates the form language to ensure recognition may also contribute augmented, relevant understanding—for example, the geometric simplification of a fish's scales /**E**/ not only captures a fundamental aspect of their structure and surface, but suggests a kind of armoring.

Purposeful, dramatic alteration of a base subject may give rise to powerful, complex narratives that obviate the need for explanatory text /**F–M**/. An extremely neutral, identifiable subject (for instance, the Earth, visualized by its continents) may take on exceptionally compelling visual qualities and impart stirring, emotional understanding that far exceeds what is offered by a photograph.

F–M The effects of manipulation on a neutral, commonplace image can be startling, offering tremendous opportunity for rich and immediate communication. / Estudio Diego Feijóo *Spain*

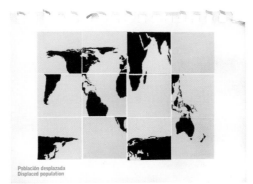

Población desplazada
Displaced population

F Displaced population: ordered fragmenting

Población excluida
Excluded population

G Excluded population: obscuring

Sequías
Droughts

H Droughts: texturization

Solidaridad
Solidarity

I Solidarity: repositioning

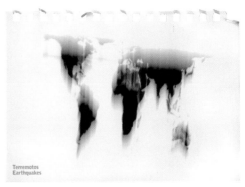

Terremotos
Earthquakes

J Earthquakes: shaking and blurring

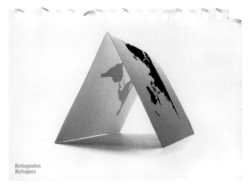

Refugiados
Refugees

K Refugees: iconic allusion

Hambrunas
Malnutrition

L Malnutrition: form distortion

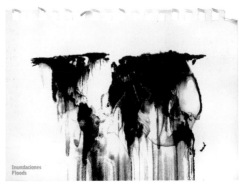

Inundaciones
Floods

M Floods: drips and washes

Allusion, Symbol, and Metaphor

Trading on audience's cultural, political, historical, and personal experiences by merging or altering commonly agreed-upon symbolic or allusive meanings is a strategy to which designers may turn to deliver startling messages—startling and eminently powerful because they not only tend to necessitate unique inventions of form but, more importantly: because they draw upon deeply-ingrained under-standing, memory, and social themes, provoke exaggerated responses that resonate deeply in a target audience.

The possibilities are endless.

Allusions are references to subjects or experiences made without calling them to mind explicitly, a signification which is also called indexing. Visual forms or styles associated with particular events or cultural contexts may be invoked to create a form language that makes this connection for the viewer—whether of a vernacular experience with a common game /**A**/, reference to a cultural festival and its emphasis on death /**B**/, or period styles that pin social, historical, or philosophical meaning to the message for a contemporary audience /**C**/.

Symbols are signs that hold meaning that comes to be understood through socialization, an "agreed upon" signification in which the members of a social group participate. Symbols have ritual depth and significance; simply juxtaposing certain ones /**B,D**/ or constructing one using other, equally symbolic or allusive

A A common metaphor for dominance and role reversal, applied to portraits of romantically involved artists Frida Kahlo and Diego Rivera. /Carbone Smolan Agency *United States*

B An icon representing the Mexican Day of the Dead—though subject and decorative allusion—is given new meaning through the substitution of a notorious logo. / Un Mundo Féliz *Spain*

C Pop-cultural styles situate a communication—and its subject—in a particular time, place, and social context. / Modern Dog Design Co. *United States*

D A group of symbols influences each others' meanings, all characterized symbolically by the foreboding icon from which they emanate. / Studio 360 [Vladan Srdic] *Croatia*

E The hyacinth, a symbol of rebirth in the Persian new year, takes on a menacing quality when constructed of grenades. / STIM Visual Communication *United States*

images /**E**/ is bound to elicit a dramatic response by virtue of association.

Visual metaphors are messages of parity; a subject, cast using a particular form language, becomes equivalent with the source of that language and so incorprates whatever narrative attends it /**F–I**/— whether the presence of the sinister in the everyday /**F**/, the personification of local heritage and noble cultural aspirations /**G**/, a provocation inherent in personifying the audience as unwitting prisoners /**H**/, or the surrealism of a peeling, melting letterform that evokes a painter's iconic work /**I**/. Viewers may appreciate a metaphor after being directed toward it by some symbol or allusion as a starting point: returning to the playing card /**A**/, one understands the card's metaphor only after appreciating its reference to the contentious relationship between two artists.

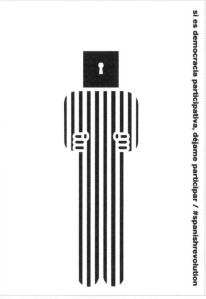

H The poster's headline makes a statement about participating in the democratic process, but the replacement of forms with others suggests that participation may not be forthcoming. / Un Mundo Féliz *Spain*

F Revealing a word that suggests concealment through changes in typographic color—within text that is styled to appear computer-generated—alludes to intrigue or identity theft in a digital environment. / Topos Graphics *United States*

G Period styles of pictorial representation and calligraphic typography allude to a winemaker's heritage; the character depicted, a Medieval bishop, becomes a metaphor for culture and craftsmanship. / Massimo Pollelo: ABC Atelier *Italy*

I The peeling type form is surreal by itself; it also refers to an iconic painting by Salvador Dalí, the subject of this poster. / Martino *Argentina*

Storytelling in the Abstract: Messages through Form, Structure, and Rhythm

Nonpictorial drawing expresses meaning through the purely visual qualities of abstract forms. While interpretations of abstract imagery are often emotional, a quality used by designers subliminally to underpin more concrete imagery, abstract form languages may be used independently to communicate any number of concrete subjects, not only intangible ones. To accomplish this, designers use their knowledge of viewers' universal responses to visual stimuli that stem from common human experience: Asked to project meaning onto a simple geometric form—a circle—all viewers will offer the same responses: the earth, sun, or moon; unity, continuity, the cycles of nature—all that which is organic. In contrast, the universal responses to a square will be associations with the intellectual or man-made: shelter, order, mathematics, and so on /**A**/.

Ever more specific interpretations deriving from cultural context, individual experience, and emotional life compound the common and universal. Every level of interpretive response mutually colors the others. For instance, among a group of design students tasked with abstractly representing a primal emotion such as rage /**B**/ or an opposing emotion, comfort /**C**/, the form languages that result will be individual (shaded by personal interpretation), but will still all exhibit one archetypal identity (informed by the universal). The more primal an intended message, the more common will be its form language and its reliability in communicating to a diverse audience. The more intangible or culturally specific a communication, the more variable will be its form language, and the fewer reliably similar interpretations.

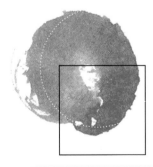

A The simple circle and square embody a wealth of narratives all by themselves. /

B A telling sample of visual responses to the emotion "rage." Top to bottom:
Kei Tsukuhara, Parsons: The New School
Alan Tung, School of Visual Arts
Carlos Baquero, Parsons: The New School
Hayan Chong, Parsons: The New School
United States

C Equally informative, a sample of responses to the feeling "comfort." Top to bottom:
Alan Tung, School of Visual Arts
Kei Tsukuhara, Parsons: The New School
Hayan Chong, Parsons: The New School
Kelly Chew, Parsons: The New School
United States

The beginning point for nonpictorial narratives is the form language established by the mark and the shapes that grow out of them in accumulation. Meanings communicated by the identities of the form language's syntactic elements may vary from the elemental, biological, and organic, to the intangible, emotional, and psychological; and even the concrete and prosaic. In the context of a communication system—for instance, a series of DVD packages—a language of linear, geometric images /**D**/ evokes narratives specific to the respective films.

Forms acquire new meanings as a result of their gesture; how they participate in spatial and structural relationships; and how they share or oppose each other's mass or textural characteristics. More so than in pictorial images, structure and positive/negative rhythm influence viewers' construction of meaning. Structure, in providing a basic framework, sets up primary conditions of overall energy—vertically-emphasized structure imparts energy and confrontational quality, while horizontally-emphasized structure results in a restive, passive quality. Grids suggest order; the behavior of elements on that structure will convey a specific meaning /**E**/. Lines, rhythmically grouped, may signify sound; organized in decisive patterns and masked into arcing shapes, the general meaning of sound or vibration may be directed to the specific meaning of music /**F**/.

E The behavior of the dots—coalescing on a grid—conveys the idea of orderly assembly. / The Luxury of Protest *United Kingdom*

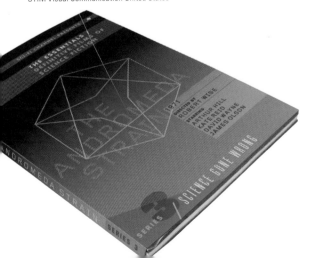

D In one series of DVD covers, ellipses in different configurations refer to extraterrestrial encounters (above); in another series, angular configurations suggest molecules and dangerous science (below). / STIM Visual Communication *United States*

F Line rhythms of varied densities, arranged to create rising and falling, arcing gestures, communicate a sense of vibration, sound, and constructed music in this identity for a digital music producer. / Hort *Germany*

Gesture, rhythm, and directionality enhance the perceptions of meaning already established by form language and structure.

The rhythmic pulse of positive/negative interplay delivers information about movement and energy. Rapid alternation between the two visual states increases a viewer's sense of activity, while the opposite occurs when fewer intervals are present, or are more generously spaced. Along with the degree of energy, the kind of structural interval and positive/negative rhythm both add information. Repetitive structures and proportionally related spaces create order and a sense of mathematical relationship, and may suggest the mechanical or intellectual. Progressions suggest evolution and process, or directional energy. /**A–D**/.

A A field of options for reaching a goal, all worthy of consideration

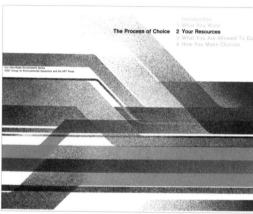

B Outside input narrows the number of options and isolates stronger from weaker.

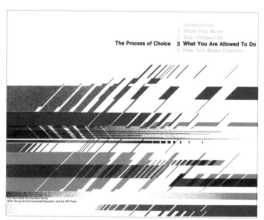

C A complication: consideration of (possibly unexpected) new conditions

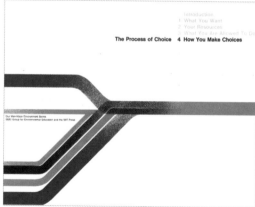

D Final decisions and streamlined, singularity of focus

A–D Changes in positive/negative proportion, rhythm, and directionality—even with a limited syntax, can communicate subtly shaded meanings, or complex intangibles. / Steff Geissbuhler, C+G Partners LLC *United States*

E The waving of tree branches in rain / Eva Surany, UArts *United States*

Through the combination of form language, structure, and positive/negative interaction, nonpictorial imagery may capture a feeling or represent a physical activity; it may connote a time or place. In place of pictorial subject, such narratives are often suggested by simplified allusions to physical experience, in effect, translating shapes or actions in a diagrammatic way. Linear, branching forms may evoke a tree or even suggest an entire orchard /**E**/, and arcing or swirling mass- and line-formations capture the influence of wind on branches; a repeating sequence of strokes and rippling forms may encapsulate the action of swimming /**F**/; masses compressing against each other and expanding may tell a story about breaking through a barrier. /**G**/.

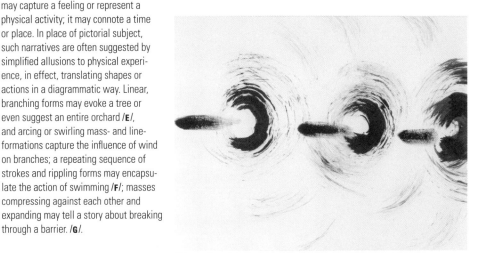

F The stroke and ripple of a swimmer / So Won Lee, UArts *United States*

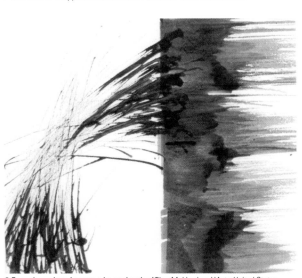

G Force brought to bear on a heavy barrier / Tina Mukherjee, UArts *United States*

H Logo for an environmental hiking trail conference / Kate Erickson, School of Visual Arts *United States*

The specificity of the form language is critical for delivering the right narrative in branding situations, where the viewer will rely primarily on its visual qualities to interpret a client's identity—not so much what service the client provides (although this may be suggested through allusion similar to those activities previously described) but a sense of its culture and context. Form and gesture may team up to communicate the efficiency or reliability of the client's services; they may establish reference to environment and cultural heritage /**H**/ (for instance, a mark that suggests pine forests and Native American textiles, moving in a rhythmic pattern that connotes exploration and expanding horizons).

British French German Swiss

Narratives in Typographic Form

A Typeface styles carry cultural and historical baggage, no matter how seemingly neutral.

C Extremely stylized type forms may take on the quality of images; in this case, shaping and details become architectural constructions. / Strange Attractors *The Netherlands*

Both pictorially and nonpictorially derived narrative strategies may be used to powerful effect in manipulating typography, whether found or invented. The intrinsic form language of a typeface, established by its stroke-and-counter alternation, weight, width, and details automatically carries nonpictorial narrative. These attributes first situate a typeface in a particular historical and regional context /**A**/; oldstyle typefaces are from the Renaissance of French, English, or Italian derivation, for example, while geometric sans serifs are typically from the twentieth century and most often of German or Swiss origin. Such contextual messages are subconsciously apparent to viewers; they will interpret a typeface's historicism and cultural associations as appropriate relative to its use in a particular communication /**B**/. The more stylized the type form, the more specific its message is likely to be, as its form language will impart only particular interpretations, whether organic, mechanical, or architectural /**C**/.

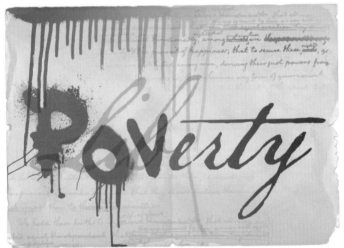

B Changes in typeface style here exploit their cultural baggage to communicate: the script, specific to Age of Enlightenment documents, is supplanted by spraypainted graffiti, suggesting an unforeseen, and unfortunate, turn of events. / Pettis Design *United States*

The rhythmic and stylistic attributes of a typeface drawing, however, usually trump historicism in communicating feelings or associations. Interpretations of elegance, romance, or sensuousness attend typeface styles that are lighter and more linear, express fluidity in the modulation of weight in their curves. Light, extended typefaces /**D**/ seem graceful, open, and calm, while bold ones read as aggressive, authoritative, or loud /**E**/. Oldstyle serifs lend an organic and human quality to communications; clean, detail-less sans serifs are often associated with science, mathematics, and the mechanical.

EgAajGnNtP

D An extended face seems more contemplative and restful, despite the joint and terminal details. / Ali Sciandra, SUNY Purchase *United States*

AgGtNaPjEn

E A bold, condensed typeface is perky, energetic, even aggressive. / Phil Wong, SUNY Purchase *United States*

When inventing a new typeface, or even a limited character set for a magazine masthead or film title, designers are free to manipulate the weight, width, positive/negative rhythm, contrast, and terminal details at will to impart those evocative characteristics that best deliver an intended message.

Distortions or deviations from archetypal form—away from "neutral" toward stylization—are invaluable resources for discovering new form qualities. An intricately constructed face with industrially-evocative details may augment the sense of iron architecture /**F**/; irregular contours and weight changes may give rise to a stone-like quality /**G**/; sharp, partially edited outlines may suggest the unknown in a difficult experience /**H**/. The specific tool or method used to make the forms will itself add its own language of effects—in concert with, even independent of, the designer's choices of proportion and formal detail. The diagonal linear pattern of a brush over a textured surface may lend a sense of connectivity, as well as environment, to a bold, authoritative face /**I**/.

Further the tool or method used may itself derive from some commonly understood source—a vernacular experience. Developing type forms that evoke the printouts of sales receipts or grocery store signage /**J**/ construct additional narratives through association.

F For a park reclaimed from an elevated train track / Phil Wong, SUNY Purchase *United States*

G For a rock-climbing organization / Andrew Scheiderich, SUNY Purchase *United States*

H For a cancer treatment/management center / Donald Brady, SUNY Purchase *United States*

I For a humanitarian, medical aid organization / Jaime Justen, SUNY Purchase *United States*

J The typography for this design event poster draws on the vernacular of hand-painted supermarket signage. / Under Consideration *United States*

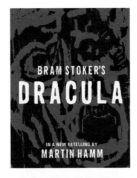

K Symmetry (top) is typically associated with classical or historical aesthetics and considered formal; asymmetry (bottom) usually connotes modernity and accessibility / STIM Visual Communication *United States*

The compositional qualities of typographic presentation follow similar conditions of effect with regard to structure and rhythm as do both pictorial and nonpictorial imagery. The layout of a headline or a body of text may very directly allude to a pictorial idea by replicating the shape or behavior of a physical object or environment. The structure of a text layout will also connote ideas related to its aesthetic strategy: a symmetrical layout will signify the classical, historical, and academic while an asymmetrical one will connote modernity /**K**/. Further, creating formations of columns of text that behave with a particular gesture or rhythm may visually signify ideas or subjects in support of the text, or simply shade or color the reader's interpretation of what is being read—much as they would with any other drawing language.

Narrative
Effects
of Medium

The choice of medium is profoundly
influential on pictorial narrative. This
influence is primarily an overlay of
emotional tone, expressed by the textural
qualities of the tool and its gestural
application. This may range from an
academic, journalistic, or studied feeling
/**A**/ to the strangely analytical /**B**/ as
methods are combined, to a more casual,
intuitive, or friendlier tone /**C**/ as softer,
or liquid, media are introduced. It is
sometimes the case that the medium's
presence is so pronounced that it
becomes the defining essence of the
form language—and so of subjects,
ideas, or associations to the subject
being depicted. A newspaper rendered
with dust /**D**/ relies on the medium for
its narrative about the ephemeral; in

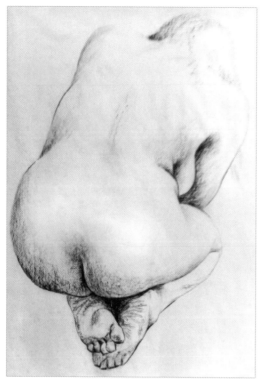

A Empirical images drawn with typically academic media, such as the
figure here is, in pencil, present an objective, journalistic quality. /
Fang Chen *United States*

C A light wash, escaping the confines of the linear figure,
communicates a lightness of being. / Richard Hart, Disturbance
South Africa

B The answer to an age-old question—"Which Came First?"—is visualized in all its ambiguity through
different media which all attempt to suggest dominance and physical manifestation, from analytical pencil
drawing to collaged objects and bold icon. / Steff Geissbuhler, C+G Partners, LLC *United States*

Drawing
/ for Graphic
Design

Discovery

**Meaning
and
Message:**
Creating
Narrative

E–J From fragility to the material translucency of glass, to distortion, to the sense of the glass's function, to double-vision, and beyond to agitated intoxication—a treasure trove of stories waits to unfold from the medium alone. / Erica Peterson, UArts *United States*

a second investigation, rendered with minute figures, it suggests the narratives of everyday life. Similarly, a delicate linear drawing of a wine glass /**E**/ or one made with a controlled wash as a translation /**F**/ reflects the quality of the glass's craftsmanship, as well as its lightness and fragility; another made with loose, spattered ink washes /**G, H**/ may suggest intoxication from drinking the contents, while an aggressively, roughed out image made with charcoal evokes a disturbed state of mind and the dangers of alcoholism /**J**/.

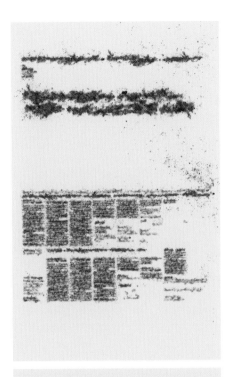

D An image of neutral content relies on two contrasting media to communicate different ideas. / Grafikum: Marion Mayr *Austria*

Communicating With Color

Last, but certainly not least, is the potential for color to communicate further narrative meaning. A designer may make use of color for this purpose in three ways, often in combination: to create associations with concrete experience; to evoke emotional response; and to code or organize components in layouts, both visually and conceptually.

Empirical associations between represented forms and either their colors in real life (what is called "local color") is a common strategy, but it is often more useful, and compelling, to apply color for the purpose of adding information; the potential of this strategy to create specific, or augmented, understanding is evident in the series of leaf studies /**A**/ and more so in the advocacy poster, where color interaction suggests a causal relationship /**B**/.

With color comes a variety of psychological messages that can be used to influence content. This emotional component of color is deeply connected to human experience at an instinctual and biological level; however, such properties also depend highly on a viewer's culture and personal experience. This subjective quality introduces the potential of widely varied interpretation /**C**/, so designers must proceed with caution—understanding the specific psychology of the intended audience is critical in attempting to achieve as universal a response as possible.

A Color relationships designed to specifically support different verbal concepts applied to the same image: complementary hue and extreme value difference (left); complementary, overall warm, close value (middle); closely analogous and nearly no value contrast (right) / Allanah Curran, San Diego State University *United States*

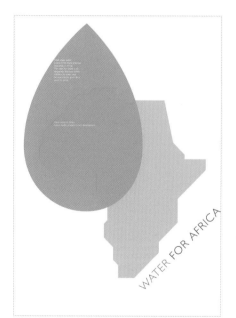

B A fundamental mix of two primary colors tells a very complex story concretely and with immediacy. / Paone Design Associates *United States*

C Color can be intangibly evocative of mood, and its interpretation is highly subjective. One might read the transition from somber, cooler tones at the right to warmer, lightr, more intense tones at the left as hopeful; or one may interpret the starkness and simplicity of the palette as melancholy. / Sean Ryan *United States*

RED

Stimulation / Arousal / Hunger /
Anger / Violence / Blood / Biology

YELLOW

Sun / Heat / Happiness /
Wealth / Clarity / Energy / Alertness

BLUE

Water / Sky / Calm / Quiet /
Dependable / Intellectual / Spiritual

VIOLET
Mystery / Compromise / Wealth /
Nostalgia / Drama / Magic

GREEN

Nature / Growth / Energy / Safety /
Freshness / Earthiness / Toxicity /
Illness / Finance / Prosperity

ORANGE

Vitality / Friendliness / Adventure /
Irresponsibility / Luxury / Quality /
Exotic

BROWN
Earth / Wood / Comfort / Timelessness
/ Value / Ruggedness / Hardworking /
Durability

WHITE

Authority / Purity / Cleanliness /
Clarity / Omniscience / Wholeness /
Spirituality / Restfulness / Quiet

BLACK

Unknowable / Dominance / Night /
Death / Nothingness / Outer Space /
Exclusive / Superior / Dignified

GRAY
Formal / Elegant / Aloof / Untouchable
/ Luxury / Technological / Precision /
Control / Competence / Noncommittal

Drawing
/ for Graphic
Design

Discovery

**Meaning
and
Message:**
Creating
Narrative

Along with color's spatial qualities—useful for organizing material compositionally in layouts or enhancing hierarchy in drawn forms—designers may also use color to code information. This strategy is typically employed to differentiate similar products in a line, or headlines from subheads, or labels from text, within typography; or to create associative links between a logo and coloration of backgrounds or image elements in a branding situation /**D**/.

D The logo's two-color palette is extended into such applications as business stationery and mailing materials shown here / Pettis Design *United States*

E A historical subject is situated temporally in the past—relative to the present time of the photographic image—by virtue of its light, neutral, stone- or sand-like coloration. / STIM Visual Communication *United States*

At other times, it may be used to characterize the content of individual forms, relative to others—as in the page spread from a brochure for a private school /**E**/. In this publication, the educational experience is framed as a kind of fulcrum between learning about historic cultural achievements and students' eventual application of that learning to future achievements of their own. Each grade is described as a developmental level corresponding to a particular historical achievement; contemporary images of student experience, presented as color photographs, connect readers with the school's present. In contrast, graphic translations of the related historical event—itself a decision that delivers narrative—are colored in a light, neutral beige, or stone hue, signifying the drawing's subject as existing in the past and governing the contemporary philosophy under discussion.

This section explores various drawing processes and their integration into design and production—including practical application through a series of selected real-world case studies.

Pro-
c/
...ess
es/

Drawings come to be through an intensive dialogue between intuition and analysis. The opening stages of their evolution initiates a period of play in which a designer first confronts unlimited possibility for subject matter, means of representation, and form language. In this initial investigation, the designer must leave preconception behind to test spontaneously the available options; to to evaluate what results from these first attempts; continually to add, subtract, alter, and rediscover; and eventually to resolve the forms that contribute to the fulfillment of the designer's purpose.

The process takes place through creating, obliterating, and reworking. Each idea, each form, each structure, as it manifests in the accumulation of marks and gestures, presents information to be incorporated or refuted. The process almost cinematically records its development for contemplation, accepting missteps as necessary components upon which to build the right elements. In that sense, the drawing process is very forgiving; it is assumed that accidents will happen and allows them to become part of the final work.

So often, designers who don't typically draw are paralyzed by the fear of not getting it right in one shot. It's important to recognize that the process of drawing defines "failure" as a clear direction toward improvement; only by seeing what isn't right can one then conceive of any possible appropriate alternatives. That recognition builds skill and then confidence in exercising it. The very idea of failure transforms into the idea of discovery, liberating designers to actively seek out the true depth of their creative sensibilities. This fear is also often compounded by the misconception that the purpose of drawing is to accurately reproduce observed reality. Considering the works of such fine artists as Alice Neel or Henri Matisse—which certainly are not accurate depictions but, seem somehow "right" because of the artists' gestural confidence and their decisive demonstration of universal principles— reveals the limitation of this idea.

The process itself, while more or less universal, is unique to every designer and, very often, to the context of each individual project. Some designers favor intuition over analysis and allow form to live as it comes into being, freely altering as it develops; others approach drawing from a highly structural and analytical standpoint, architecturally planning and constructing it in discrete stages. Only through experiencing the process can one define one's own methods and how these may be applied in any given situation.

Beyond the process of making the drawing itself, a designer must also integrate this act into the overall ideational process of design with regard to other design elements and the process of production. How the drawing comes about, its medium and method (whether physical or digital, or both) must be considered in the context of photographic and existing typographic structures or styles that may be used, as well as how these will be incorporated in the environment of the software being used to prepare the completed work for print or screen-based publication. Drawing, as will be seen, happens literally in image-making but also informs a conceptual process of manipulation in composition and content interaction at many stages during the development of a total project.

The Search: Ideation and Resolution

Many designers, despite the individuality of their approaches, tend to follow a staged process that leverages basic notions garnered from early formal training, even if they are very experienced. The fundamental idea of this process is to define the simplest aspects of the image first—the broad strokes, as it were—and then, through successive stages, to clarify and enhance more complex aspects with increasing specificity; in effect, building a rough foundation and then filling it in. Although this process may be described and understood intellectually as linear, it is usually reiterative and circular, meaning that it often necessitates stepping back as a result of going forward. Intuition guides the exploration; analysis of what results defines a particular direction; intuition returns to test variations; analysis guides the drawing toward its final form.

Modeling Creative Processes

The design process may be mapped using a few different models. As seen here, such models typically incorporate similar stages of inquiry that act in different relation to one another.

Exploration

The designer examines a range of different approaches to understand their respective potentials in the given context: visual brainstorming to discover possibilities.

Focus

Comparing the results of the exploration, the designer evaluates which possibility—or combinations thereof—may yield the most interesting and clearest direction for the visualization of the subject.

Construction

The designer integrates and "builds" the components of the form and composition, working with the attributes he or she has selected.

Testing

As the drawing takes shape, the designer experiments with variations—in scale, rhythm, position, and so on—to determine how these options confuse, clarify, or augment the constructed image.

Refinement

Not to be confused with "clean-up" or mere simplification, this stage concerns editing the form to clarify relationships—to bring them to a state in which they appear purposeful and somehow "complete."

Converging Tree

Visualized as a series of stages in which multiple alternatives are compared, and some selected for further refinement, in successive rounds; at each juncture, the choice of alternatives narrows until only one refined state remains.

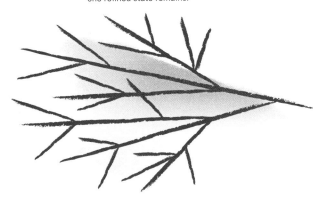

Focus Target

Similar to the tree model, each set of alternatives directs the designer to the next level of specificity; in this model, however, only one option is given focus at a time and future directions selected from testing and refining it alone.

Iterative Spiral

The path of exploration is generally linear, a path of gradual, simultaneous exploration and refinement that iteratively circles back to incorporate and test understanding from previous phases.

Staged Augmentation

A continuous, linear evolution in which each stage is formed directly from, and incorporates, the previous one.

Emphasizing Exploration

In some sense, every stage of the creative process is one of exploration, so it's important to really understand what it means: investigating, without preconception, as thoroughly and objectively as possible. To envision an end result and work only toward that usually results in a formulaic response, even cliché; it blinds a designer to potentially more inventive solutions. Cutting the exploration short before seeing an exhaustive diversity of approaches similarly denies comparison of all the options—the best one may be unknown. At every juncture, the designer must accept the exploration's results, whether these support an intended goal or reveal limitations, even failure: the point is to discover what is effective and discard that which isn't, rather than force the visual solution to conform to some predetermined desire. Being open to rethinking is critical. Try not to like anything in advance: find what works and then like it because it does.

Refinement and Resolution

The process of clarifying form language, compositional structure, spatial relationships, and so on works toward achieving a state of "resolution," a condition in which the drawing's visual attributes have become somewhat singular—indisputably embodying a particular quality such that their relationships seem "decisive," or that they appear intentional (two forms clearly aligning, for instance, or clearly not).

The work of refinement, or making specific editing decisions (such as smoothing a curve so that it actually appears to curve fluidly) should not be equated with trying to achieve the apparent "cleanliness" or reductive quality of an icon or translation. Gestural drawings that announce their medium explicitly may be highly refined; sometimes they show this process of refinement as "leftover" sketch marks, or elements that have been erased and redrawn, which become part of the resolved language. There is no right or wrong to be found in a form language's resolution. It simply exists one way or the other and, in the context of all its parts, seems the one best way to be.

Nonpictorial or pictorial?

Naturalistic or stylized?

Profile or head-on view?

Optical or isometric perspective?

Close-in or distant?

Horizontal, square, or vertical proportion?

Planar or volumetric?

Mass or line?

Field or singularity?

Focused or dispersing?

Energetic or passive?

Same or different size?

Repeating or always differentiated?

Curvilinear or angular?

Equidistant or not?

Parallel or diverging?

Aligning or not?

Gradual transition or abrupt change?

Touching or overlapping?

Staccato or fluid?

Consistent thickness or modulating?

Rising or falling?

Tight curve or open and steady?

Alternating or progressing?

Darker or lighter value?

Soft or sharp?

Diagonal or orthogonal?

Multihued or monochromatic?

Concentric or radiating?

A Early studies focused on line, complex detail, and regular positive/negative alternation.

Investigating contrasting line, mass, and scale detail revealed dramatically different options for identifying each kind of space, with different tools—pens, round and flat bristle brushes, sponges, and white paint—exaggerating these variables /A–E/.

As greater foreground mass accumulated from study to study /A, B, C/, the designer returned to incorporate flat, planar forms for the mountain face and then, subsequently, tested sharp, small-scale linear detail in both positive and negative /C, D/. Heavier textural and linear motifs /F–J/ later merged as evidence of discoveries made in previous studies.

Exploration for the Sake of Experience

Outside of an academic setting, it's a rare luxury to be able to study a subject in great depth. Even so, it's important for a designer to set aside a significant portion of a project's schedule to thoroughly investigate as many different possible approaches up front, even in a limited time frame. The experience thus gained ultimately allows the designer to make faster, more reliable decisions at later stages.

What is an adequate exploration?

The study of a mountain scene shown here, an academic exercise, nonetheless reveals the thoroughness and diversity of process toward which designers would be well advised to strive. This open-ended study began with illustrative, naturalistic attempts at differentiating the scene's three spatial areas (sky, mountain face, and landscape), but the designer knew intuitively that something more inventive was possible.

B Greater contrast in weight and positive/negative distribution

F Line weight concentrated on the mountain form and a textural sky area

I Another evolution exaggerates approaches seen in F, G, and H

C Lines become masses; finer detail emphasizes the mountain, now in negative.

G Combining strategies from studies such as A, E, F encapsulates a preliminary phase

D An evolution toward heavier marks overall, contrasted by reversed line detail

All images on this page spread:
Andrew Iskowitz *United States /*
Completed in the advanced class in graphic design, Basel School of Design: Peter Olpe, Instructor; Basel, Switzerland

E Maintaining weight contrast with overall heavier line motifs

H Again reversing strategies for weight distribution along with reduction in the mountain face

J A test of the planar mountain and reversed line detail combines with strategies in H.

K Less controlled gestural marking

N The light, linear foreground contrasted by heavy marking strategies from **D, H,** and **L**

Drawing
/for Graphic
Design

Processes

**The Search:
Ideation and
Resolution**

L Loose gesture with greater specificity of weight distribution

O Another variation merges sky and mountain, separated by loose reversed lines.

R A return to generally heavier marking with the simplicity of study **Q** but more foreground detail

M An evolving emphasis on the lightness of the foreground again integrates textural marks

P Further spatial merging tests negative detailing seen in studies **D** and **J**

S A late-stage study returns to generally even line weights throughout.

This exploration ended when the designer achieved what he considered an adequate level of understanding. Had there been a defined, practical goal, the designer would have a tremendous body of research on hand from which to make further, directed decisions to support it.

On the following pages, studies that inhabit varied geographies of drawing concisely demonstrate fundamental processes and their seamless integration of intuition and analysis.

Reaching such conclusions drove the designer to reverse the positive/negative logic, focusing weight in the sky and mountain contours while articulating the landscape with light-weight traces /**K, L, M**/. Seeing this possibility suggested another combination: returning to heavy, geometric shaping that joined sky and mountain in opposition to an open, primarily negative foreground /**N–R**/... and thereafter, uniform weight among all the parts of the image, whether dominated by line or mass, and in varying degrees /**S**/.

Q A dramatic simplification combines aspects from **K, N,** and **O**

Empirical, Volumetric Drawing / Timothy Samara *United States*

The author's goal was to understand and represent complex, structural relationships in architecture using a typically academic, perspective-based approach.

Exploration

Quick studies /A/ compared different vantage points and their effects on the overall proportion of masses, distribution of axes, and the relative clarity of understanding—what would be revealed or obscured at a given angle and how the structure would break the space of the format.

Focus

A relatively low, close-up viewing angle was chosen /B/ to emphasize the height of the vertical tower and horizontal thrust of the adjoining hall. The relatively symmetrical perspective of this view overcame potential confusion of more detailed structures inherent in the dramatic, asymmetrical perspective of other studies; setting the main vertical axis to the left of the format's center counteracted a potentially static quality in the symmetry.

Construction

Major axes and contours were drawn first /B/, establishing the compositional structure and defining the relative measures of heights and widths among the building's components. After the most general, large-scale measurements were verified through comparison, more intricate axes and contours /C/ were continually added to articulate subordinate structures.

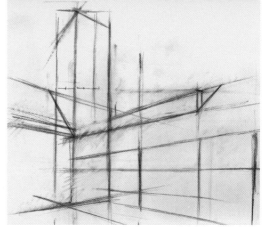

B The selected vantage point best reveals the building's structure; major axes break the format into dynamic proportions and establish rudimentary divisions between the building's components.

C Extrapolating axes provides reference for more complex divisions and helps confirm relative distances among forms.

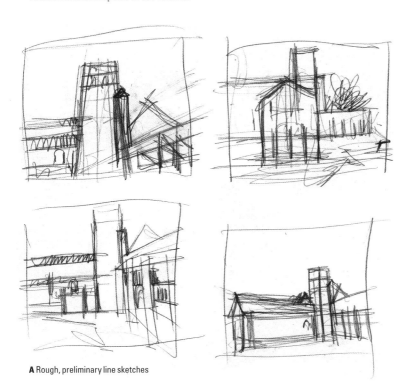

A Rough, preliminary line sketches

D Darker line weights confirm desired lines and begin to emphasize specific components; as weight builds within the tower structure, the designer darkens the buttresses at lower right as a counterpoint. Other embellishments acknowledge repeating, triangular axis connections.

Testing

Upon achieving a spatially-accurate armature of forms /C/, the designer tested additions of texture and deeper value /D/ to see which emphases helped clarify perception of space and structure, as well as lended dynamic rhythm and movement across the format. A light touch with the tool permitted removal of undesired emphases with a kneaded eraser, while still adding evidence of the drawing's evolution.

Refinement

Determining an overall progression of value (light to dark) along the vertical axes from exterior to interior created a dramatic visual pull inward. Rather than remove exploratory lines, the designer embellished some and used the eraser to hazily disintegrate others, exaggerating the sense of movement. Textural, diagonal strokes that follow the angles of the pitched roofs impart further movement, as well as help define their spatial relationships to vertical and horizontal planes. Erasing and slight smudging of specific axis lines helps resolve the unfinished exterior of the form by integrating them into the untouched areas of the format /E/.

E Further erasures at the left, extension and embellishment of seek lines along the tower, and controlled alternation of darkening and diagonal erasing all clarify value progressions and axis relationships.

Drawing
/ for Graphic
Design

Processes

**The Search:
Ideation and
Resolution**

Nonpictorial Language Study
Catherine Harvey *United States*

The designer's goal was to invent a series of non-pictorial images, unified by syntax and gestural logic, that would also demonstrate the language's versatility.

A One of many preliminary studies investigates combinations of syntax—here, overlapping open and closed squares.

B A later, preliminary study shows a progression toward a more specific syntax in simpler configurations.

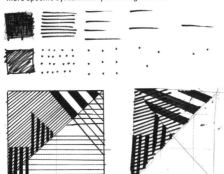

C In focusing, the designer visually "outlines" the variables with which to work: line weight, spacing, and geometric axes.

Exploration
The designer roughly sketched a number of form languages /A, B/. Many of these seemed too complicated; two examples show a greater restraint toward the end of this phase, focusing on a single form element (squares, versus lines) acting in varied relationships (overlapping versus separate).

Focus
Deciding to pursue a language of lines, the designer focused the study even more specifically by mapping out a family of weights and densities, along with a rotated 90° axis as a compositional device /C/.

Construction and Testing
Working with cut paper and casein paint (drawn with brush and ruling pen), the designer built each layered study as a kind of test, blurring two phases /D/. Among nearly 150 variations, she often repeated compositions, changing one element for comparison. She also explored versions based on a dark background /E/, ultimately discarding them as too heavy.

While testing a black marker, the designer noticed a new kind of staggered rhythm /F/; she expanded upon it, introducing differences in spacing and a heavier diagonal element—all aspects she had previously examined. But now, leaving behind the 90-degree axis afforded a looser, more fluid kind of geometry the designer felt was fresher and less rigid.

D Construction variations test the variables, further limited.

E An alternate series constructs the drawings in negative and with simpler conditions of overlap.

F What began by testing a marker suddenly revealed a new direction that was both simpler and more organic in rhythm.

G A controlled version of the new language, using ruling pen

K A refined composition merges aspects of **G, I,** and **J.**

Drawing
/ for Graphic
Design

Processes

**The Search:
Ideation and
Resolution**

Refinement

From among roughly 30 versions, the designer selected three /N–O/ whose basic compositions together suggested a progression from light to dark. She refined the language by defining a set number of line weights and spacing intervals and, from image to image, simplified the number of elements and weight changes in stark, even jumps.

H Visualizing the language with weight progression for greater contrast

L Fewer weight and spacing differences; lighter elements obscure dark ones

I Examining a greater diversity of angles, weights, and spacing

M Variables explored in **K** and **L** pushed to greater extremes

J Even more extreme contrasts combine with overlaps of light elements on dark ones for more ambiguous space.

Following this unexpected evolutionary leap, the designer continued simultaneous construction/testing of line compositions: comparing progressions in weight /H/ with alternations /I/; radically divergent angles /I, J/ with those angled more subtly /G, L/; dramatically varied weights /J/ versus similarity of weight /G, M/; differing overlap conditions between foreground and background elements /J, K, L/; and differing degrees of complexity and activity /G, I, L, M/.

N The final base composition

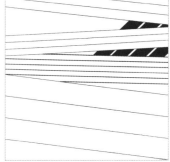

O Selecting these specific variations from among those available created a clear progression among variables to define a sequence: darker to lighter, dynamic to static, multiple weights to fewer, and increased obscuring.

Letter/Icon Logo Development
TacticalMagic *United States*

The goal was to design a logo for an animal rescue organization.

A A wall of extremely varied options produced by the design team explored pictorial and nonpictorial possibilities.

B This particular page of sketches, primarily typographic, shows a progression from complete word forms to the letter/icon concept that won out.

Exploration
A team of designers developed numerous concepts spanning a range of approaches: icons, symbols, letter marks, wordmarks, emblems, and combinations thereof. Rough images were reviewed together /A/ to compare their respective qualities; one concept was selected as capturing the essence of the organization's mission—a figure protectively holding a cat—in a bold, letter-based form /C/.

Focus
The process for the chosen concept began earlier /B/, already concentrated on typographic possibilities. In early sketches, the designer made a decision to limit the primary form to the important initial letters of the client's name and noticed that the shape of the letter's bowl and its counter could create a space for an icon. While several sketches examine the interaction of two figures, it became clear that a single figure/letter /C, D/ would make a simpler, more immeidate impression and still be meaningful relative to both of the Ps (people and pets) in the organization's name.

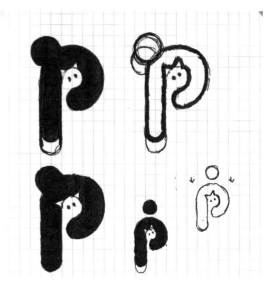

C The first constructions maintained the integrity of the *P* form most clearly.

D A rougher sketch organizes the forms with greater vitality and more clearly suggests the figural form.

Construction

The *P* form was initially built more conventionally, maintaining its strictly typographic structure and emphasizing the icon form created by the counter /C, D/. Adding a ball serif suggested the human figure more clearly, but resulted in an awkward gesture. Separating the ball as a dot freed the designer to position it above the *P* form; this strategy merged letter and figure more succinctly /D/ and produced a more stable, protective quality. The terminals of the letter were further rounded to correspond to the dot-like elements, as well as to soften the form, making it friendlier.

Testing

Once the basic form was constructed, the designer explored options for curving gesture to humanize the form. An extremely gestural version /E/ was eliminated because it weakened the letter's stroke weights and threw the figure's stability off balance. The two remaining alternatives—one with a straight vertical stem /F/ and the other with a continuously curving profile /G/—were compared together in a series of variations that explored the size and shape of the interior icon, ear shapes, and spacing.

F The designers tested shaping and proportions of the cat form's ears and head in the version with the straight vertical.

G The curved-arm version ultimately seemed more gestural and welcoming; it underwent the same extensive testing of the reversed cat form's ears and head.

E This refined, almost completely curvilinear version, was tested against earlier versions of those shown in **F** and **G**, but discarded as not legible enough.

Refinement

The curved version was chosen as friendlier and more protective; the ears of the cat icon were drawn turned to follow the gesture of the interior curve of the *P*'s main stem, itself straightened very slightly to reinforce the letter structure /H/. A sans serif with rounded terminals for the typographic component /I/ supports the curvikinear syntax of the mark and imparts a quietly playful quality.

Drawing
/for Graphic
Design

Processes

**The Search:
Ideation and
Resolution**

H The final mark offers strong gesture and contrast along with stability.

I The accompanying logotype consists of a rounded-terminal sans serif face.

Custom Display Face
Dana Tandoi, SUNY Purchase
United States

The designer's goal was to create an alphabet that would relate conceptually to an assigned client's mission—protecting waterfowl and wetlands.

Exploration

The designer determined early that conventional letter-drawing and tools /A/ might not yield as interesting or conceptual a face as she felt was needed, experimenting instead with other methods. Ink and toner, interacted upon by water /B/, as well as letters made from bread, ripped leaves, and grass /C, D/ introduced unusual contouring, along with narratives about the environment and eating habits of waterfowl.

Focus

One of the letter constructions made from heavier grass and twigs was inked, then printed and dragged /E/ to create a dramatically organic contour whose details also seemed reminiscent of bird tracks, legs, and beaks; the designer chose this direction as most interesting.

A Early study with a flat brush

B A drawing with felt pen subjected to water

C Forms made from ripped bread (top) and ripped leaves (bottom)

D Forms made from grasses proved overly light in weight.

E When inked and printed, the grasses yielded very interesting new forms.

F The designer made an extensive "library" of stroke and detail shapes, both by direct impression and dragging.

Construction

It quickly became clear that trying to construct the letters "at a stroke" (in one shot), would be nearly impossible—especially if also attempting to achieve proportional and stylistic unity among them. The designer instead created a library /F/ of printed forms—straight lines, angles, curves, splotches, and independent details—then scanned them at high resolution. She selected basic elements for the primary character shapes, cutting and pasting details in various positions to support each letter's structure.

Testing

Once both sets of uppercase and lowercas eletters were constructed, the designer began a process of altering individual stroke weights and placement of details /G/ to establish a consistent rhythm of variation among the letters for stylistic unity /H/.

Refinement

In the final stage of the alphabet's development, the letters spelling the client organization's name were ordered in various ways to compare rhythmic relationships; details were further enlarged or reduced, strokes thickened or thinned, and edges simplified for a stronger impression. The designer composed a sample configuration as a kind of logo /I/ in which changing letter sizes, baseline relationships, and the introduction of alternate characters create a lively, organic form.

G After roughing out each letter's structure with elements from the library, the designer adjusted the combinations, scales, and complexity of elements to create a consistent variation in texture across the alphabet.

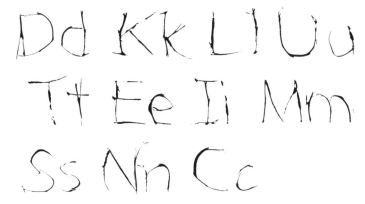

H The final set of uppercase and lowercase characters

I The designer constructed a logotype to experiment with the refined forms.

Stylized Translation
Lauren Reese, UArts *United States*

The goal was to represent the essence of an object's form and express its function.

Exploration
With translation, exploration distills the essential structure of a subject—in this study, a fish—as a unique, expressive form whose reductive syntax conveys a relevant idea. The designer began by attempting to understand the fish's basic attributes with studies from reference /A/.

A Photocopy of a photographic image used for reference

B The first quick study captured useful detail, but the form's structure was unconvincing and in need of study.

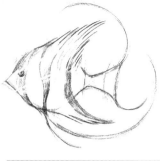
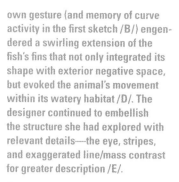

C Naturalistic study of the form

D Extreme reduction focuses on circular line movement and defining overall contour.

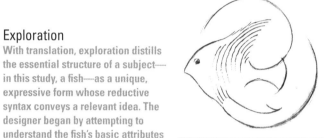

E Merging qualities of **A** and **B** with greater weight contrast in the lines

A first sketch with pen proved illustrative and demonstrated misperception of the subject's proportions /B/. Careful construction, comparing each part's relationship to others, resulted in an accurately naturalistic structure after in-depth study /C/. At the same time, the designer's own gesture (and memory of curve activity in the first sketch /B/) engendered a swirling extension of the fish's fins that not only integrated its shape with exterior negative space, but evoked the animal's movement within its watery habitat /D/. The designer continued to embellish the structure she had explored with relevant details—the eye, stripes, and exaggerated line/mass contrast for greater description /E/.

Focus
Having gained this understanding of the form at a more complex level, the designer focused on the basic mass of the fish's contour and the extension of the linear curves as the most fundamental expression of the form.

Construction
Working with casein paint and alternating between black and white, the designer composed the primary shapes /F/, adjusting the proportions of positive and negative shapes and the modulation of weight among the curves to arrive at a sturdy, generally resolved template for further development. With respect to the source subject's structure, and to enhance a sense of its typically forward movement, the lower fin's terminus was shifted to the left of that of the top fin; the lower curve curls back upward to optically flow into that of the upper fin; and the upper curve was weighted to pull the eye from the tail back into the form's origin at the left.

F The base form, constructed with black and white paint, then photocopied as a template for further study

Testing

The designer photocopied the constructed base and, again working back and forth between both black and white paint, altered details, weight relationships, and tested embellishments to the surface plane of the fish's body for detail that could bring visual contrast, as well as greater description, to the form:

textural motifs /G, H/ graduated from dark to light to suggest the fish's scales; stripes to capture characteristic markings /H–L/, visualized as progressions of line weights and as continuous lines that modulated in thickness.

G Heavier masses combine with textural surface activity

J Testing fewer curve elements in the body

M The final translation

H A test of the line pattern to help articulate surface and structure simultaneously

K Waving lines and greater mass in the face more decisively integrate parts

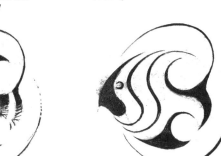

I Merging (and simplifying) the linear elements of **H** with the heavier masses of **G**

L Pushing and pulling the weights among lines and masses in the body and tail

Refinement

As a result of her tests, the designer found a language that was primarily linear, changing in weight and approaching planar mass at times, which would create rhythmic contrast and more cohesively integrate the large area of the body with more delicate structures. Articulating curved lines across the body's surface as waves /K, L/, rather than following the front curve established by the head /J/, added greater movement and continuity among the elements. Even the eye, for example, is linear, yet creates a perception of spherical volume while corresponding to the surrounding syntax.

Weight emphasis was pushed downward in the face, rightward in the lower fin, then upward out of the tail to ensure continuous optical circulation; the eye is encouraged to circle reflexively around the form, emphasizing the impression of the fish's movement in water /M/.

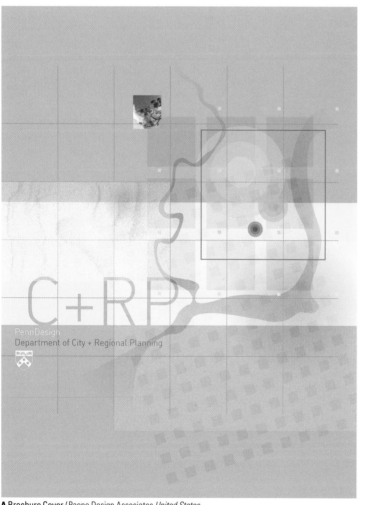

A Brochure Cover / Paone Design Associates *United States*

From Pencil to Mouse and Beyond: Integrating Drawing with Other Image-Making and Production

In a professional practice, so dramatically influenced by digital and photographic media, using drawing as an approach is challenging in many respects. There is, of course, an often-perceived disconnect between imagery that is generated by hand, with its characteristic roughness and gestural spontaneity, and what is slick, hard-edged, or photographic. Overcoming this disconnect is simply done by attuning the form language of the drawing to best correspond to that of other pictorial material, while considering the two simultaneously for how they will interact when juxtaposed. Corollary to this perception is another, that a drawn image must remain separate from digital and photographic forms as a kind of sacred element that can not influence, or be influenced by, the latter. Once a drawn image is brought into a digital environment—and further, given that drawing may be accomplished digitally and photographically—it affords a designer new opportunities for investigation and refinement, in which digital tools may be used to alter the original work, or the drawing hybridized with photographic elements as a totality.

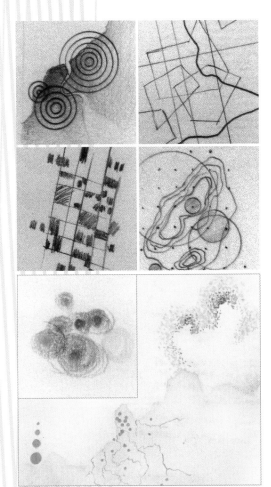

B Hand-drawn studies of visual languages derived from a study of geographical and survey maps at small scale, both in graphite and colored pencil

C A photograph of snow with grain enhanced and a charcoal tracing overlaid

D Translations of mapping syntax drawn with vector-based tools in a software program

E Vector-drawn translation of a local river

In this cover for a brochure promoting a university program focused on regional planning /**A**/, approaches that originated in research and sketching were translated into other media. The designer explored visual languages derived from mapping elements—topographic contours, spatial grids, and graph data associated with surveying—first in sketch form and then as vector elements /**B, D**/. A reductive translation of a river /**E**/, local to the university, was drawn in a software program. Population density images were simplified and re-envisioned as vector dots. A photograph of snow /**C**/, on the other hand—which imparted seasonality as well as a dual interpretation as a landscape—was used as a photograph; its textural contours and gestural rhythm clearly embody qualities seen in the designer's sketches, almost acting as a drawing as-is, but the designer enhanced it with an overlayed charcoal tracing. Together, these components—because of their identity as drawn images, but evolved through the respective media of their execution—integrate seamlessly in the realized cover.

Another, more practical concern is how to translate effectively a drawing digitally and to manipulate it with regard to production, specifically in print. Different methods yield not only varying degrees of finesse for desirable reproduction and an impact on file size, but also limitations and possibilities for layout, coloration, and printing techniques. Some methods are more appropriate for retaining fine detail and authenticity; others for keeping file size small, or when the designer intends to use it in a particular way. The nature of the drawing itself directs the designer toward best practices with regard to production, as its form language and composition do with regard to conceptual and visual unity in the final, designed expression.

Production
Mechanics

The first act of integration on a purely mechanical level is scanning. For drawings that will remain in their original form, or either will be reconstructed or form the basis of some further manipulation, scanning is the obvious first step in bringing the drawing into the production-focused phases of the design process.

Most flatbed scanners currently available in the mainstream market, at very reasonable prices, are capable of capturing images at extremely high resolution, usually far in excess of what is needed or even used by high-end imagesetters that create separations and make plates for printing. However, such high resolution capability—upwards of 3000 dpi—is still important to ensure the accuracy of the captured image, especially for textural, finely detailed drawings with extremely subtle variations in tonality.

The more information included in the scan of such images the better (for more subtle control during editing), even though much of this information will be discarded by the imagesetter during output. A scan resolution of at least 1200 dpi, possibly greater, is usually desirable.

A Comparison of an enlarged detail of the same image at different scan resolutions: 300 dpi (top); 600 dpi (middle); 1200 dpi (bottom)

When comparing a print-resolution (300 dpi) scan, with others at 600 dpi and 1200 dpi, respectively, you can easily see how much more minute textural detail is evident /**A**/. This textural detail, though very small, will help designers retain areas of very light value and delicate detail should they need to adjust the image's contrast and tonality levels in an image-editing program. Without this information, the potential to eradicate subtle areas may become a problem.

For drawings that will be used as a template to trace or remake with vector drawing tools, scanning at a very high resolution is also important. This is particularly true for highly refined translations and letterform designs /**B**/ where weight proportions, the fluidity of curves, and transitions between curved and straight forms are finessed to extreme tolerances. Scanning at a lower resolution—even at 300 dpi—is unlikely to capture the hair's-width changes in a letter's stroke weights, critical for optical balance; it is equally unlikely to accurately translate curves (especially very subtle ones), given that these are captured in an orthogonal grid of pixels; the more pixels available, the more detailed the curve translation.

B The information in a low-resolution scan (top) may not be sufficient to accurately trace subtle forms with vector drawing tools; note the detail that is present in a 2500 dpi scan of the same form (bottom) and its implication for the vector tracing.

Screen-based environments are infinitely forgiving and flexible when it comes to working with images— their low display resolution obviates the need for the pixel detail described above, and in terms of manipulation and display, anything is possible. Print, on the other hand, requires great attention not only to resolution, but also to the choice of file format so that images appear the right way when ink hits paper.

There are only two reliable file formats for images in a print context: the bitmap format (pixel-based, or TIFF) and the Postscript format (vector-based, or EPS). Each is used for specific purposes, and each has particular ramifications for production.

Bitmap files, or TIFFs, replicate continuous tone through changes in grayscale or chromatic value of pixels; this format is best suited for textural, continuous-tone drawings of a photographic nature.

The EPS format encapsulates the parts of an image as vector-drawn objects; it is best suited for reductive images because it can not typically render gradation without drastically increasing the file size; further, it describes contours as mathematical algorithms defined by point- and line-segments, and so usually enhances the fluidity of forms, especially curves. For these reasons, font drawings and logos are most often rendered in this (or a very closely related) format.

There are two basic kinds of TIFF format: one integrates numerous values (gray-scale, CMYK, or RGB), and the other is composed of only two values, black and white (bitmap TIFFs). The CMYK and RGB TIFFS /**c**/ can not be edited within page layout software, while grayscale /**D**/ and bitmap TIFFs may be colorized and manipulated by changing their blending modes. The bitmap TIFF /**E**/ is also transparent: while its black pixel content (the image positive) is opaque, its white pixel content is invisible. Only images of this format may be placed over objects below them and remain see-through. When converting an image from continuous tone (which must be of grayscale mode) to bitmap, the designer may employ different rendering options: the threshold option interprets gray values as being lighter or darker than 50 percent black and converts each accordingly, resulting in a high-contrast image; the halftone option allows the designer to specify a screen shape and resolution for a print halftone; the dithering options create halftones of randomized texture, rather than grid-based formations of dots or lines, which may appear more organic /**E**/. At high resolution conversions, the bitmap TIFF retains all the detail of the original, but also radically reduces file size.

C CMYK TIFFs render images in process color (top), used for printing; RGB TIFFs render color optically using light-based primaries (bottom) and often present printing problems.

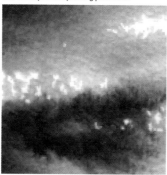

D Grayscale TIFFs are typically used for black-and-white continuous tone images.

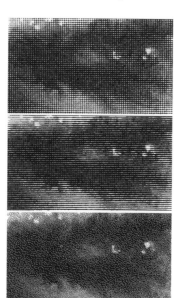

E Bitmap TIFFs represent only pure black or white. Tonality achieved during export: dot halftone (top), line screen (middle), or diffusion dither (bottom).

F The vector-based clipping path allows an image to be silhouetted from its background.

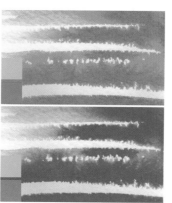

G Duotone variations, in which each of two ink colors is more or less dominant, must be gray-scale images saved in the EPS format.

The EPS format may include color, render tone, or be pure positive/negative. While it can not be altered within a page layout program, its outer contour may be defined as a clipping path that allows it to be silhouetted as an irregular shape /**F**/, and saving files in this format typically results in relatively smaller file sizes. In spot color printing applications, continuous tone images may be colorized with two, three, or four ink colors (using the duotone mode function /**G**/ of image-manipulation software); despite such images' tonal variation, this format is the only one that will translate spot-color, ink-specific coloration as applied to the image's tonal values. The designer may select not only which ink colors to use, but also how each ink color's density is applied to corresponding tonal, value-based densities in the image.

In creating vector-based EPS files from a scanned drawing, it's usually important to not auto-trace the source image; this will result in extremely complex vector shapes made up of hundreds, if not thousands, of points and line segments and consequently, files of huge size that will often become corrupted. When tracing a scanned image, it is therefore desirable to render the form with as few points and line segments as possible. The designer must look for the places around the form's contour where a single point, whether an angle, curve, or transition point, can be placed to allow for the most extensive control of the surrounding contour. /**H**/.

H Compare the results of auto-tracing a complex form (top) and tracing it manually using the Bezier pen tool (bottom); fewer points, with specifically controlled line segments, result in cleaner images of lower file size.

**Production
Techniques
and Aesthetic
Integration**

Form language
parity

Because the designer is free to construct a drawn image to not only capture a subject or convey meaning in the most appropriate way possible, the most direct strategy for unifying drawing with photographic image material is to purposely develop its language and compositional structure to reflect the latter's formal qualities. Approaches to creating such parity may trade on very broad, immediately recognizable structural and compositional relationships or, alternatively, call attention to more subtle elements within the photograph—exaggerating them or, perhaps, restating them indirectly.

Two versions of an advertisement shown here illustrate these extremes of approach. The first pairs a photograph with a gestural figure drawing /**A**/ whose major axes, as well as distribution of overall linearity and mass, echo those seen in the photograph. The second version takes a textural approach, paring the photograph with a composition of non-pictorial elements /**B**/. While the irregular, dot-like formation of ink-blots relates more literally to the flower details in the tie, diagonal linear forms reproduce the tie's sharply detailed linear patterning, but in a less direct way.

A Drawing and photography related by similarity of shape and axis

B Creating a more subtle relationship using tonality and texture in a drawing that is similar to those in a photograph

Juxtaposition, overlap, and transparency

Drawn image elements that are—or must remain—clearly different in form language than that of accompanying photographic or digital image elements may be integrated simply by clustering them /**C**/; the viewer's consideration of the grouping as a whole promotes a perception of synergy among the formal attributes of the cluster's components, while each retains its inherent language difference. Allowing drawn elements to cross the boundaries of inset, cropped photographs and so exaggerating their contrasting qualities, establishes a similarly dynamic, interactive dialogue.

Following the logic of juxtaposition, overprinting drawn elements /**D**/ with photographic ones will enhance the apparent relationship between the two. As the drawn image seamlessly joins a photograph's space by appearing to pass through it in to the surounding area, it will become simultaneous with the photograph and the compositional space. Affecting the relative opacity of each element /**E**/ may further contribute to their visual unity.

C Simple clustering creates an integrated totality from disparate elements.

D A drawn element overprinting a photograph

E A photograph made digitally transparent over an underlying drawing

Masking

Drawn images may be digitally masked into larger, environmental forms within a photograph (opaquely or with transparency applied) /**F**/, or within vector-based planes or typographic forms; and photographic imagery may also be masked into drawn or typographic forms /**G**/—even those that are exceptionally textural or gestural.

F Drawn elements masked into a silhouetted photographic form

G Photographic imagery masked into a drawn typographic form

Manipulation Strategies

Whether by importing an independently generated drawing /**A**/ that has been scanned, or working directly into a photographic image file with the drawing tools available in image-editing software /**B**/, the native character and texture may not only be simply influenced, but dramatically altered by drawing. Mark-making, collage, and montage strategies all may be used in any combination.

Conversely, the photographic filters available in image-editing software may be applied to a drawing /**C**/, either in its entirety or selectively. Warping, skewing, scaling, distorting, blurring, and extreme contrast adjustments /**D**/, as well as color balance, all offer compelling possibilities.

A A hand-generated ink drawing scanned and embedded into a photographic image

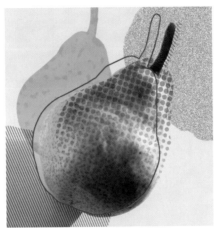

B Drawing and textural effects created within a photograph, using the tools available in an image-editing program

C An original drawing, distorted and repeated in overlap, takes on photographic qualities.

Type and image congruity

One of the most challenging unifying conditions to achieve in any design context is a visual relationship between type and image. Whether in response to a photograph /**D**/, or to an image that is also drawn /**E**/, a designer's first focus may be one of selecting typefaces that express some formal quality to be seen in the image—similar rhythms in bold and light, softness and sharpness, stroke-and-counter alternation, and so on.

D Textural and shaping relationships between details in various typeface drawings and those in a photograph.

E A designer may also define similar relationships between typefaces and other drawn imagery.

F Text elements may be sized, shaped, and positioned to literally restate elements within an associated image.

G Formal elements in the image may also be extended outward, reinterpreted—or even contrasted—by text composition.

Given that text often is designed neutrally to accompany supporting images, the designer may also look to the composition of the text forms—column widths, high/low position, axis logic—to achieve unity between image and type within the format's space. Such interplay may be accomplished by repeating the shapes of existing elements or spatial breaks within the image /**F**/. But another option is to extrapolate the image's compositional qualities into surrounding space: not simply restating them, but reinterpreting them in variation—at different scales or values; with similar gesture or shaping, but in different positions; and even evoking clear contrasts between the text and image elements /**G**/.

Color language

Enforcing similarities—and clear optical relationships /**H**/, whether analogous, complementary, or value-, saturation-, or temperature-based between photo-graphic, drawn, and typographic elements also accomplishes aesthetic unity among these disparate forms while maintaining their individuality. Systematic approaches allow for variation and spatial separation with greater complexity /**I**/.

H Clear hue and saturation relationships help unify drawn and photographic imagery.

I A similar progression in temperature and value is expressed by a photograph, drawing, and typograpghic hierarchy within a layout.

Posters/
Identity
programs/
Typeface
design/
Editoral/
Environmental
graphics/
Animation/
Signage/
Website
experience/
Packaging

Selected

Cas/e stu_d_ies

Following are five project case studies that demonstrate the use of drawing as a design process that, while following some expected similarities, are as unique to the designers and as to the projects themselves. These projects present a diversity of application for comparison, from posters and editorial, illustrative work to the development of logos, animations, and online website experiences. Each is shown in its entirety, from initial research to concept development through successive stages of reiteration, refinement, and final solution.

Bizu Design
São Paulo / Brazil

Visual Identity and Applications for a Cultural Festival

Graphic designer Ana Starling, with the support of colleagues in the studio BIZU, was asked to develop an identity for the South American Festival of Arabic Culture in 2010—the festival's inaugural year. With an eye toward creating a brand that could be implemented immediately and updated in subsequent years, Starling framed the problem as a search for a language that could be easily updated, as well as one that could be flexible for the tremendous number of applications the festival would require. Furthermore, the diversity of Arabic culture necessitated a unifying, non-culturally specific visual style.

Starling immersed herself in the culture by studying photographs of people, art, and architecture. Almost immediately (and luckily, given a short deadline), she was struck by a consistent aspect of Arabic alphabetical ornament: repeating hexagonal and triangular axes /**A**/. Starling distilled this geometry into a grid of diagonals and horizontals, providing an essential building block— a triangular module—that she could reconfigure endlessly.

A Typical examples of Islamic decoration
Photographs ©Thomas Samara

Upon defining this atomic element, she set about using it to build the festival's primary logo /**B**/. By filling in the triangular modules, she explored a variety of patterns that were contemporary, but clearly rooted in the tradition of Arabic imagery. Numerous sketches resulted in a basic logo form that exhibits line/dot contrast in a lively, rotational, and interlocking movement. The festival's name was aligned to mark along a diagonal grid line to integrate it with the mark's dominant visual structure /**B**/. Attempting to build a logic of flexibility into the identity from the ground up, Starling determined that the base mark could itself be varied: first, by reorganizing its internal parts /**C**/; and second, by allowing its elements to be colored in different ways. From among the collection of images she had studied, Starling extracted an extensive palette /**D**/ of 70 hues typical of the desert environment, architecture, textiles, and artwork (a selection is shown).

B The designer's base construction grid of diagonals and horizontals underpins the symbol and typographic components of the logo.

C The modular language allows for a logo that can be reconfigured without confusing its identity.

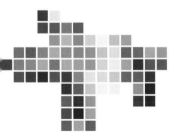

D An extensive palette of colors was extracted after researching photographs of Arabic art, textiles, architecture, and street scenes.

A brief series of further tests revealed the diagonal drawing grid's potential to generate compositions of elements whose mass and linearity could radically vary—all while remaining indisputably related to each other /**E,F,G**/. With the deadline approaching, Starling and associates from BIZU set about applying the new language to the festival's myriad promotional and collateral materials /**H**/.

E The designer briefly experimented with color and compositional possibilities based on the underlying grid, color palette, and the logo's modularity.

F A study with type to test compositional ideas in relation to the diagonal grid

G Repeating and overlapping the logo side-by-side, demonstrates continued recognizability even though the logo is no longer explicitly present.

H A fine arts print, made for sale, experiments with transparency and overprinting.

A One of several posters designed to announce the festival

Early print applications produced for the first festival hint at the identity's potential to be endlessly refreshed in coming years. While an intuitive expression of the triangular grid module as a mosaic pattern dominates /**A**/, radical changes in its scale—creating planar forms—introduces great variety in that syntax alone /**C**/; it further gives rise to linear, ribbon-like structures /**B,C**/ that offer added contrast.

Throughout the applications, color—anchored by a deep, historical brown—traverses a range of vibrant and subdued green, turquoise, and blue; taupe, violet, and pink; and oranges, ruddy reds, and mustard-yellows.

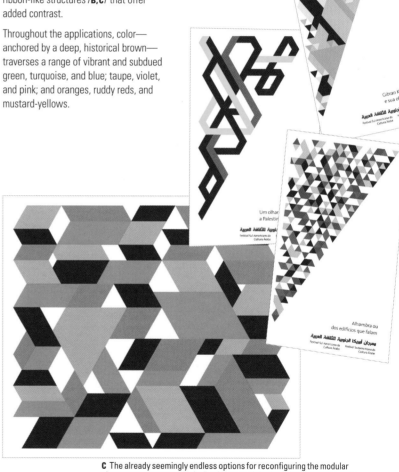

C The already seemingly endless options for reconfiguring the modular element to create new scale, line/mass, and rhythmic ideas become even more pronounced in this limited selection of festival program covers (upper right) and one of the endpapers (above).

B These two flyers demonstrate the pattern-based language and a new linear option created by linking strips of triangles with color.

The logo and graphic language come alive through animation, seen in the festival's promotional TV ad /D/. Accompanied by contemporary Middle-Eastern music, the symbol first draws itself in and then expands outward in a continually shifting arrangement of plane and line forms. Although completely nonpictorial, the language succinctly identifies the culture and, through the movement of its changing attributes and extension outward into the frame space, suggests the evolution and far-reaching influence of Arabic culture.

F These screens show alternate color schemes that are randomly applied as the user browses.

D A television commercial promotes the festival with an animation of the logo drawing itself in and then expanding into new forms.

In the website, transparency as an effect returns in a short launch animation on the home page /E/ as the identity's typographic component is supplanted by the symbol form, fading away as content appears. The screen space itself, as well as the logo, randomly recolor at periodic intervals /F/ while users browse the pages; users also are able to repaint the logo by clicking a specific button.

E Transparency returns in the website; on the home page, the symbol form constructs itself around the typographic component, which then fades away to reveal site content.

mïöja

A

Disturbance / Richard Hart
Durban / South Africa

Branded Packaging for Bath and Skin-care Products

B

C

Disturbance, a fourteen-member design studio in Durban, South Africa, was tapped to develop visual branding and packaging for Mioja, a line of botanical bath and skin-care products. The project was led by Richard Hart who, together with his sister and partner, Susie, and Roger Jardine, a third partner, directs the studio's creative activities. From the project's very beginning, the client expressed a desire for a clean, purely typographic solution; Hart and his team obliged **/A–H/**, but as a result of the initial presentation, the client agreed that this approach didn't offer very much, freeing up the team to explore other options.

Perhaps because of a need for distinct brand differentiation in a crowded product sector and also because of his participation in a recent exhibition of prints, Hart found himself inspired to pursue drawing as a primary branding element for the packaging. Preliminary logotype studies from the typographic approach pitted organically-drawn type-faces for the brand logo against sharper, geometric sans serifs **/E, F, G/**, both potentially useful for establishing a brand voice for the products. One identity concept—a negative form of the initial M created from the organization of three petal-like forms **/G/**—was discarded as a possible logo, but did lead to a pattern that would later become a treatment for the interiors of the products' boxes **/H/**.

D

E

F

G

A–H Purely typographic, and icon/type, studies from the designer's preliminary approach to the packaging identity

H

I The fine art print that provided Hart and his team with inspiration for a new direction

With the print he had recently made for the exhibition top of mind /I/, he quickly moved to create a collection of stylized forms that he envisioned could be combined into various shapes and patterns—much like the pattern in the print that inspired him. Hart drew a number of botanical forms—leaf, petal, and tendril shapes, seed- and pistil-like configurations of dots /J/—using digital drawing software practically in one sitting, without first sketching them by hand. None of the elements were intended to empirically represent any particular plant or flower. Rather, they were conceived as expressing the archetypal notions of botany and organicism in a less literal or conventional way. Hart presented his clients at Mioja with the first rough set of images to gauge their reaction; they were, not surprisingly, excited about the new direction.

Hart spent some time carefully adjusting the internal masses, curves, and proportions of the individual elements before proceeding to developing the packages. Using a previously developed and agreed upon palette of intense, triadic hues /K/ (for coding three different series of products within the overall line) and a unifying neutral blue-green, Hart looked at the various logotype options in combination with restrained instances of his stylized botanical language /K/ and quickly decided on a neutral, geometric sans serif face for thebrand's logotype /L/. As his process evolved, he became interested in a broader, expansive presence for the botanical imagery across the package surfaces; a simpler typeface choice offered contrast and allowed the imagery to play dramatically in the format without distraction.

J The extensive family of intricate, and exceptionaly varied, botanical forms was drawn in one sitting and then refined.

K Rough studies using the botanical imagery with variations in typographic approach

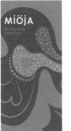

L Hart focused on a simple typographic presentation for the logo and supporting information to allow the botanical imagery to dominate the package fronts.

Each of the products, contained in jars within the boxes, required a label. Hart specified jars of colored glass to match his system, with labels carrying smaller, simpler configurations of the botanical image elements. Hart and his team tested close variations in how the details were combined /**A, B, C**/: swapping out a simpler curve for a more complex one here, adding or deleting tendril forms or dots there. Each different botanical image configuration was positioned to grow outward from its respective label's rectangular shape.

A

B

A–C Studies for labels that would appear on darkly colored bottles examined opaque, as well as transparent, options; Hart also tested variations on each label's botanical image—altering curves, swapping out more or less detail, and adjusting rotation.

C

In the final set of packaging /**D, F**/, the stylized botanical imagery flows seamlessly around the sides of the outer boxes, connecting in a continuous rhythm of decreasing scale from the largest box to the smallest; each series of boxes displays a different overall composition of this organic visual syntax. The boxes' interiors are covered with an intricate, petal-like pattern /**E**/ colored with each product sub-series' respective hue, while the colored bottles are simply tagged with a label that displays product information in a light, elegant combination of serif and sans serif faces.

D These flat schematics of the four box sizes in one product line show how the botanical imagery spans them as one continuous composition.

E The insides of the boxes are printed with a pattern that follows the color coding system. The pattern was retrieved from an early logo study (**G, H** on page 116).

Drawing
/ for Graphic
Design

Processes

**Selected
Case Studies:**
Branded
Packaging
for Bath
and Skincare
Products

F The final system of boxes and bottles

Estudio Diego Feijóo
Barcelona / Spain

Identity and Graphic Language for a Museum of Wine Making

The Vinseum, located in Barcelona, Spain, is a small institution devoted to Catalonian wine culture. In preparation for its opening, the museum's directors enlisted the talents of Diego Feijóo and his graphic design studio to develop an identity. Feijóo's body of work shows an abiding interest in typography and imagery that is decidedly modernist and, as is typical of his process, he began by defining intuitively an approach for the identity focused on a clear, simple idea: creating a custom typeface for the museum's trademark made from wine itself—transforming the neutral word into a fluid, yet stable, image that deftly captures a deep authenticity and yet, is friendly and accessible.

The designer began by selecting a relatively bold sans-serif typeface with which to work, choosing for simplicity only the capitals. He traced and then cut the letterforms from chipboard to create printing tools and stencils. Then, using actual wine as medium, he alternately soaked the cut-out letters in wine to print, and painted with the wine into the stencils—using both techniques on the surface of a heavy, absorbent printmaking or watercolor paper /**A, B**/. By adding wine for deeper color and wet, pooling effects—and also blotting with paper or thinning with water to reduce the wine's density—he created a full, custom alphabet with alternate characters /**c**/. Each instance of a given letter is unique; one may be very light and show some pooling of dark areas, while another may have a heavy overall color and a more irregular edge. A simplified, but alternate, version of each character in the museum's name was arranged to create a single logotype with subtle changes /**D**/. While the visual profile of the mark remains consistent, fluctuations in the individual letters' texture and rhythm change as different combinations of alternate characters are used. This variation within a static form suggests the both the historical context, and the continual evolution of viniculture.

A Printing a wine-saturated letter

B Stencil forms of letters cut out and used to print on paper with wine

Aula
Classroom

C The rawly printed alphabets are rich with detail and tonal changes.

VINSEUM

VINSEUM

VINSEUM

D Slightly cleaned up, the characters of the logotype nonetheless retain their alternate tonal variations.

Sala d'actes
Sala de actos
Auditorium

Recepció
Recepción
Reception desk

Aula
Classroom

Lavabos
Servicios
Toilets

E This selection of the wayfinding icons exhibits the same authentic irregularities in density and contouring as does the logotype without sacrificing clarity.

F Signage within the museum uses neutral shapes, type, and color to contrast the textural qualities of the identity and the surrounding architecture.

Feijóo used the same techniques to develop drawings for various applications. Stencils of informational icons /**E**/, first drawn in a conventionally neutral way, were used to create the final icons to be used on way-finding signs /**F**/ within the museum itself. The icon drawings were simply but carefully crafted for unity in their overall style and weight proportions but, again, using the medium of wine elevated them from commonplace symbols to fully-integrated, charming components of the identity.

An expanded repertoire of techniques—including free-form pooling of the wine /**A**/ (sometimes adding further pools after a previous layer had dried), as well as dragging it with a sponge /**B**/—opened the door to extensive imagery for other applications. Among the majority, the natural color of the wine used is that of the final piece /**A**/; at other times, the painted or stenciled form is colored for a more specific communication that may still be relatively abstract as a visualization (for instance, in the promotional cards in which overlapping lines of color create the loose impression of a vineyard /**B**/). Throughout printed materials, a simple grid with flexible column-widths organizes typographic material, set in the bold and regular weights of a gothic sans serif and alternating between black and a second color (selected from within the drawing used on a given piece).

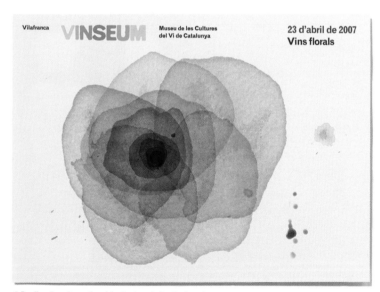

A Pooling the wine—then blotting it and allowing it to dry—creates the individual, irregular petal shapes, which were scanned to assemble the final image for a promotion about floral wines.

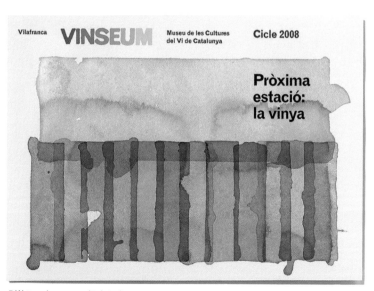

B Watercolor was used to introduce greater variety in the palette; in these cards, a flat sponge-brush is used to drag the transparent paint in linear formations.

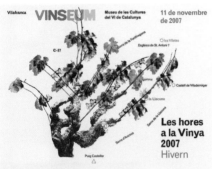

C Manipulating the contrast of grayscale photographic images imparts a drawinglike quality that is enhanced by spot-color printing techniques.

Over time, Feijóo also incorporated photographic imagery /**C, D**/ to evolve and refresh the program. Mindful of the brand language's established emphasis on drawing, he manipulated the photography to ensure that it integrated successfully. In one series of mailers, images are always of objects /**C**/, silhouetted from their photographic environments to render them somewhat more abstract and call attention to their shapes and gestural qualities—further emphasized by removing their local color and presenting them in monochrome or grayscale. Their value levels were also altered to enhance overall contrast and augment their shadow detail, which gives them an even less naturalistic, almost hand-made, look. In production, these

images are either printed directly as colored halftones or printed as black-and-white halftones and then surprinted—off-register—with a color halftone of a second hue of ink. In another series, images are cropped within icons of wine glasses /**D**/. In keeping with the idea of transparency, the full-color photographs are overlapped at full density, creating unusual illustrative effects in the overlapped area that enhances the unity of photograph and icon.

The original, wine-printed alphabet appears in other contexts than just the logotype, including as headers on the website (not shown) and as a primary typographic element on labels /**E**/ for the museum's own line of bottled varietals.

E Typographic applications that use the original raw alphabets include promotional items and labels for bottles.

D The designer integrates full-color photography into the system by cropping it into icons; overlapping the images adds to their illustrative quality.

Nakano Design Office
Tokyo / Japan

Promo-tional and Environ-mental Communi-cations for an Exhibit

As the basis of a concept that aimed to express the individuality of the creative process, Takeo Nakano established handwriting as the core element of his work for an exhibition of recent Japanese industrial design, *Prototype 03*. The first stage of the project focused on designing the exhibition space itself. Nakano devised a uniform presentation platform for each exhibitor's work. The surface of each platform was inscribed with a 5 x 5 cm grid /**A**/; Nakano asked each of the exhibiting product designers to display the stages of their work's design process across the grid /**B**/, and to then explain the process for viewers in their own handwriting, personalizing it and making it that more accessible for the audience.

A Nakano's diagram of the grid layout for the exhibitor platforms that inspired his approach to the graphic communications

B An example of the exhibitor platform in use during the exhibition

In translating this concept to the exhibit's promotional materials and on-site informational signage, Nakano asked each of the exhibiting designers to also handwrite the exhibition's title /**C**/. Further considering his idea that the exhibition gathered designers of a similar field whose work, respectively, embodied different aesthetic characteristics, Nakano sought to convey this sense of identity and difference in his design for the exhibition's poster.

Selecting each letter of the exhibition's title—but from all of the handwritten versions—and layering them transparently, he arrived at a complex form for each letter /**D**/ that expresses difference within a uniform structure. He linked this visual element with the display structure of the exhibition's platforms by overlaying the display grid. By changing the opacity and tonal levels within particular modules of the grid /**E**/, Nakano added a new level of visual interest, as well as complexity to the notion of identity and difference. The introduction of this new syntax (translucent squares in a grid formation) also provided a way to integrate photography /**F**/ when such imagery was called for—in particular for exhibitor bio information and product images that would be useful for the promotional poster (see image /**A**/, following page).

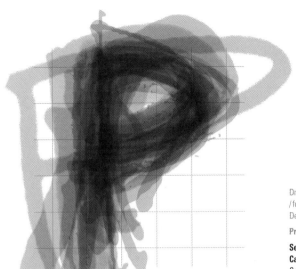

D The transparent montage of the initial *P*, representing all contributor writing samples; the construction grid is overlayed.

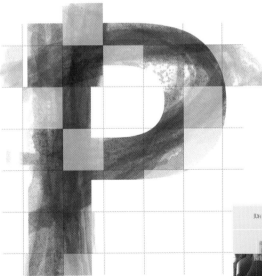

E The designer altered the opacity of selected modules in the grid, imposing a second structure.

F The grid formation helped integrate photographic elements seamlessly.

PROTOTYDE

PROTOTYPE

PROTO
TYPE

PROTO TYPE

PROTOTYPE

PROTOTYPE

PROTOTYPE

C Selected handwriting samples of the exhibition's title, collected from the exhibitors

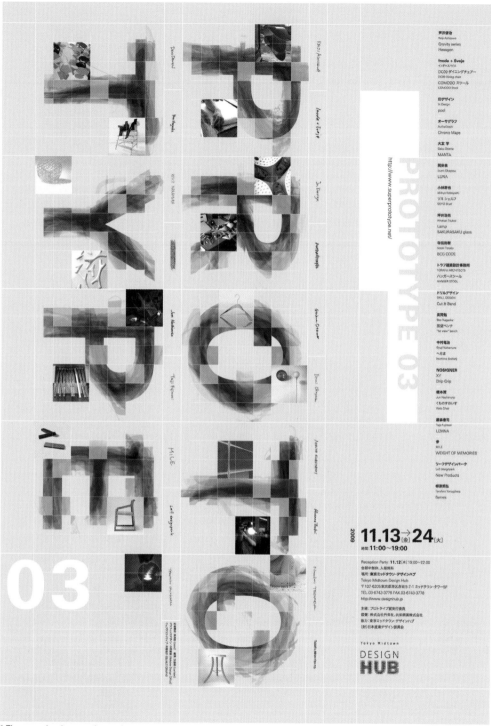

A The promotional poster, also used at
the entry to the exhibition space.

The complex, writing/grid collage drawings derived from each letter were composed into a unifying grid structure with supporting text for the final poster /**A**/. Along with the purely drawn and typographic components, Nakano incorporated photographs of selected product designs /**B**/ as images inset into the letter-grids. A strong rhythm of towering vertical structures, progressing left-to-right from regular and wide to increasingly narrow, governs the poster's layout and suggests forward directionality. The overall linear configuration, which incorporates contrasts in text weight, value, and detailing, is punctuated by the gridlike planar bocks of the individual letter collages. One version of the poster was printed for public promotion, while another was enlarged and mounted as signage for the gallery's entry.

Within the space, Nakano implemented the same strategy for profiles of the exhibitors, structuring a horizontal configuration of the letter-grids as panels across a gallery wall /**C, D**/. Each exhibitor's biography is typeset in a transparent plane defined by the proportions of the modular grid /**C**/, accompanied by additional inset images of a selected body of their typical work.

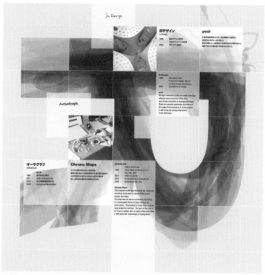

C This enlarged detail of the initial *R* composition shows the delicate quality of typography and line detail in the grid formation.

B The informational panels used in the exhibition contain biographical information about the exhibitors.

D A view of the informational wall in the exhibition space

Paone Design Associates
Philadelphia, PA / United States

Poster Announcing a Youth Orchestra Performance

The Philadelphia Youth Orchestra is an ensemble of teenaged musicians that is attached to the world-renowned Philadelphia Symphony Orchestra. Longtime consultants Paone Design Associates was commissioned to create the poster announcing a concert celebrating the Youth Orchestra's 70th Anniversary. This poster, as have others, measured 6' x 8' (1.8 x 2.4 m) and was displayed in the symphony concert hall's outoor kiosks.

Gregory Paone, the studio's principal, began his design exploration with visual research through sketching. Because the featured work in the concert's repertoire experimented with the instruments' sounds, he decided to focus on musical instruments as a subject. Initial research centered on shapes and details among various instruments—scrolls, tuning screws, keys, and so on /A/. Paone's early sketches, mostly in pencil, were quite small, especially those in which he began to test out compositional ideas while still amassing his library of shape references /B/. Working at a small size enabled him to record and compare a large number of possibilities to consider without focusing on minute details.

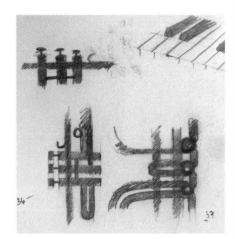

A A selection of first rough pencil studies of instruments' shapes and details

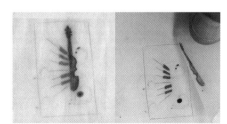

B Small-scale studies combining specific elements with trace overlay

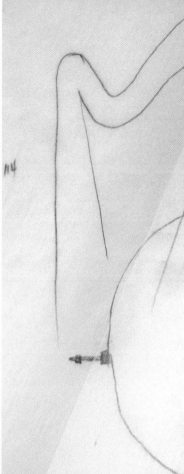

C Individual instrument contours on overlayed sheets of tracing paper

Larger sketches, which Paone often executes on tracing paper /C/, further helped him experiment with ideas for composition. Moving form elements on independent sheets of tracing paper back and forth over each other allowed him to see how the instruments' shapes interacted with each other in different combinations and positions, which, in turn, not only presented the possibility of hybridizing elements in a layered, deconstructed way, but also directed Paone more specifically toward which additional reference to collect.

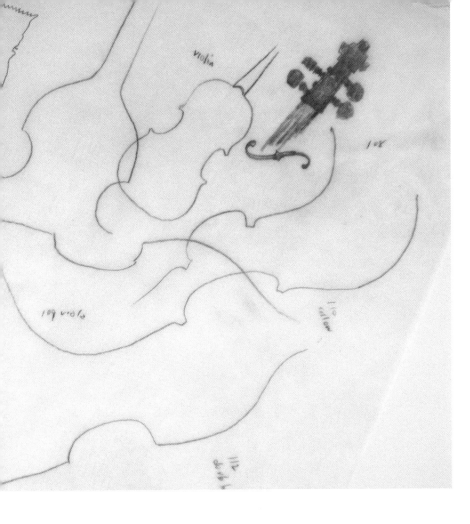

Drawing
/ for Graphic
Design

Processes

**Selected
Case Studies:**
Poster for
a Youth
Orchestra
Performance

G Traced and filled-in ink drawings
accomplished at a larger scale

The fluid, back-and-forth process led
Paone through a multitude of rough
compositional sketches /**D–F**/, building
from his ever-growing shape library.
These latter suggest Paone's relentless
experimentation with configuration and
varying degrees of detail or reduction.
Some of the sketches hint at greater
transparency and the possibility of linear,
volumetric rendering /**E**/; others test
more compressed space, opaque, and
planar approaches /**D, F**/. Within this
multitude of possibilities, Paone was
drawn to those of greater reduction; as a
result, he eventually focused on a more
iconic direction and began building a
specific palette of hard-edged instrument
details /**G**/, initially traced and rendered
in black ink at a much larger scale.

D Inked-in, reductive and
diagrammatic sketch

E A fluid, more complex layout,
possibly also suggesting a direction
toward linear rendering

F A color sketch with marker
drove the designer to focus on the
reductive approach.

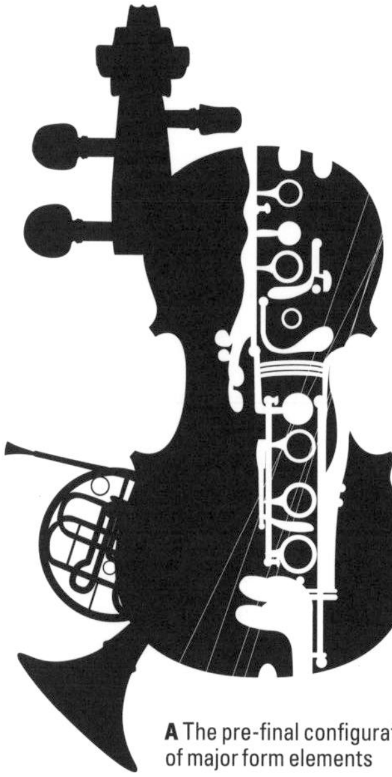

A The pre-final configuration of major form elements

Once Paone completed ink tracings of the instrument shapes and details, he scanned them and converted them to vector shapes. The next stage in his process was a similar, in-depth study of composition /**A–E**/, exploring such options as tight cropping /**B**/, complete containment /**C**/, the addition of supporting line elements /**D**/, and varying emphasis on the amount and scale of positive form versus negative space /**D, E**/. This series of studies was accomplished in black and white to allow Paone to concentrate on the specifics of positive/negative interplay. Eventually finding a dynamic tension between the overall mass of a violin's outer contour and the detailed, dot/line intricacy of a flute's keys, Paone moved to yet another, more complex stage of compositional investigation.

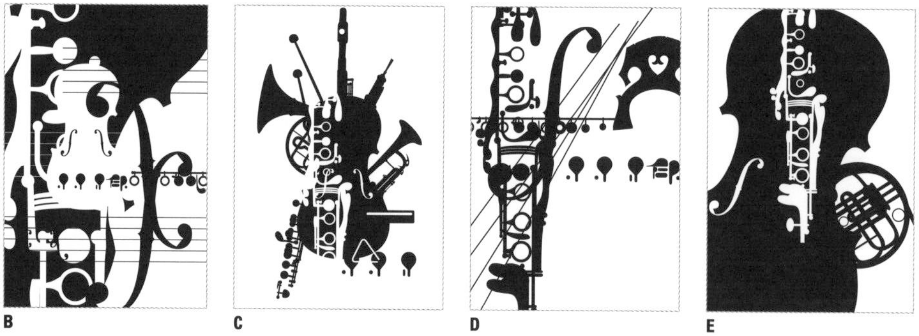

B **C** **D** **E**

B–E Black-and-white composition studies, second stage

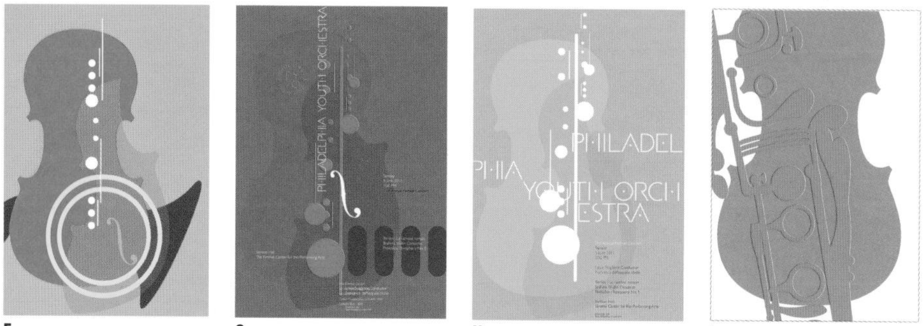

F **G** **H** **I**

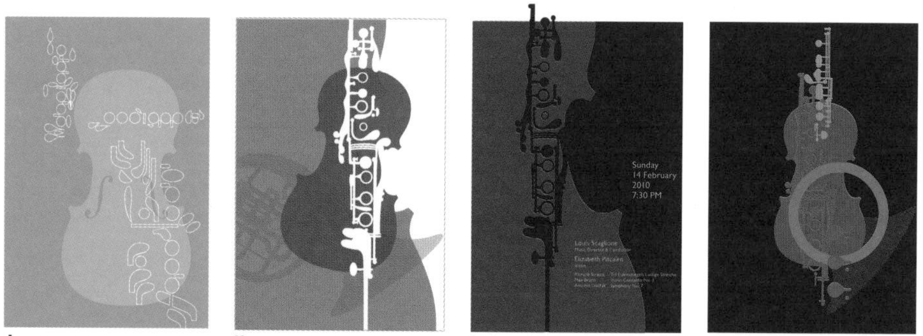

J **K** **L** **M**

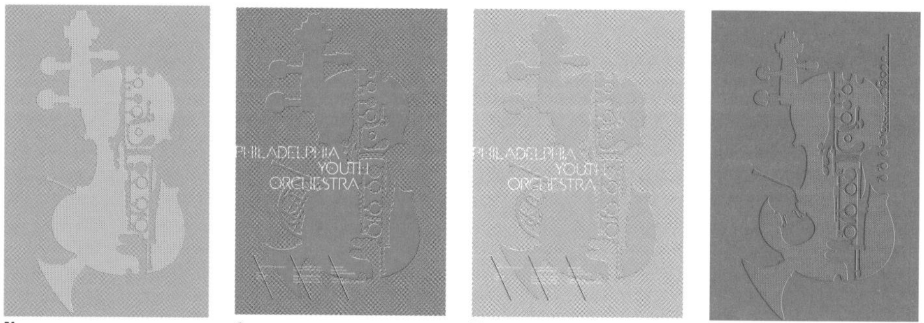

N **O** **P** **Q**

F–Q Color studies from the third stage, also integrating typography

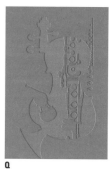

Working toward the poster's final resolution, Paone continued to consider overall composition /**F–Q**/, but also chromatic effects on spatial depth and narrative. Given the classical subject of the imagery, Paone purposely sought a contemporary color palette. Variations in this stage emphasized saturated hues; the combinations also were unusual, pairing analogous /**H, J, K, N**/ or complementary hues /**F, G, I, Q**/ to define dramatic spatial separation /**F, M, Q**/ or a vibrating, compressed space /**H, J, N, P**/. Again, Paone added other graphical forms /**F, G, M, O, P**/, but ultimately decided to forego these. To integrate the poster's typography, Paone alternately explored the contrast of sharp, horizontal breaks and staggering alignments with the flute form's dominant vertical /**G, H, L, O, P**/; and restating that vertical through rotation of the major text elements /**R**/.

Paone arrived at a detailed, reductive icon language that dynamically contrasts mass, line, dot, curve, and angles of varied scale. Overlapping positive and negative forms elicit continual figure/ground reversal. The poster expresses vertical structure, established by top-level hierarchic text elements at upper right and the major vertical axis of the flute. The title type itself is a custom face of lines and dots—suggesting musical notation and referencing the form language—designed by Paone for the Youth Orchestra years earlier. A combination of saturated complements (cyan and red-orange) evokes a contemporary connection with the past, playfully supporting the poster's tribute to the Youth Orchestra's 70-year heritage.

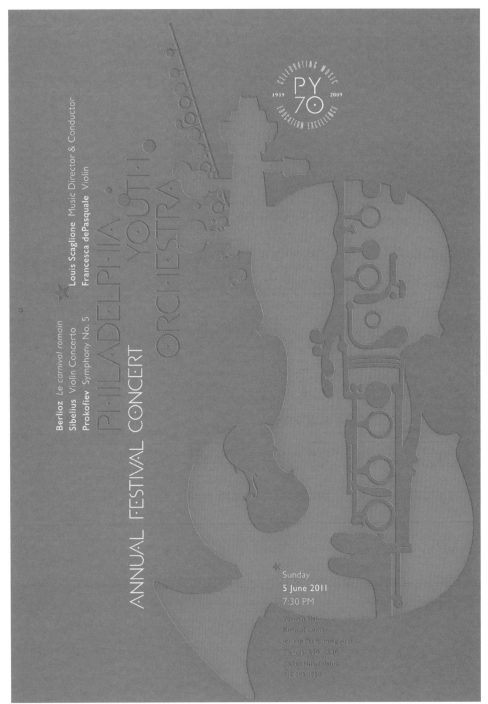

R The final poster, executed as a digital print

This chapter presents methods for overcoming timidity—facing the blank page!—and exploring, hands-on, the development of skills from basic mark-making and gesture through structure, composition, description of pictorial form, and creation of non-pictorial narrative.

In/ven?t—tion/

Drawing is a skill that, like any other, can be learned. Some people demonstrate a superlative native talent for it, just as they might for playing football or cooking, working with typography, or taking photographs; others must actively work on honing it as they would for any of these latter activities.

It's interesting to consider that children draw intuitively as part of their early development—and, perhaps not surprisingly, are extremely accomplished at it, even at the early age of three. Research has documented both a universal instinct among children to make images and an equally universal process of evolution in their approach, regardless of culture.* It begins with the discovery of gesture and then, almost immediately thereafter, the articulation of a first, purposeful form: a mandala, the child announcing the understanding of self and location in existence. From there, all children vigorously express themselves through nonpictorial means with increasingly complex shape-based forms that eventually result in pictorial depiction. Even more fascinating is that, in looking at childrens' drawings, one confronts an undeniable consistency in resolving the aspects of the universal principles discussed earlier—a remarkable level of visual sophistication.

This realization has nothing to do with condescending to accepting childens work as "good" simply because of their age. Comparing nearly any drawing by a child with fine art works (of any genre) that hang in the world's most prestigious museums—or, for that matter, with any of the posters, brochures, book covers, or website layouts that captivate us in myriad graphic design journals and showcases—will immediately prove otherwise. Being completely objective, one will recognize a powerful cohesion among gesture, form, structure, and space that seems to have simply occurred in a state of complete resolution, without the effort that is evident in works made by adults. The issue here is confidence; young children are fearless when they draw. They accept their skill and the expression that results without the judgment that adults impose on themselves. Somewhere along the way, though, many of us—even those who go on to be image-makers for the rest of our lives—lose that fearlessness and, eventually, the desire to even explore drawing as a vehicle for communication. In effect, our intellectual development cuts us off from one of the most provocative, compelling, and human modes of storytelling and narrative.

Uncovering, or rediscovering, the creative possibilities of drawing is empowering. The assignments that follow are accompanied by suggestions for translating their exploration of specific concepts and skills in their day-to-day job or projects; corresponding real-world examples give evidence to this same practical potential. For beginners, assignments in this chapter may be approached with photographic reference through tracing or scanning and working digitally; once some level of comfort with these activities have been achieved, revisiting assignments to work directly through observation or from memory will further enhance budding skills. Designers or draftspersons with greater experience are encouraged to engage in both the simpler, more fundamental studies and those of a higher level of complexity. Drawing skill is like a muscle: It needs continual exercise to keep strong and flexible and, eventually, able to be called upon powerfully and instinctively.

*Rhoda Kellogg with Scott O'Dell.
The Psychology of Children's Art.
[1967] CRM, Inc.

Getting Started: Tools and Prep

Basic drawing requires a little space, some paper, and a pencil or pen. The most important tool, however (and the hardest to come by), is time. Drawing is labor intensive; it necessitates a clear mind, unencumbered by other concerns—to understand and respond to the process as it unfolds. In a commercial context, it's wise to add hours to a project proposal to ensure the work is compensated. But whether project-driven or independently explored, drawing demands a period of freedom. Rushing the process or fitting it among other tasks usually results in unresolved form, incomplete understanding, and frustration. A free mind fosters contemplation and deeper creativity.

On a more pragmatic note, there are a few items (beyond the basics) a designer will find useful. Many are available at office supply or craft stores, hardware stores, and even pharmacies; all should be found at professional artist supply stores. For specialized techniques and effects, there are hundreds of tools to explore. It's not critical to have every item described here, but absolute necessities for a basic tool kit are noted. The more diverse a range of tools on hand, the more seamless the process becomes.

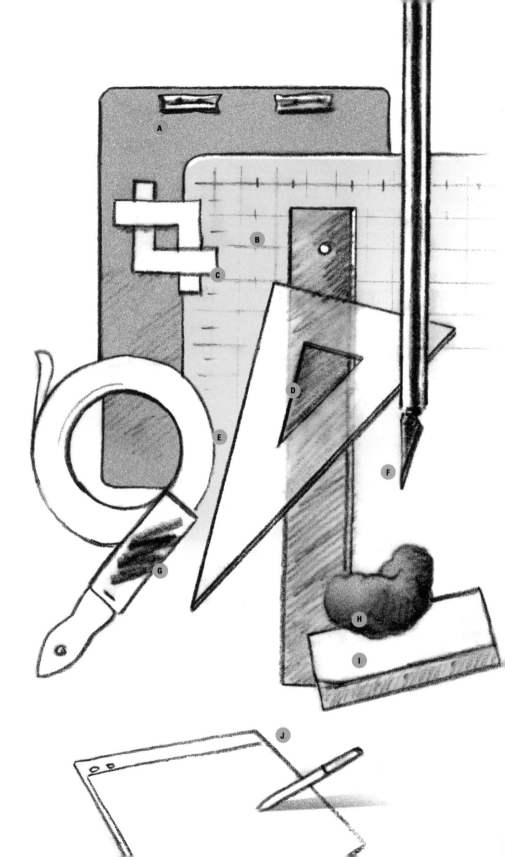

A A masonite drawing board provides a smooth surface to which paper may be clipped or taped. It can be leaned against a wall to protect work between sessions; and it can be used outside. A 16" x 20" (41 x 51 cm) board will accommodate small-format work associated with design, as well as larger drawings.

B A vinyl cutting surface prevents cutting on the drawing board to avoid creating grooves that may be revealed in a drawing. A size similar to that of the drawing board allows them to be clipped and carried together.

C A viewfinder is useful for planning compositions. It may easily be made from two L-shaped pieces of heavy paper or board that can be reproportioned and taped together to create different formats.

D A straightedge, ruler, and triangle are always useful, and should be givens in a design studio.

E White artist's tape is strong enough to steady paper during vigorous work, yet less damaging to most paper surfaces than are other kinds of tape.

F In addition to cutting paper, using a studio knife (any brand) to sharpen a pencil reveals more of its core and creates a more dramatic point than does a conventional pencil sharpener.

G Rubbing a pencil point across a sandpaper pad will sharpen it to a more controlled point when needed; the pad may also be used to sharpen the edge of a piece of chalk or crayon.

H, I Two kinds of erasers will be needed: a soft, gray kneaded eraser **I** (for delicate work) and a hard, white graphic eraser **H** (for more durable surfaces and cleaner erasures).

J Bearing in mind the dramatic potential of digital drawing (and standard production processes), having a computer with drawing applications is essential. While a mouse provides exceptional point-based control, a tablet and stylus will capture gesture more authentically.

K Drawing pencils come in various hardnesses, rated from 8H (the hardest and lightest) to 9B (the softest and darkest), as do mechanical pencils and woodless pencils; having three or four in a range of densities typical.

L The most ubiquitous tools of all, ballpoint pens are excellent for drawing. Testing various brands will reveal subtle differences in their marks and fluidity over alternate surfaces.

M A set of colored pencils in ten or twelve basic colors is usually adequate.

N The graphite stick is an edge tool used for rougher and broader mark-making than are pencils.

O Vine charcoal is soft and fragile; it makes ethereal, hazy marks of generally lighter value.

P Compressed charcoal is a tightly-formed stick; its marks are a very deep black.

Q Charcoal pencils, also available in different hardnesses, offer the depth of compressed charcoal's blackness in a controlled point.

R Conté is a clay-based chalk, available in sanguine (red), umber (brown), terra cotta (rust), black, and white varieties.

S Pastel is a dry chalk, similar to compressed charcoal. Oil pastel is a moist chalk, closer in feel to a crayon.

T Crayons are colored sticks of wax. China markers are similar, but come in pencil form.

U Felt (or "magic") markers are available in staggering variety, all yielding marks of a similar wet, translucent quality that bleeds on absorbent papers. A small selection with different nib shapes and sizes will be adequate to start.

V Brush markers also are magic markers, but with flexible, pointed nibs that mimic the marks of brushes with varying pressure.

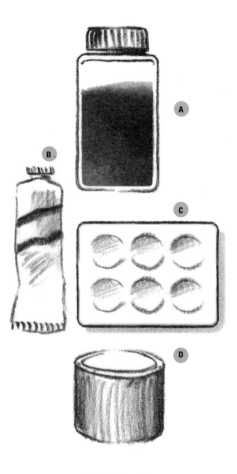

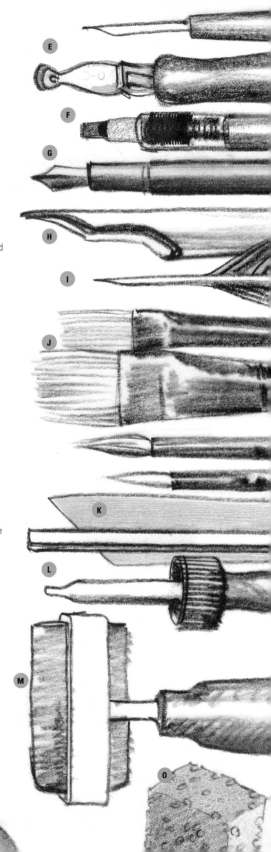

E–I Calligraphic pens are available in an assortment of nib shapes and ink-delivery methods that all yield different effects. Among these are automatic pens **E** (and their modern equivalent, parallel pens **F**), fountain pens **G**, reed pens **H**, and quills **I**.

J A single brush will produce myriad marks based on its shape, the pressure or angle applied, and its wetness or dryness. A set of three or four rounded brushes (of different sizes) will address large areas and detail work. Similarly, it's good to have a small selection of narrower and wider flat brushes for different needs and more varied possibilities.

K Sticks and spatulas of balsa wood are excellent for drawing with ink or paint, as are twigs, sturdy leaves, and hard vines.

L A dropper produces a variety of interesting marks with ink that change with varied pressure on the bulb and the speed at which it is dragged over a surface.

M Rollers, usually used for inking printmaking plates, make dramatic marks. Ones of softer rubber will accept water-based paint, while harder ones require oil-based inks.

N Spraypaint, available at hardware and home improvement stores, creates a characteristic mark; it also requires a lot of space and adequate ventilation.

O Sponges are useful not only for making marks when dipped in ink or gouache, but to absorb excess water or redistribute it across a surface for pooling and bleeding effects.

A Black India ink or Chinese ink is suitable for most needs: it works with brushes, pens, and droppers; and may be diluted with water for wash and bleed effects.

B Gouache is a rich, high-end paint that is typically opaque. It leaves a velvety finish, and its colors are super-saturated. It's also quite expensive; tempera paint is an adequate alternative.

C Watercolor, similar to gouache, offers an assortment of vibrant colors, but the pigments are naturally translucent. They are available in tubes or in cake form.

D Plaka, a casein-based paint, is most useful for drawing where continual refinement will take place—once it dries, it can be painted over without reconstituting and mixing (as gouache will do). A jar or tub each of black and white is essential for icon and translation work.

P

Q

R

The most important aspects of paper to consider are roughness and weight. Smooth papers **S** accept pencil, pen, marker, and some wet media well, but don't work well for chalk or charcoal, which need "tooth" (grain texture) to hold onto. Rough papers **T** are also good for wet media; the tooth will be more or less evident depending on how much water is used. Wet media requires heavy paper to prevent buckling from moisture.

S Examples of common media on a smooth paper stock: graphite (top) and a graduated ink wash (bottom).

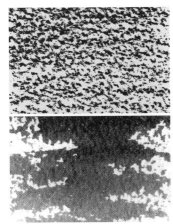

T Examples of graphite (top) and ink wash (bottom) on a heavy-weight stock with a lot of "tooth," or rough grain texture.

P Scratchboard is a heavy stock covered in black emulsion that is scratched away to reveal the white substrate underneath, resulting in dramatic, negative-like images.

Q, R Linoleum-cutting and woodcutting are ancient printmaking techniques. An image, created by cutting away the surface with specialized tools, leaves a relief to be inked and then pressed onto paper **Q.** Engraving is more complex, requiring heavy pressure to force ink, from within lines scratched into a metal plate, onto paper **R.** All three techniques can be accomplished with even a small 9"x12" (23 x 31 cm) press.

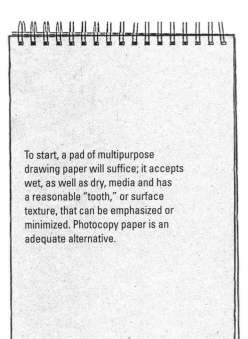

To start, a pad of multipurpose drawing paper will suffice; it accepts wet, as well as dry, media and has a reasonable "tooth," or surface texture, that can be emphasized or minimized. Photocopy paper is an adequate alternative.

Bristol board is similar to card stock, and is available in hot-press (smooth) and cold-press (rough) surfaces and several thicknesses.

Illustration board is a chipboard base covered in a veneer of bristol or clay-coated paper.

Printmaking papers, in a variety of heavy weights and surfaces, yield the best results when working with graphite, charcoal, and conté; they are also good for wet media. Most brands are available in several neutral colors.

Transparent papers, such as tracing paper and mylar (a plastic), aside from allowing a designer to work over an existing drawing to make corrections, or to transfer an image, are also useful in collage to create layers of differing opacity.

Ex/
er
cise
/s

The studies in this section are presented in a progressive sequence; they begin at a simple level to establish familiarity with tools, media, and basic techniques, and eventually segue into advanced studies that integrate complex combinations of strategies, concepts, and techniques (logotypes and typeface design, and transformational narrative).

Even before these latter, high-level exercises, the most fundamental of them offer absolute beginners a number of techniques for creating unique imagery that can be used right away at an empowering level of accomplishment.

Although developing conventional hand skills is greatly encouraged, those who aren't as comfortable working by hand may approach most of the exercises with digital drawing software before committing to pencil or brush.

Every exercise also includes suggestions for evolving the technique in different ways, to greater effect, and in combination with others for more varied possibilities of approach.

Practical Example: Cover Design

Throughout, this hypothetical project is presented in specifically redesigned iterations to show how the concepts, skills, and methodologies that the reader encounters in each study may be applied in a real-world context.

In each case, analyze how the given strategy is used to communicate a narrative of the book's subject matter.

The Organic in Architecture: Sources, Conditions, and Approaches to Building the Next Millennium

Rubbing

This study establishes familiarity with basic tools; creating directly from a physical source helps build confidence.

Find a rough surface: for example, a wall or sidewalk. Lay a sheet of paper on the surface and rub the drawing tool across the surface with varying degrees of pressure to transfer a relief of the surface's texture. Thinner, lighter-weight papers work best. Harder graphite will capture greater detail /**A**/; softer tools, such as charcoal or wax crayons /**B**/, will capture less and add more of their own textures. Test different kinds of tools to see their varied effects.

As an alternative to existing surfaces, try creating one; build a relief by overlapping bristol board or cardboard; tape or glue down bundles of cord or thin wires, thin plant stalks or hard leaves; then proceed with the same rubbing method as for a found surface.

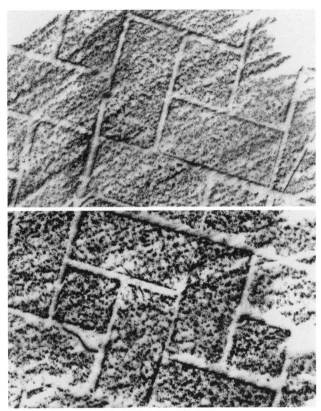

A Results with hard graphite (top) and soft crayon (bottom)

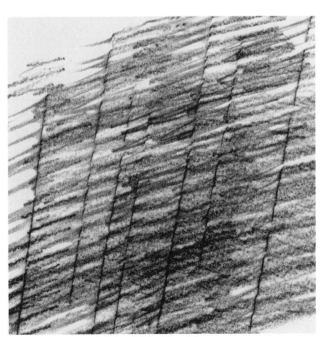

B A rubbing made from a built-up relief of cardboard pieces

Ideas for Development

Name the source of each rubbing; scan and use the image masked into, or to replace, a photographic element related to it.

Consider the rubbing for how it feels or associations it may suggest; use the image as a background in a context in which this feeling supports the project's overall message.

Scan the image and dramatically enlarge it; combine it as a layer with other kinds of imagery, using photo-manipulation software.

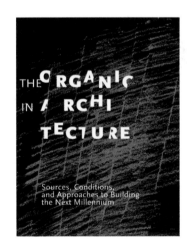

Isolating Marks and Forms

This study focuses on observing and editing; it also provides a way of exploring automatic mark-making.

Place a sheet of tracing paper over a photograph. Identify a specific element or shape in the image (dotlike or circular forms, lines, triangles, etc.). Using any kind of tool, trace and/or fill in all the instances of that element you are able to locate /**A**/. Be specific, isolating only forms that are related. This exercise can also be accomplished by scanning the photograph, tracing with vector or brush tools on a layer above the image. Repeat the process on new layers or sheets of tracing paper, each time beginning with a different kind of form element, a new tool, or by imposing stricter limitations— for example, isolating only lines or edges of shapes that are running parallel /**B**/.

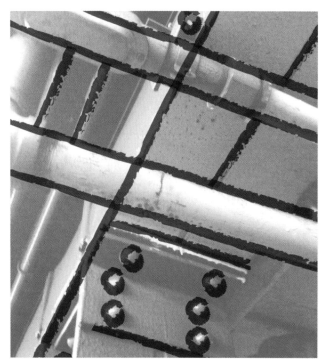

A Overlayed comparison of a source photograph and isolated marks

B A subsequent study showing stricter limitations

Ideas for Development

Lay multiple isolation studies on top of each other to build more complex form languages.

Assign feelings or ideas to each isolation study's form language; use them in place of other image media to express these ideas.

Choose a single isolation study; using the same form language as a motif, explore multiple variations in their compositions, scale relationships, and so on. Maybe a story develops.

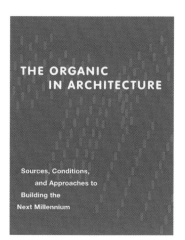

THE ORGANIC
IN ARCHITECTURE

Sources, Conditions,
and Approaches to
Building the
Next Millennium

Positive/Negative and Dark/Light

This study trains the eye to distinguish form from space and contrasting levels of value.

This study may first be made on tracing paper over a photograph (or digitally, on a layer over an imported image); after gaining confidence, attempt the study again but through direct observation of a physical object or a photograph.

Using a dark, opaque medium—whether compressed charcoal, ink, or cut/torn black paper—draw the negative spaces that surround, as well as exist within, an object /**A**/. The chosen object should be relatively complex, with several parts and/or an unusual contour; for example, a coffee cup, a chair, and so on. Consider the outer boundary of the drawn negative forms in relation to the contour of the object itself, defining a shape in which the positive form is revealed.

In a second stage, using different values of magic marker or pencil, diluting black ink as washes, or by changing pressure, define three or four levels of value /**B**/ that you observe in the source—including black (shadow), gray (midtone) and white (highlight). Add each level independently, beginning with shadows. In each reiteration, increase the number of levels between black and white.

A The subject's negative spaces drawn with ink, establishing an outer contour for the negative field that plays off the subject's form

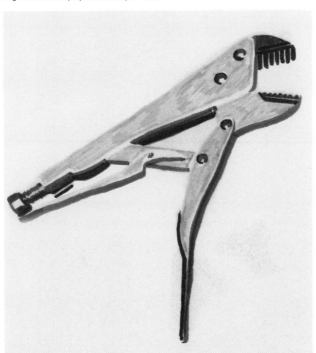

B An example of the exercise's second stage, using three levels of gray produced with magic marker

Ideas for Development

Use the positive area of the first stage drawing as a mask for a rubbing or photographic image whose subject creates a meaning in context.

Develop the negative form's outer contour as the silhouette of a related subject. Note any meaning suggested by the juxtaposition.

Revisit the second stage study in color; explore alterate palette approaches each time: all warm or cool hues, values made by mixing complements, one hue in varied values or saturations, etc.

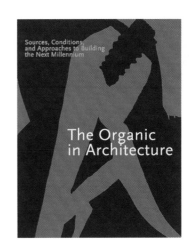

Form Language: Motif and Evolution

This study initiates original mark-making. It cultivates conceptualization and specificity of intent; analytical sensitivity to composition; and further awareness of media.

Work on an 11" x 14" (28 x 36 cm) sheet or larger. Choose any medium to define one set of conditions for a gestural motif, or form language: one way of using the tool (edge only of a chalk /**A**/, for example, or twisting a brush /**B**/); a specific movement (rotational /**C**/, wavy, single upward motion /**D**/, etc.), application of pressure (generally light or heavy, or varied /**E**/ in a purposefully distinct way), and, potentially, a complicating aspect (encountering an obstacle under the paper, perhaps /**F**/, or drawing off the edge of a table). Apply these "rules" together over and over, very rapidly and in one general area, to build up a rhythmic expression of the motif /**G**/. Continue until the composition reaches an "ideal" state: neither too little nor too much. Repeat the same motif and process on new pages, stopping earlier or continuing past the final state of earlier reiterations to compare their differences.

In a second stage, approach the study with the goal of developing a textural field by repeating one, smaller-scale motif—filling the area of the page /**H**/ so that the motif remains individually clear and the field created through its accumulation seems balanced and stable. The motif should retain its individuality, but no instance of it should optically disconnect, or be emphasized, more than

any others; the field of texture it builds should seem continuous and undisturbed to produce an optical calm. As each instance of the motif is introduced, respond to it by varying the position or orientation of subsequent instances, building the field outward to the format's edges.

In a third stage, define the motif as before, but repeat it at different scales, using different media, and in different values /**I**/ to develop a single composition in which negative spaces are active and integrated with the positive forms' clear size and position relationships.

Number the reiterations in each stage and date the sets; periodically revisit this study using different motifs to build a library for reference. As with other studies, each stage of this exploration may be accomplished digitally, using cut/paste functions and layers to make adjustments.

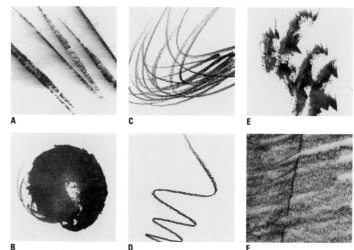

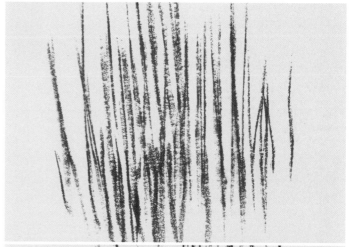

A–F Examples of a variety of motifs, both tool-based and action- or gesture-based

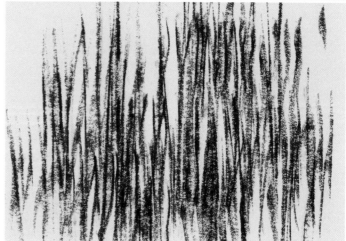

G A repeated motif composition that has been ended early (top); the same motif applied repeatedly over a longer duration (bottom])

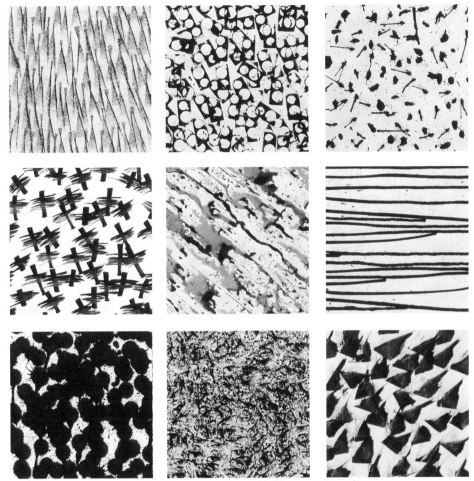

Drawing
/ for Graphic
Design

Invention

Exercises:
Beginning
Level

Ideas for Development

Analyze the forms of first stage motifs and associate each one with an action; use an appropriate one by itself or in combination with others to create a kinetic sequence.

Alternatively, combine a single motif with photographic imagery to help convey a relevant action.

Scan or photocopy a first-stage, single-gesture motif; splice it into a grid and rearrange the modules to create a new composition.

Scan second stage field drawings and use them as backgrounds or masked into shapes as compositional elements to support other kinds of imagery.

Isolate fundamental form elements in the field; redraw the field as a vector pattern using the basic form elements at the same size.

H A student's examples of varied motifs applied to create continuous fields, filling a square format. /
Eva Surany, UArts *United States*

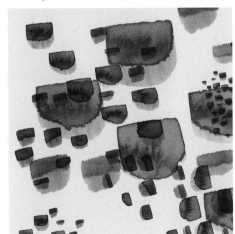

I Examples of a motif used at different scales and orientation (left) and with obliteration (right) in the exercise's third stage

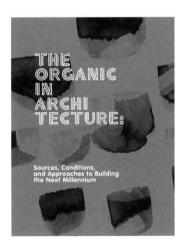

THE ORGANIC IN ARCHITECTURE:

Sources, Conditions, and Approaches to Building the Next Millennium

Rough Traces:
Mass and Contour

This study helps to understand how to connect gestural language and pictorial depiction; it introduces the notion of stylization at a basic level.

Choose a photograph of an object, figure, or scene. On tracing paper, or digitally on a layer above the image, quickly rough in the subject's masses (simply, then with increasing complexity) using any medium or drawing tool /**A**/. Work with the image at a reduced size so that the medium, no matter how controllable, captures essential mass shapes as bluntly and directly as possible. Explore using a combination of media, or multiple values or colors for different masses, as further options.

In a second stage, focus on the image's contours, outlining its major shapes /**B**/. If working conventionally (or using a digital tablet with stylus), define the contours in a continuous line without lifting the tool from the surface, creating a loopy network of connective contours, supporting those that are essential to describing the subject's form.

Attempt both stages through direct observation once you have become more confident in your skills.

A Rough-mass tracing from a source photograph using a fat oil pastel

B A contour drawing derived from the same source image with a medium-weight graphite pencil

Ideas for Development

Use a rough trace as the basis for an icon or logo; maintain its gestural qualities and shaping, but clean it up in a vector drawing program.

Use a rough trace as a mask for a rubbing, texture, or motif pattern.

Combine rough tracings of different subjects to create a simple narrative.

Combine the same subject's rough tracing and contour drawing as a two-layered image; explore options for coloring each layer.

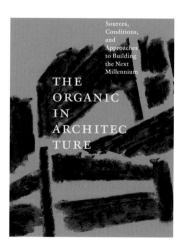

Flat Plane and Axis

This study builds facility with analyzing the fundamental geometry of form for building pictorial representation; it also enhances compositional sensibility with regard to layout.

While this study in particular will build greater skill in working from direct observation, it may be approached using tracing, whether conventional or digital. Choose a relatively complex subject (physically before you or a photographic image). Using planar masses, define the simple, geometric forms /**A**/ that you determine as defining the naturalistic objects or elements within the image: circles, squares, triangles, rhomboids, and so on. Any medium that produces planar masses is appropriate.

In a second stage—either directly on the plane drawing or, alternatively, as a second drawing—use lines to define the image's major axes /**B**/. Draw the horizontal and vertical axes of each object or form component, as well as axes that appear to connect them across the format of the image. Add as many as you see; darken or colorize the ones that seem most important and lighten or erase those that seem less important as you progress.

A A simplified geometric plane study created in an image-editing program, shown on a layer over the source image

B The same source image (lightened with transparency) beneath an overlay of its major geometric axes, created in a vector-based drawing program

Ideas for Development

Develop the flat plane drawing using the source image's color palette.

Combine the flat plane drawing with a single-gesture motif.

Use the flat planes as masks for other images, rubbings, textures, or field-motif patterns.

Fill the areas between axial lines in the axis drawing with colors from a limited palette.

Use the axis drawing as compositional framework for a layout; arrange typographic and pictorial elements according to the structure.

Drawing
/ for Graphic
Design

Invention

Exercises:
Beginning
Level

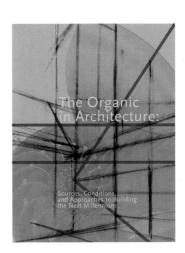

Volumetric Form: Planar Object

This study builds fundamental skills in observating, analyzing, and structuring pictorial depiction; along with form structure, it also confronts compositional structure and perspective.

This classical approach to drawing centers on alternately looking and marking; while the medium may be conventional (pencil on paper) or digital (the pen and various line tools in a software program), the subject should not be traced.

The first stage of this exercise concerns only a single subject. Choose one that is made up only of rectangular planes that meet at right angles—a thick book, a box, or even a very simple chair. Position the subject on a surface a few feet away, in front of you when drawing; this will allow you to compare the subject and your drawing without having to turn away from either as you work. The subject should be lower than eye level, but not so low as to create an extreme overhead view. Further, rotate the object left and right so that its closest vertical edge is not centered between its outermost edges, and so that its left- and right-hand forward sides appear different in proportion to each other. These conditions prevent difficulties in analyzing structure at a beginning level of exploration.

Observe the subject to determine which of its proportions is dominant. If it is predominantly vertical, developing its structure will focus first on defining vertical edges and planes; if it's a flatter, more horizontal form, like a thick book, the process will first focus on its width-related edges.

For a tall form, first define its closest, vertical fore-edge with a line /**A**/; it is fine if the line is sketchy or rough. Then define its left- and right-most edges in the same way. For a more horizontal form, focus first on the angles that its base edges appear to describe—the kind of "V" they make as left and right base edges meet /**A,B**/.

Use your pencil to compare relationships: in a vertical form, to understand how far the left and right edges are from the original, fore-edge vertical; in a horizontal form, to see the difference in the two base-edge angles. As you define each set of edges, continually use the pencil to compare your drawn lines with those of the actual subject /**B**/. If you find disparities, use the kneaded eraser to lighten (but not erase) the incorrect elements to see how to correct them. Darken lines that are correct; you may choose to keep the earlier seek lines as part of the drawing as it progresses,or not, as you like.

By comparing the beginning structural edges to those of the opposing proportion (vertical edges to base edges, or vice-versa) and, by using the pencil to establish relative distances and angles among them, build the cube- or boxlike rectilinear volume of the subject /**C**/.

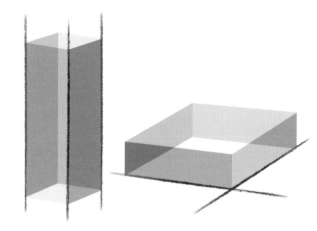

A Comparison of the first stages of a vertical planar volume and a horizontal planar volume

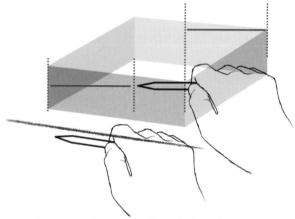

B Comparing distance and angle relationships of a horizontal planar volume using the pencil measuring method

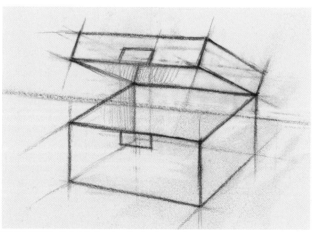

C A completed volumetric drawing of a simple, open box

Proceed to the next stage: a grouping of three objects. Introduce the new objects into the setup with the first one and then work them into the original drawing; or arrange the grouping in a new way and begin a second drawing. Consider the objects' placement within the format for the interaction of their contours and axes; and the shapes, proportions, and directional movement of the negative spaces among them.

The base-edge angles and top-edge angles of the original drawing together create a perspective structure based on two vanishing points /**D**/. Find the horizon by extending these angles outward from the subject until each set converges on a point; draw a horizontal connecting each point. Whether adding to the existing drawing, or developing a new one with all three objects together, discover the horizon and all the objects' vanishing points by quickly and loosely sketching their various edge angles and axes—using the same process as for the single subject /**E**/. Use the pencil to compare angles and distances between edges. If the subjects are stacked with their edges aligning, they will share vanishing points on the horizon; if they are positioned at differing angles to each other, their vanishing points will be different. Use the eraser to help correct as before—but, again, consider that preliminary seek lines, no matter how rough, may richly contribute to the drawing's quality and continue to provide valuable information as it continually evolves /**F**/.

Ideas for Development

Use a refined volumetric drawing as a template upon which to explore rough tracing, flat plane drawing, positive/negative drawing, or as the basis for a nonpictorial, geometric composition.

Combine a volumetric drawing with a photograph of the same subject as a graphical support.

Integrate a single-gesture motif that reflects some action or movement related to the object's subject.

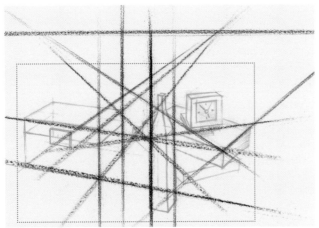

D Roughing in the major axes of a group of objects to discover the horizon and define their vanishing points; note that the horizon and vanishing points may truly exist outside the defined edges of the page format, as seen in this zoomed-out view.

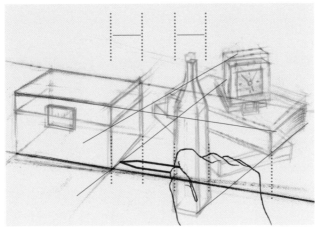

E Comparisons of angles, distances between edges, and relative sizes made using the pencil measuring method; note the erasures and corrections

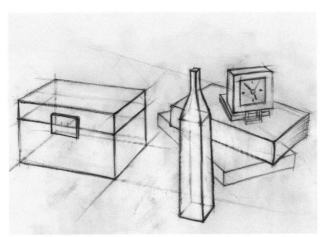

F The completed drawing of the object grouping. As simple as the objects are, their arrangement creates an extremely active contour, tightly interconnected axis structure, and negative spaces that continually change in proportion.

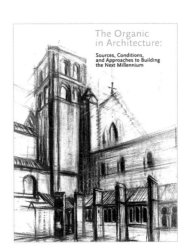

The Organic in Architecture: Sources, Conditions, and Approaches to Building the Next Millennium

Alphabet Investigation

This study develops knowledge of formal typographic (letterform) structure and proportion; it also builds skills in axis and measurement comparison, gesture, and sketch quality.

Begin this exercise by drawing the roman square capitals diagrammed at upper right /**A**/. Use a 3B pencil and work on horizontal 14"x17" (35.5 x 43 cm) pages. Begin with horizontal guides to define baseline/cap line rows, 2" (5 cm) tall as shown; when you feel ready, continue without the guidelines to further evolve your skill.

From left to right, draw an alternating sequence of the full-square, capital H and N; the spaces between the letters should be half their width /**B**/. Use any line quality you like, but keep it consistent. Continue row after row down the page. The goals at this stage are to ensure that: vertical strokes are truly perpendicular (90° to the baseline); both letters appear square in proportion; the horizontal stroke of the H appears centered on its height; letters appear evenly spaced, never getting closer or further apart. Due to letters' varied shapes, most of these attributes must be determined by eye. If they are constructed mathematically (for example, the H and N both measuring 2" [5 cm] wide), the N will appear as extended compared to the H.

Once you achieve these desired formal consistencies, keep adding letters in random order, alternating between characters of different proportions and shape/structure /**C**/. Consider the drawing successful when the following conditions are met: all verticals are truly vertical and (without guides) clearly the same height; the baselines remain consistently horizontal; the spaces between letters and between rows appear consistent; full-square and half-square proportions are clear and consistent; all curves are clearly circular, not ovoid (except the S, which is more of a wave); joints appear optically centered; upper and lower counterspaces in such letters as A, R, P, H, B, K are the same size.

The second stage of this exercise repeats the process using modern proportion /**D**/. Establish a width for the capital M that is roughly 80 percent of its height, noting the proportional alternation between its strokes and counters. Draw the other letters with the same spatial rhythm; this will create the appearance of all the characters being the same width. The curves will become ovoid but, other than that, all the same formal consistencies achieved for the roman square capitals should be achieved here.

In the third stage, introduce the lowercase letters, also drawn to exhibit the same width/stroke/counter rhythm as do the capitals. Define a height for the lowercase (the x-height) roughly 75 percent the height of capitals. This height varies among all typefaces, but the 75 percent proportion is a good average starting point. The distance between the x-height and the cap line determines the height of ascenders in letters such as f, h, k; descenders in letters such as g, p, q should drop a corresponding depth below the baseline.

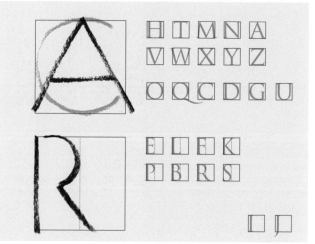

A The roman square capitals are grouped by their structural proportions: full-square, half-square, and single stroke.

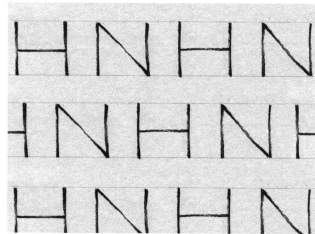

B A sequence of full-square N and H drawings shows the desired evenness of spacing, proportion, and verticallity to be achieved

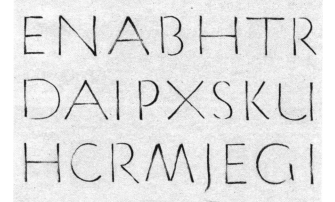

C Example of continuous stroke-writing using a pencil; alternating curved, angled, full-square, half-square, and single-stroke letters

The last stage of this study is to explore the effects of other media, beginning with black ink and either a flat brush or flat-nibbed calligraphic pen. Using this method helps first to understand the historical distribution of thicks and thins in typefaces with contrasting stroke weights. For the established cap-height, a 0.25″ (6 mm) flat brush works best to start. Hold the brush at an upward angle of roughly 30° off horizontal; draw the letters as you have previously, but without rotating your wrist or hand— keep the angle consistent, even when drawing curves. Note how the brush's angle uniformly creates thick and thin strokes depending on their respective directions /**D**/; compare your results with the model at right. Aside from the capital *N*, *Z*, and lowercase *z*, the thins and thicks in all typefaces (even sans serifs) appear in the same locations. Changing the angle of the brush alters the degree of contrast.

Experiment with different overall character proportions (condensed/extended) in combination with different degrees of contrast. For bold forms, whether uniform in stroke weight or contrasting, add weight outward from the core of each stroke. Finally, expand your study to include drawing with a variety of media, but always honor the logic of the stroke weights as defined by the flat brush /**E**/.

D Characters of modern proportion drawn with a flat brush, showing historical distribution of thins and thicks among letters of different structure; note the effect of brush angle on the degree of contrast in the strokes.

E Further exploration with various media demonstrates the potential effect of the tool on the overall stylistic quality of the letters.

Ideas for Development

Scan or photocopy related sets of letterform drawings; cut and paste them together to assemble callouts or title treatments. Alternatively, splice components from sets with different drawing qualities together to create hybrid forms.

Combine a single letter (or word made using the strategy above) with a photograph of a subject that seems related to the letter's visual qualities.

Combine a single letter, word, or grouping (using the same strategy as above) with a drawing from one of the previous exercises to establish a formal (visual) and meaningful (narrative) relationship.

Drawing
/ for Graphic
Design

Invention

Exercises:
Beginning
Level

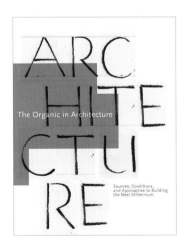

Obliterating
and Obscuring

This study attunes sensitivity to subtractive drawing and the editing of form in preparation for studies of reduction; it also builds further awareness of positive/negative interplay.

Obliterating and obscuring, or hiding, present interesting visual possibilities that may influence a form's recognizability or alter its meaning. This exercise may be accomplished conventionally or digitally using a variety of sources, including ones you may have created in previous exercises. Choose some to photocopy these or scan them and print out several copies. Test different methods to see not only how they evolve into an existing form language but, more importantly, to discover how much of the source can be hidden and still be recognizable. Images may be painted onto with white gouache or plaka, or covered by either opaque or transparent paper /**A**/; or they may be smudged or erased /**B**/ if they are original pencil or chalk drawings. Experiment with pictorial and nonpictorial drawings, as well as with letterforms or words—with these latter, obliteration and obscuring have a dramatic impact on legibility /**C**/.

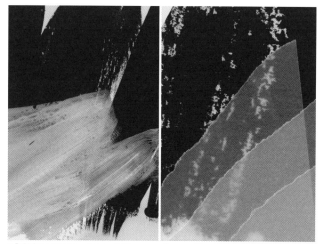

A Painting out and overlaying with transparent paper offer numerous possibilities.

B Erasures made with graphic (left) and kneaded (right) erasers have pronouncedly different effects on various marks.

C Obscuring pictorial and typographic material

Ideas for Development

Use a rough-trace or positive/negative drawing, converted white, to obscure a photographic image or another positive drawing, rather than obscuring directly.

Use a drawn letterform to obscure an image of any kind.

Mask a secondary image into the area of a drawn object or figure that has been obscured; maintain the obscured object's outer contour.

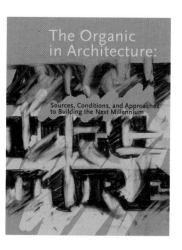

The Organic
in Architecture:

Sources, Conditions, and Approaches
to Building the Next Millennium

Letterform Manipulation

This study expands creativity with regard to type, and integrates techniques from previous exercises. It reinforces understanding of type as image; and it promotes iterative investigation.

Choose a single capital or lowercase letter with which to work. Draw the letter at a height of 4" (10 cm) in bold, sans serif and neutral, regular serif styles. From this point, make dozens of copies of each; you may also add new drawings of specific styles, or freely drawn interpretations of the form as you go forward.

Alter the letter any way you like /**A**/; perform a different manipulation on each copy, or on originals when appropriate; make sure the results of each manipulation are clear and dramatic. Employ as many different manipulation strategies as possible, using physical, digital, and photographic methods—individually and in combination. Keep each manipulation separate, on its own page (or layer within a file).

scribbling
rough tracing
outlining
contour drawing
erasing
altering contours
filling
shredding
smearing
folding
tearing
disintegrating
photocopy degeneration
slicing/dicing
shifting parts
masking
cropping
scratching
scoring
rubbing
stenciling
texture mapping
placing onto or dropping out of a field
cloning
roughening
contorting
warping
bloating
skewing
ornamenting with "foreign" elements
merging different type styles' elements
extruding
light effects
blurring
making with found materials
moving during scanning or photocopying
soaking
puncturing
perforating
burning
spattering
hybridizing with a pictorial image

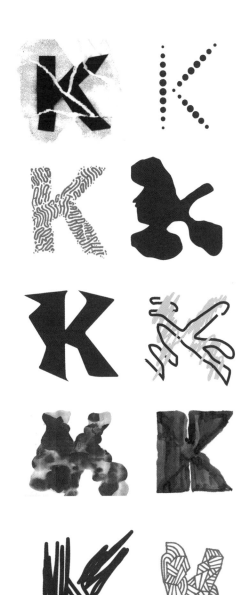

A This edited selection of a study barely hints at what is possible with letter manipulation. /Kevin Harris, School of Visual Arts *United States*

Ideas for Development

Use manipulated single letters as initial caps (for instance, as drop caps) in an editorial layout.

Assign feelings or associations to each version of a manipulated letter; use one as a typographic image to represent that idea or a related subject in place of pictorial imagery.

Combine a manipulated letterform with a photograph or other pictorial image to create narrative.

Use a manipulated letter as a logo for a client.

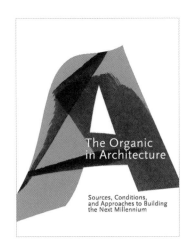

The Organic in Architecture

Sources, Conditions, and Approaches to Building the Next Millennium

Drawing /for Graphic Design

Invention

Exercises: Beginning Level

Silhouetted Icon:
Naturalistic

This study develops skill with simple pictorial reduction and stylization.

Choose an animal or common object as a subject. The goal here will be to achieve an important distinguishing characteristic of an icon that it is nonspecific. An icon of a clock, for instance, should not identify it as a certain kind of clock, nor an old-style or modern one—but instead, capture the neutral, universal aspects of all clocks. What defines its "clock-ness"?

Find three to five photographs of the subject, of different kinds and from different angles; trace their outer contours and fill them solid black to create silhouettes /**A**/. Work digitally; use black markers or use black plaka or ink. Use white plaka to refine or edit elements. Compare the versions: Which is most recognizable? Which has the most dynamic contour and positive/ negative interplay? Which aspects of its silhouetted contour are universal, as opposed to specific? Combine aspects to meet these goals /**B**/. Reduce the icon to a very small size /**C**/; remove any distracting elements and exaggerate important ones weakened by the reduction. Analyze the inward/outward movement of the contour and transitional rhythm between changes that occur; adjust these with the goal of establishing a clear logic.

A Icons generated from different source images of the same subject show varying degrees of recognizability and contour interest; desirable characteristics were selected and combined.

B A refined icon based on the initial study

C Extreme reduction helps isolate important elements for exaggeration and unimportant ones to be edited out.

Ideas for Development

Explore visual and narrative effects of color on the silhouetted icon.

Use the icon in place of a photograph in a relevant context.

Digitally redraw the icon using only available line and shape tools (not the pen tool) to create a super-simplified, stylized version that retains essential information.

Mask other drawn or photographic imagery into the silhouetted icon's shape; note how the meaning of the icon changes.

Manipulate or alter the icon using a variety of strategies (as in the Letter Manipulation study, page 151) to create a visual narrative.

THE ORGANIC IN ARCHITECTURE

Sources, Conditions, and Approaches to Building the Next Millennium

Gestural Translation

This study further explores reduction by enhancing observation and editing skills; it integrates mark isolation, gestural motif, and icon strategies for expanded visual and narrative potential.

Choose a subject of any kind. If the subject is small, you may decide to work from empirical observation. Alternatively, you may work from photographs. Analyze the subject to understand its essential attributes: plane and axis structure; contour shaping; angularity and curvilinearity; surface activity and texture; materiality; opacity or translucency; and so on. Also consider the subject's function— what it does, how it works—as well as any metaphor or association it evokes.

Isolate characteristic form elements as potential sources for marks. Using any medium and method, define one, two, or three gestural motifs that may express different attributes; use them to rapidly articulate the subject's form /**A**/. If desired, edit reiterations through obliteration to reduce and clarify. Note how each unique form language supports understanding of the subject matter or seems unrelated; further, consider how such visual changes suggest new meanings.

A Numerous studies of a single subject alternately exploit the textural qualities of the tool, gestural movement in the marks' application, and subject details to express different qualities.

Ideas for Development

Integrate a gestural translation with a silhouetted icon of the same subject; explore color differentiation for each of the layers. Alternatively, colorize the gestural translation as white and use it to obliterate the same silhouetted icon.

Use a gestural translation over a photographic image.

Combine the gestural translation with a contour, rough-trace drawing, or flat-plane drawing.

Support the gestural icon with a single or field-pattern gestural form language motif.

Drawing / for Graphic Design

Invention

Exercises: Beginning Level

Sources, Conditions, and Approaches to Building the Next Millennium

The Organic in Architecture:

Volumetric Form:
Cylinders and Polyhedra

This study further develops skills related to observation and analytical depiction first explored in with planar form (p. 146).

For the first stage of this exercise, choose a simple cylindrical object, such as a can or bottle. Position it in front of where you are drawing, similar to how you did with a simple planar object, so that it rests somewhat below eye level. Standing the object upright initially may complicate analysis, but not dramatically so; decide whether you'd like to proceed with the object in this position or by its lying down on the surface. If you opt for the latter, rotate it so that its forward circular base isn't oriented toward you head-on.

A cylinder is essentially a tubular box. Although the ends of this shape are circles, and its circumference curvilinear, underlying these attributes is a cubic shape. Begin by defining its outer contour edges, which run parallel to each other (or, alternatively, may converge very slightly as they recede in perspective from near to far). Check these edges' angles in your drawing against those of the object, using the pencil method.

Next, envision and construct the invisible, planar structure /**A**/, approximating the interior edge of the "box" and the upper and base edge angles of its ends, which are squares rotated in space. Roughing these in loosely and, determining somewhat intuitively if these planes correspond to their actual positions on the subject is a process of trial and error. After the planar volume is constructed, the next step is to draw guidelines that describe the central vertical and horizontal axes of the end planes, using them

to construct the arcs of an ellipse on each plane's surface, as shown /**A**/. An ellipse is a circle that has been rotated away from a direct, head-on view. You may add the diagonal axes of these same planes as further support to help maintain fluid, symmetrical curves around the ellipses. The front and rear ellipses should appear identical in size, although the rear one may actually be slightly smaller if using the converging angles of perspective.

While a paint can, for example, is composed only of one cylindrical structure, an object such as a wine bottle is constructed of two cylinders—the wide one of the vessel itself, and the narrower one that describes the neck—joined by a sphere whose diameter is the same as that of the large cylinder /**B**/. The sphere is drawn by constructing an ellipse in the opposite direction, along the cylinder's central planar axis. Multiple, smaller ellipses help describe the details of the neck's end and the lip of the bottle's opening. It is then a matter of connecting the cylinders using curved lines that approximate the transition between them that is observable in the bottle.

A Building the planar understructure of the subject; Constructing the ellipses on the frontal and rear planes; note how the arcs of the ellipses, from axis to axis on their planes, are mirror images of each other

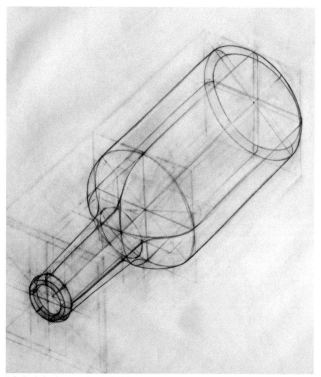

B Articulating in secondary cylindrical structures

The second stage of this exercise is to employ both the planar and cylindrical structural approaches in combination to draw a much more complex, intrinsically geometric object—a sauce pan, a toy truck, a garlic press, or some similar object. The components of all objects, no matter how seemingly complicated, can be built using this process /**c**/. Triangular, trapezoidal, and polyhedral forms of greater intricacy are, in simplest terms, clusters of cubic forms and, in some cases, can be conceived of as being formed by edges that cut into cubic forms, deviating inward from the outer contour edges and planes at specific junctures. The pencil-measuring method helps locate the junctures at which cubic and cylindrical masses are joined, as well as their relative angles.

As complex as this strategy may be at first, it becomes easier as the ability to perceive planar and cylindrical structure improves through each attempt. Ultimately, it becomes a point of departure for more intuitively describing volumetric forms, especially when the subject is no longer explicitly geometric—as is the case with organic forms such as vegetables, animals, and figures.

All images this page spread:
Paone Design Associates *United States*

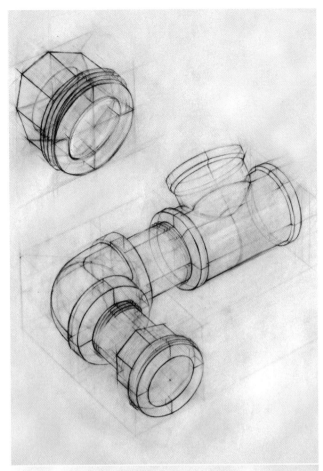

Ideas for Development

Use a complex volumetric drawing as a template for investigating more rendered, or naturalistic, pictorial representation.

Combine the volumetric drawing with a positive/negative or dark/light value study, in either black and white or color.

Integrate a form language motif whose gesture complements the volumetric drawing's structure and supports its meaning.

Overlay two or more volumetric drawings to create a dimensional "wireframe" composition.

Drawing
/for Graphic
Design

Invention

Exercises:
Intermediate
Level

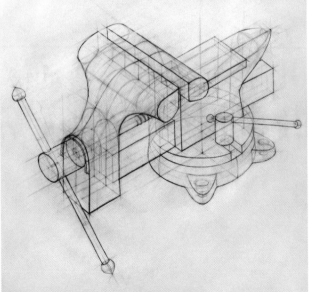

C Similar stages are used to construct a relatively more complex object whose structure consists of both cylindrical and planar/polyhedral volumes.

The Organic in Architecture:

Sources, Conditions, and Approaches to Building the Next Millennium

Nonpictorial Narrative: Gestural/Field

This study explores communication through nonpictorial form; it enhances sensitivity to form language resolution. Before beginning, have an array of mark making tools and media, along with a stack of smaller-format drawing paper (as from a sketchbook, or a ream of copy paper) within easy reach.

In the first stage, represent emotional states with purely non-pictorial drawing, avoiding even symbols—hearts, stars, etc. Consider an opposing pair: anxiety and joy /**A**/. Develop as many possible variations for visualizing each on separate sheets of paper, taking into account the possibilities offered by different media /**B**/. Compare the two sets, noting which characteristics in their respective form languages identifies them and their quality of opposition. Eventually, choose one from each set and refine them; edit, exaggerate, and clarify relationships in shape, size, gesture, spacing, and movement. Continue with another pair, perhaps anxiety and comfort; or more subtly shaded pairs.

In second and subsequent stages, explore concepts. Always work in pairs or groups /**C**/—doing so creates a context for comparison to help judge the specificity and relevance of the images' form languages. Concepts may be concrete (technology and nature, for example), or intangible (intimidating and welcoming).

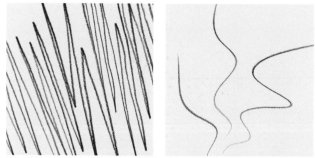

A Considering a pair of emotions to start helps compare the qualities of their respective visual languages, relative to their opposed meanings (anxiety/joy).

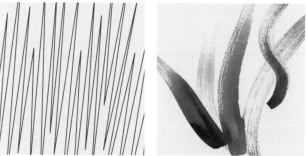

B The medium may contribute to the expression of meaning, adding its physical or textural qualities to those established by the syntax of marks.

C A grouping of related subjects (the seasons)

Ideas for Development

Use this exercise as an approach to visualize moods or concepts in a poem or prose text.

Revisit the study using color media to further enhance the form language's intended meaning.

Develop a series in which the form language is unified among different messages, expressed in variation.

Combine narrative form languages with other pictorial imagery to support or alter its meaning.

Sources, Conditions, and Approaches to Building the Next Millennium

The Organic in Architecture

Nonpictorial Narrative:
Reductive/Singularity

This study develops facility with nonpictorial representation; it hones editing skill, perception of positive/ negative relationships, and form resolution.

Working only in positive and negative— using black and white plaka and brush, or digital drawing tools—undergo a similar process of representing emotions, then concepts, as in the previous exercise. This time, develop the images as self-contained units (independent of the surrounding compositional space), and work to radically simplify the elements, as one would for a logo. Pursue this study with opposing subject pairs as before /**A,B**/; or consider subject groupings: the seasons, the senses, the elements, geographic locations, world cities, and so on.

Use black, positive marks and shapes to evolve the forms of the language; use white elements (or the vector points in a digital context) to refine and simplify. You may consider imposing a particular limita- tion /**B**/ on the reduction; for example, to accomplish the image with only five or six elements, or using only line or only dots.

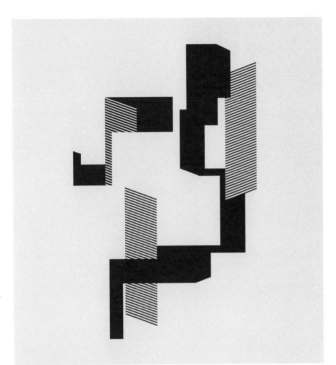

A The concept of "building" is expressed here as a self-contained unit, or singularity, of nonpictorial marks.

B The notion of "organicism," also reduced to a singularity; as an added limitation, it is composed only of one kind of syntax and restricted to three repetitions.

Ideas for Development

Use the reduction as a primary image in place of a pictorial one.

Apply color to selected elements within the reduced image to test changes in spatial depth, hierarchy, and internal contrast.

Combine a reduced, nonpictorial singularity with other imagery to support or evolve narrative.

Use a reduced, nonpictorial image as a logo for a client.

Combine several reduced images to create a visual narrative; consider basing their development and combination on a text as a source for visualization.

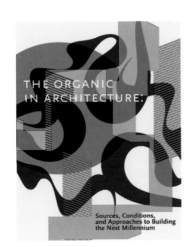

Drawing / for Graphic Design

Invention

Exercises:
Intermediate Level

Area Map

This study improves spatial analysis and clarifying part-to-whole relationships; it promotes hierarchical simplicity; it raises awareness of diagrammatic form language options and type integration.

Find an existing map of an urban or rural locale; select a portion on which to focus from within the entire territory it shows. Scan the map in grayscale mode at high resolution to preserve values and details; place the image into a drawing program and, on a layer above it, trace the map's features in black and white, using the program's available tools /**A**/. As you work, consider such qualities among lines and masses as: angularity or curvilinearity; line texture or weight; value or pattern differences; and degree of naturalism versus abstract simplification—all relative to clearly distinguishing the identities of the various features. Apply value changes also to optically calm or simplify the presentation so that key features (as you may define them) are emphasized more than others /**B**/. The hierarchy must be explicit, and contribute to a totality of presence that prevents optical busy-ness.

As a last step, integrate typographic labels /**c**/ for the features, establishing a system of specific styles, sizes, values, and structural relationship among them so they are not only legible, but also clearly indicate which feature they name.

A Blocking out major areas and differentiating features through shaping; changes in line weight indicate the relative traffic volume of different roads.

B Value and intensity changes help merge or emphasize features.

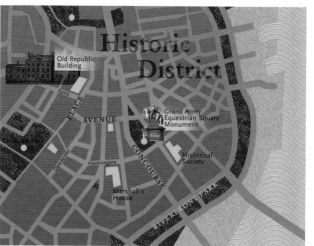

C Typographic labels are styled and colored for maximum legibility and unity with the map's form language; textures and patterns impart greater interest and distinction.

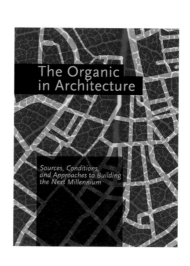

The Organic in Architecture

Sources, Conditions, and Approaches to Building the Next Millennium

Detailed Icon:
Naturalistic, Stylized

This study expands on skills explored in the Silhouetted Icon exercise (p. 152) in greater depth and complexity.

For this exercise, work with the same subject as for the silhouetted icon study, or choose a new one—arrive at a black silhouette using the same process. Then, also articulate components of the subject that are both more detailed and dimensional: surface features, limbs or parts that exist spatially in front of the silhouette's contour, and so on /**A**/.

Keep in mind the desired universality to be achieved. Add details that help identify, as well as augment essential characteristics; refine and simplify, exaggerate and discard, elements as you did with the simpler, silhouetted version.

In a second stage, revizualize the icon using a highly exaggerated form language /**B**/—only lines or planar forms, for example, replicating the structure with a pattern, or applying strategies from previous exercises, such as mark isolation, blunt tracing or contour, and so on.

A Comparison of a flat, sihouetted icon used as a beginning point and the detailed icon that resulted from introducing more information. Note how dimensionality is indicated by the use of changing line weights and figure/ground reversal.

B Using the detailed icon above to experiment with stylization in the second stage

Ideas for Development

Manipulate the icon using a variety of strategies to alter its perceived meaning or narrative.

Juxtapose several icons, of different subjects, in a composition to create a narrative.

Combine the icon with other pictorial images to create simple narratives.

Explore the application of color to enhance the icon's expression of its subject, or to alter that expression.

Use the icon in place of a photographic image of the same subject in a relevant context.

Mask related (or unrelated) textures (rubbing, nonpictorial motif, decorative pattern, or photographic) into the icon to enhance or alter its meaning.

Drawing
/ for Graphic
Design

Invention

Exercises:
Intermediate
Level

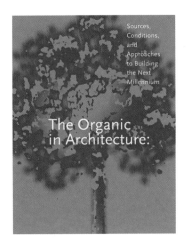

Letter/Letter Combination

This study increases sensitivity to letter structure with respect to its limitations and potential for alteration; it enhances understanding of form-language, composition, and positive/negative interplay.

Sketch a variety of capital and lowercase letters—or, alternatively, review research from the Alphabet Investigation exercise (p. 148) to find structural similarities and contrasts that might prove useful in selecting two characters to combine in a reductive monogram (much like one might for a logo). Once you make your selection, explore myriad possibilities for how they may be juxtaposed and integrated with each other to express a simple, clear, and compelling visual relationship /**A**/. Using only black and white, test an array of possible relationships, separately and together: relative scale, weight, width, position, stroke contrast, type style, capital versus lowercase, rotation, parallel or conflicting angles, curve versus angle, overlap, slant, directional thrust, complexity, figure/ground reversal, and so on. Be conscious of legibility as a concept takes form: both letters must remain clearly recognizable.

The goal of this exercise is to develop a simultaneity and singularity of experience between the two letters /**B**/, exhibiting a decisive logic of shape, positive/negative interplay, structure, and form language.

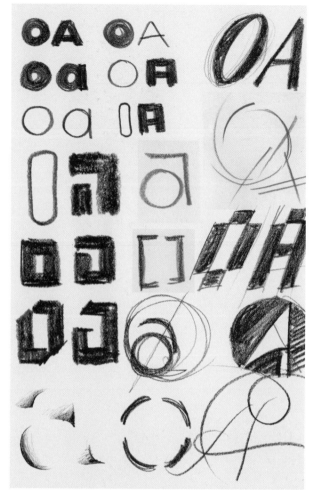

A Various studies of proportion, structure, composition, and detail between a letter *A* and a letter *O* to discover ways of unifying the two very different forms

Ideas for Development

House the letter combination in a geometric or organic shape; unify the compositional relationship between the two forms.

Support the letter combination with pictorial imagery or non-pictorial form language to create narrative.

Manipulate the letter combination using a variety of drawing strategies to test their effects on both its form and potential meaning.

Apply color to selected elements in the combination to enhance or alter its existing positive/negative and spatial qualities.

Use the letter combination as an identifying primary image, instead of a pictorial image.

Use this strategy to create a letter-based logo for a client.

B A refined combination of the letters *A* and *O* following the initial study, painted first by hand and then traced in a vector-based drawing program

Letter/Icon Combination

A Experiments with an icon and the initial letter of its name; note the differing, specific relationships between the two with regard to formal parity and contrast, given the style, size, position, and interaction of the letterform.

This study supports analysis of formal relationships between typographic and pictorial imagery; it further enhances the skills addressed in the letter/letter combination exercise at left.

For this exercise's first stage, work with one of the icons you have developed in previous studies—integrating it with the initial letter of its name, or with another letter of your own choosing. Analyze the icon's overall shape and structure first to determine if it shares a fundamental, structural relationship with a letter; this may sometimes be true and at other times, not—depending on the letter's style. The existing icon may need to be adjusted slightly to better integrate with the letterform /**A**/.

In a second stage, develop the combination of icon and letter of its name in tandem /**B**/. Draw both forms at the same time, as a seamless image; allow the shaping of both the icon's and letter's proportions, gesture, and detailing to mutually respond to each other. Be sure to note possible similarities between parts, or all, of the icon's form and those of the letter's counterspaces in and around the strokes; these offer possibilities for figure-ground reversal. It may also be interesting to extrapolate details from within the icon itself—markings, textural elements, etc.—beyond the icon's boundaries and into the letter where the two overlap.

Drawing
/for Graphic
Design

Invention

Exercises:
Intermediate
Level

Ideas for Development

House the letter combination in a geometric or organic shape; unify the compositional relationship between the two forms.

Support the letter combination with pictorial imagery or nonpictorial form language to create narrative.

Manipulate the letter combination using a variety of drawing strategies to test their effects on both its form and potential meaning.

Apply color to selected elements in the combination to enhance or alter its existing positive/negative and spatial qualities.

Use the letter combination as an identifying primary image, instead of a pictorial image.

Use this strategy to create a letter-based logo for a client.

B Here, a different icon and the letter *A* were combined to create an integrated form.

The
Organic
in
Archi
tecture

Sources, Conditions,
and Approaches to Building
the Next Millennium

Volumetric Form: Organic Subject

This study reinforces skills explored previously with simpler volumes; it further facilitates a transition from studied, structural drawing to more direct, intuitive drawing.

Choose an organic subject: fruits and vegetables of simpler, more appreciably geometric form are excellent to start; such complex subjects as branches, flowers, animals, or figures are better subjects once you become more proficient. Following similar logic, begin with graphite or charcoal pencil before proceeding to media whose form languages may introduce greater complexity. Position the subject with the same considerations as you have in previous exercises /**A**/. Construct the subject as you would a planar or cylindrical form, using the pencil as an analytical tool to compare volume proportions, distances between edges, and so on. Establish the simplest planar structure first /**A**/, articulating components and details with increasing specificity. Use both the kneaded and white erasers to lighten and choose darker values to obliterate, minimize, or emphasize seek lines and confirmed lines /**B**/.

In the second stage, place tracing paper over the structural drawing and redraw the subject gesturally, using the structural drawing as a guide /**C**/. Explore several reiterations on this template to test alternate value, line-to-mass, gestural, and detail relationships. Consider the surface of the subject and the play of light across it: the gestural tracks of the tool you're using can describe these conditions, as can purposely drawn details. Note how

surface elements often appear to follow the "direction" of the volume's planes or curvatures; whether explicitly describing the surface or expressing the syntax of the tool, orient marks to follow this same direction. This strategy will usually enhance the form's volumetric quality.

For the third stage, reposition the same subject so you are viewing it from a different angle. Having analytically built its structure first, and gesturally represented it with the support of that structure, draw the new configuration intuitively, merging structural understanding with gestural vitality and intuition /**D**/. Particularly at this stage, experimenting with medium, gesture, obliteration or obscuring, and motif will present new options for more specifically attuning the formal language of the drawing to the structure being articulated and, alternatively, imposing stylistic conceits which may be relevant to narrative or not.

Revisit this exercise periodically with increasingly complex organic subjects. The human figure, notably, is quite complex /**E**/ and may be explored both structurally and gesturally in the same sitting. If you pursue the figure as a subject, you may work equally well from photographs as a source (by tracing or direct observation of the photographic image), as well as from a model—drawing a friend or colleague, sitting in a park and drawing passersby, or by visiting a figure-drawing group or class. Drawing the figure is no different from drawing any other organic subject.

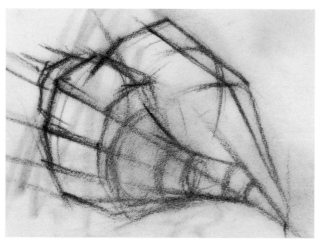

A Describing the subject's essential geometry and positioning the subject's volume in the format for dynamic compositional relationships

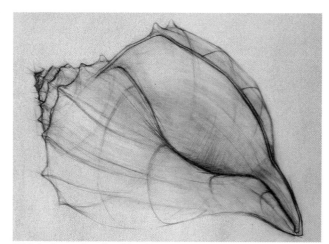

B Refining the organic quality of the subject through observation of transitions between volumes Paone Design Associates / United States

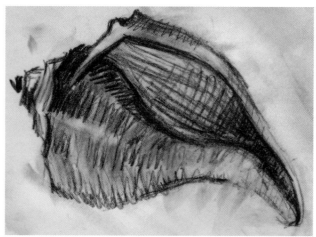

C A gestural version traced over the analytical drawing in the second stage of the study

D The subject was repositioned and then gesturally drawn using the same basic approach as before.

E Following the same construction process for other organic subjects (such as a figure), but emphasizing gesture and line quality, can inform even the drawing of simpler objects—to develop a more intuitive, personal approach as skill and confidence grow over time. Paone Design Associates / United States

Ideas for Development

Work from a planar, structural drawing of the subject to develop more rendered, naturalistic versions.

Experiment with color, using cool tones to accentuate shadow areas and warm tones to emphasize highlights.

Combine a gestural drawing with flat-plane drawing, using the geometric forms as transparencies in color or tones of gray to add depth.

Drawing
/for Graphic
Design

Invention

Exercises:
Intermediate
Level

The Organic in Architecture:

Sources, Conditions, and Approaches to Building the Next Millennium

Depiction: Spatial/Landscape

This study reinforces skills developed throughout all previous volumetric, pictorial depiction-based exercises; it further promotes intuitive, gestural drawing skill initiated in the Organic Subject exercise (p.162).

The complexity of intricate still lifes, interior scenes, and landscapes can seem overwhelming, but the same fundamental process for evolving form and composition prevails: defining large-scale spatial and volumetric structures first; and then evolving subordinate structures of decreasing relative scale, but increasing intricacy.

No matter the subject, and whether working from reference or direct observation, first establish the scene's horizon and basic axial structure /**A**/. Because the spatial field in environmental scenes is all encompassing and vast, relative to the viewer, the empirical horizon will tend to fall around eye-level; this intuitively corresponds to the format's central horizontal axis. Placing the horizon here positions the viewer at a natural and expected vantage point, but this symmetrical spatial break also may initiate a passive composition. Test alternatives for the horizon's location: very low and very high positions will significantly change the vantage-point experience; also consider the proportions of format space created above and below the horizon with regard to their rhythmic potential.

The horizon in a complex still life (unless viewed head-on at eye-level) will usually be located above the central area of focus, possibly beyond the format's upper edge. The further away from the grouping of subjects, or the less extreme the angle at which they are viewed, the lower and more central the horizon will tend to be.

Once the horizon is established, rough in major features' vertical axes and contours left to right, and their relative heights (as compared to each other and their respective proximities to the format's upper and lower edges), using the pencil-analysis strategy /**B**/. These relationships are critical to finding perspective angles that will influence how individual volumetric structures are developed, as well as creating rhythmic structural intervals. Continually comparing these relationships, use the kneaded eraser to lighten tenuous seek lines and darken corrected ones as you approach confirmation of the structure.

Next, articulate subordinate subjects' individual structures as you would when drawing a single object. Work back and forth between them, noting the heights of their respective horizontal axes and edges to ensure that their vertical positions and their respective vertical height proportions are accurate.

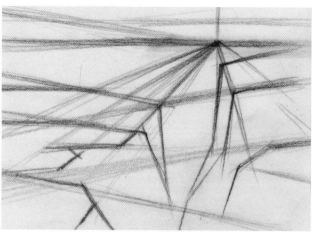

A Selecting a location for the horizon and roughing in major axes for a landscape image

B Constructing secondary structures' basic forms and, subsequently articulating their internal structures in greater detail

C Adjusting value and textural relationships to enforce a hierarchy and emphasize subjects within the field

Once both environmental and secondary structures evolve, begin to assess which foreground, middle ground, and background components require emphasis or simplification; adjust values and embellish as needed to accentuate relevant areas in general /**C**/, as well as such components of secondary forms, and strategically downplay others. The role of value here cannot be underestimated. A viewer's ability to immediately appreciate distribution of light, medium, and dark areas permits them to rapidly analyze the scene's complexity—and in so doing, understand its hierarchy. Use value change to differentiate areas and objects, but work to focus dark values in one area and light values in another; introducing an element of opposing value in these areas adds contrast and helps integrate each with the other.

Along with landscapes, explore interiors /**D,E**/ following the same basic procedures. Drawing interior scenes allows for more numerous vantage points and, therefore, presents a wealth of opportunities to experiment with their effect on perspective and subject emphasis. You may also wish to revisit object groupings (still lifes) explored during the latter stage of the Planar Object exercise (p. 146), but from vantage points that will similarly introduce greater complexity.

D An interior scene, drawn from a central, eye-level vantage point

E The same scene, drawn from a low vantage point that is positioned to create extreme angle divergence in the perspective

Ideas for Development

Experiment with naturalistic and invented color schemes.

Scan the drawing; explore extreme adjustments to its contrast and tonal levels using digital filters. Further, test the effects of various filters on selected areas of the drawing.

Replace areas of the drawing with nonpictorial motifs, such as rubbing or field textures.

Introduce iconic pictorial forms orphotographic elements to create a surreal presentation and suggest new kinds of meaning.

Explore scenic drawing as both full-format fields and as self-contained singularities, considering the outer contour of the drawing's boundaries with respect to the composition of interior elements.

Gestural Typographic Composition

This study boosts confidence with letterform structure and style; sensitivity to form interaction and contrast; and analysis of compositional and positive/negative relationships.

A larger format—18" x 24" (46 x 61 cm)—is best for this activity, as is a less precise medium (ink or paint, charcoal, cut paper, found collage materials, etc.). To begin (and before each subsequent drawing), define limitations to guide you: for example, drawing only capital letters, a set number of forms to draw (vary from three to perhaps twenty) and a time limit—perhaps five minutes. Once these variables are set, begin every drawing the same way: choose a character to introduce into the format /**A**/. Analyze all the formal information this first character provides: scale, weight, width, value, rotation, lateral position, edge proximity, angularity, curvilinearity, stroke uniformity or contrast, stroke directionality, parallelism or divergence, location of joints, stylistic details, and so on.

In consideration of this information, add subsequent characters in a sequence of intuitive responses to these conditions—until the limitations have been met, and a dynamic, unified composition with strong contrast and active spaces results /**B,C**/.

A The first character introduced into the format sets up basic conditions to which subsequent characters must respond.

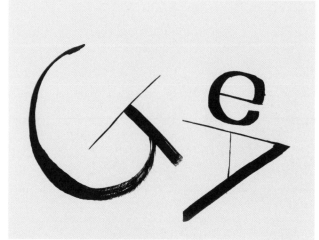

B The composition in progress; try to describe the specific relationships that occur between each of the charcters and the format.

C The completed drawing, timed to five minutes and including dots and lines.

Ideas for Development

Also include lines and dots, along with letters, as elements within the drawing; assign limitations to their number and behaviors as you would for the letterforms.

Before beginning a drawing, make a number of gestural marks on the surface with your eyes closed.

Respond to these forms compositionally and as a source for constructing letters in the drawing.

Accomplish the study using a full word or short phrase as a source for the characters; develop the drawing as spontaneously and gesturally as before, but maintain legibility.

Use colored media and varied hues to enhance the composition's dimensional quality as it is developed.

Introduce a pictorial element, such as an icon or volumetric drawing.

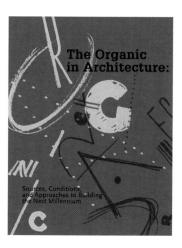

Final image at left:
Hyung Kyu Choi, School of
Visual Arts / *United States*

Form Language: Action

This study further enriches knowledge of, and confidence with, nonpictorial drawing; it provides added opportunities for conceptual development, visualization, and the creation of narrative.

Approach this exercise in exactly the same way as in the emotions/concepts version (p. 156)—but this time, represent a physical, environmental, or mechanical action or activity with purely nonpictorial form. The empirical subject(s) that are performing the action are only important with respect to how they perform it. Analyze the action and break it into distinct segments or sub-actions: How many are there? How are they each different? How long does each sub-action last, relative to the others? Does one sub-action cause the others? Is the action intricate or bold and aggressive? How much force is needed?

Translate the qualities of movement, force, and intricacy that you are able to distill from considering the action in your choice of medium, mark, and gesture /**A**/. Capture the physicality of axial rotation, thrusting, lifting, pushing, scraping, breathing, and so on through the structure of the marks, their axes, and their textural qualities.

A Various studies of the action evolution or germination and growth

Ideas for Development

Differentiate sub-actions using different languages or color.

Support the action gesture with another nonpictorial motif.

Combine alternate versions of the action gesture to create a kinetic sequence or suggest a process.

As an alternative, combine different gestural actions to accomplish the same goal in a more complex way.

Introduce a volumetric or other pictorial image related to the action gesture to create a context for understanding it.

Compose the action gesture in a relevant photographic image to clarify or alter its meaning.

Drawing / for Graphic Design

Invention

Exercises: Advanced Level

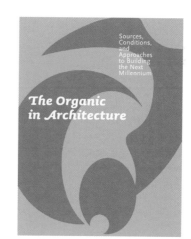

Reductive, Naturalistic Translation

This study hones editing skills; it integrates structural drawing, gestural marking, obliteration, and approaches to stylization; and it further develops control over positive/negative interaction and form language resolution.

This exercise may be completed digitally and from photographic reference for preliminary explorations; but drawing from observation and by hand will result in greater understanding of form, as well as improved eye/hand and tool control. Whichever approach you take, you may elect to bypass the first stage (volumetric drawing) to investigate form spontaneously with positive/negative media (black and white plaka).

Any subject may be graphically translated—mechanical or otherwise volumetric objects, organic objects, figures, animals, and environments— which, similar to creating an icon, means to present it in a highly edited, purely positive/negative form. While a translation also seeks essence (and may be approached to achieve universality), it is more commonly directed toward specificity: not simply "monkey" or "perfume bottle," but a precise species of monkey, or a particular perfume bottle's shape and materiality.

The first stage of developing a translation proceeds simultaneously along two paths: researching possible viewpoints for presenting the subject and, from there, constructing a descriptive, volumetric drawing /**A**/; and engaging in gestural research (see Gestural Translation, p.155, to discover and test mark-making that may be useful in

creating a unique, but essential language to articulate the structure /**B**/. Rather than pure information, a translation is intended as an expression of fundamental characteristics. The designer must define which characteristics are important— and how a given form language may best describe them. This may establish a relevant semantic or conceptual association, or narrative. Even if the intent is neutral description, the gestural research will still help reveal basic characteristics and offer possibilities for articulating them: for example, a loose, ink-wash study of the textural or modeled surface of a ceramic vessel could influence how its surface will be treated to enhance a sense of its volume.

Bring the descriptive and gestural aspects of initial research together /**C**/, working with only black-and-white form to articulate the subject's volumetric structure and grant it liveliness and specificity. As you introduce positive elements in black, be conscious of how they add to, or obscure, understanding of the form; obliterate elements that distract from the unity of the form language, or induce spatial confusion. This second stage concerns structural clarity, form language unity, and the rhythmic alternation of positive and negative both within the subject and with regard to its outer contour.

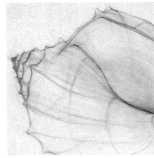
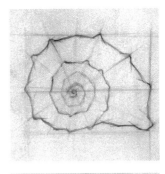

A Study of the subject's structure and volumetric form /
Paone Design Associates *United States*

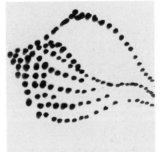

B Gestural studies of the subject; be aware of similarities between syntax generated by tools or gesture, and surface details of the subject, such as markings or protrusions.

During the third stage of this process, once form language, structure, and positive/negative are in dialogue, the refinement of the form and rhythmic logic begins. Now, the goal is to arrive at decisive qualities for each of the form's parts; curves should clearly be curves, and of a particular slope and rhythm, not appearing flat; the distribution of mass and line throughout the translation should follow a clear pattern of alternation and transition; overall distribution of dark and light should also exhibit a clear logic; the weights of linear elements (and whether they are uniform or modulated) should be clearly differentiated; and so on /**D**/. Work back and forth between adding, with black, and removing or carving, with white, until these qualities become as clear as possible.

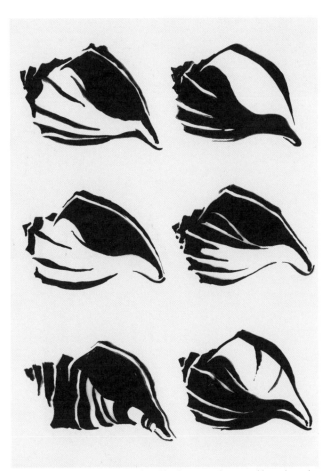

C Comparing options for articulating the subject's structure in pure positive and negative to construct the translation's base form; discoveries made during gestural sketching inform the development of the translation's syntax.

Ideas for Development

Use the final reductive translation as a template upon which to explore less precise media or techniques such as rough tracing.

Apply color to selected forms in the translation, as well as its negative space, to enhance the expression of its subject or alter its dimensionality.

Manipulate the translation using a variety of strategies to suggest new meanings or create associations.

Mask a texture or pattern (both drawn and photographic) into the translation to express meaning.

Combine the translation with a symbolic element, icon, or other pictorial subject to create a simple narrative.

Drawing /for Graphic Design

Invention

Exercises: Advanced Level

D Refinements made with black and white paint evolve the form language and clarify relationships of weight, rhythm, and dialogue among syntactic elements to arrive at a final, resolved translation.

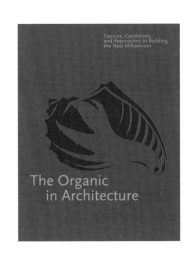

Sources, Conditions, and Approaches to Building the Next Millennium

The Organic in Architecture

Letterform Manipulation: Wordmark / Titling

This study merges concepts from previous exercises with typographic form, as well as icon, translation, and nonpictorial languages; it enriches facility with typographic drawing; through resolution and unification of disparate formal issues, it prepares the designer for future investigation of custom typeface design.

For this exercise, investigate any and all prior strategies for letterform drawing to transform initially neutral, verbal typographic form into an image of what it means. Combine physical, digital, and photographic media and processes as seems appropriate.

In a first stage, select a single word as a verbal subject. This word may be of concrete meaning (for example, architecture or explosive) or it may signify something less tangible (music or evolution, for instance). Begin by drawing the word in a relatively neutral, uniform-weight, sans serif style; or, set the word in a neutral typeface and print it out. A neutral style necessitates more radical alteration to derive meaningful narrative (avoid relying on typeface style, except as seems intrinsically useful to support meaning or formal logic later on; doing so early usually results in a facile, unoriginal solution). You may want to also draw or set examples in light and bold weights, as well as condensed and extended widths; make multiple copies with which to work.

From here, explore alterations and manipulations to the forms as they exist, along with redrawing, as you did for the single letter exercise [see p. 151]. The letters of the word need not remain on the same baseline; they may be rotated and scaled independently; each letter, or groupings thereof, may be manipulated in different ways; letters may be replaced with icons or stylized translation elements; they may be deconstructed or diagrammed; and both pictorial and nonpictorial elements may be integrated.

The manipulations should communicate with each other visually, creating a unique form language of shaping, gesture, texture, weight and spacing rhythm, position, and structural formation that unifies the components of the word as a singularity, much as would be the case with a logotype. At the same time, these aspects of the form language should support the meaning of the word itself; work to avoid decorative or stylistic approaches that are simply "eye candy."

Last—and most significantly—the logo must remain legible. Even though some visual aspects may challenge immediate recognition, if it seems the average viewer would need more than two seconds to figure out what it says, it has essentially failed as type.

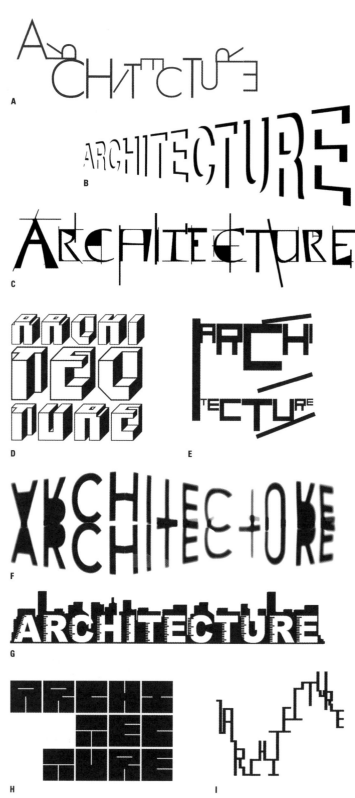

A

B

C

D

E

F

G

H

I

As a further challenge, if you like, constrain the drawing to pure positive and negative—translate textural or tonal effects using pattern, or exaggerating them dramatically at high contrast. Considering it in the context of a logo's functionality, refine it further so that it will reduce to an extremely small size (perhaps 0.5" [1.3 cm]) without sacrificing any information. This condition requires careful attention to spacing intervals and the weights of delicate elements, along with the relative scale of small details to the whole. Negative spaces, or negative elements that intrude upon positive masses, must be generous enough to not fill in as the image shrinks; line weights and small details must not dissolve or disappear, yet clearly retain contrasts that differentiate them.

J

K

L

M

N

O

P

Q

R

S

A–S Student explorations of wordmark concepts for 'architecture'; all from the School of Visual Arts, New York

A Ben Grandgenett
B Rachel Kim
C Aksana Berdnikova
D Chiu Hyung Yip
E Sean Glissman
F Diane Wilder
G Hee Won Cho
H Saebom Bae
I Shawfay Guo
J Rebecca Liebert
K Yoojung Kang
L Ha Young Kim
M Eri Chi
N Bo Rim Kim
O Jihyun Park
P Sooim Heo
Q Alexandra Stikeleather
R Jeong Hyon Kim
S Rosa Gazarian

Ideas for Development

Apply the same strategy to the title of a film or book, adjusting all aspects of the forms as seems appropriate—not with the goal of creating a typeface, but as an overall, unified custom treatment.

Support the wordmark with non-pictorial forms that derive from, and that you further evolve, from within the wordmark itself.

Combine the wordmark with a relevant pictorial image of a closely related form language.

Mask photographic or nonpictorial textures into the wordmark's positive areas to enrich both its visual and narrative aspects.

Experiment with color to augment the wordmark's form and meaning.

Drawing / for Graphic Design

Invention

Exercises:
Advanced Level

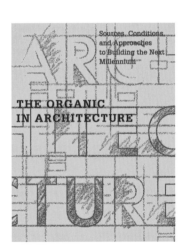

Stylization: Deconstructed or Kinetic Narrative

This study investigates stylization in greater depth; it reinforces the relationship between form and meaning; and it augments sensitivity to form language resolution, structure, spatial depth, and positive/negative interplay.

Combine a variety of stylistic, pictorial formal strategies and nonpictorial motifs that you have explored in previous exercises to communicate a complex meaning. The purposeful nature of this study suggests that you have an intended concept to convey before beginning; but as a preliminary first stage, working with a group of individual drawings you have already created may be very enlightening.

If you pursue this latter strategy to start, collect examples from the previous exercises so that you have them on hand to consider; you may want to scan and print, or make photocopies of, them in case you discover a useful combination and would like to manipulate further. On a surface before you, such as a larger sheet of paper, bristol, or illustration board, arrange a selection of three pictorial images, each representing a different form language or degree of naturalism or stylization. If you have studied a particular subject several times in different ways, one possibility is to juxtapose three or more versions of it.

Look for concepts, feelings, and associations (meaning) that come to mind as a result of this juxtaposition. If working with reiterations of the same subject /**A**/, does its changing form suggest a particular idea? If so, is it a causal relationship—the quality of meaning in one image seems to "lead to" the quality of meaning in another—or is it kinetic—the suggestion of an action or transformation? Three formal variants of the same flower, for example, may suggest its life cycle, from germination, to bloom, to decay.

Whether juxtapositions of the same or different subjects, perhaps a symbolic meaning presents itself: the two or more images clustering conceptually, by virtue of their stylistic qualities and respective subjects, to suggest a meaning that isn't explicitly depicted (a kind of signification called indexing) /**B**/. They may refer to some common narrative, notion, or current topic of discussion, as in the combination of a fish, an ethereally gestural figure, and a structural drawing of an ape, which could suggest a specific discussion about theories of human origin.

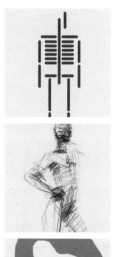

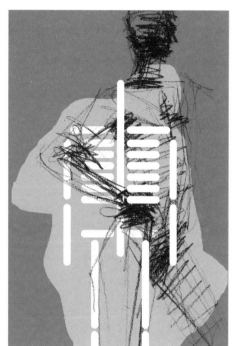

A Combining three versions of the same subject, each with very different formal qualities, suggests a close-in narrative about the subject.

B Images of different subjects suggest a meaning that joins them when brought together in juxtaposition.

If you have chosen to communicate an intended message from the beginning, consider both pictorial and nonpictorial strategies as sources for representing pertinent ideas /**C**/. Test not only different combinations of subjects for their effect on the intended narrative, but also different options for each subject's form language. In both cases, overall composition is the next concern. Side-by-side positioning may suggest parity, or equivalence of meaning—as will similar scale or orientation that calls out similarities of structure between them. Scale changes introduce contrast and also suggest meaning; the value of a smaller image is less than that of a larger one, a progression in sizes may suggest evolution or causality. Overlapping or clustering may suggest dialogue; transparency may hint at transformation, or that the meaning of one subject underpins that of another. Nonpictorial motifs may convey meaning as subjects by themselves, or be used as both formal and conceptual "connective tissue"—visually unifying areas of a composition of parts or, further creating a meaningful context for a grouping by suggesting a relevant physical environment or psychological state. As the image develops, simplify or attenuate each component image's respective form language to maintain the contrast they each bring, but to encourage greater visual unity /**D**/ in structure, tension, and positive/negative interplay within the composition as a totality.

Ideas for Development

Integrate photographic components with drawn elements as an added-strategy; manipulate photographic-forms as seems appropriate to unify them with the drawing.

Experiment with color: use specific, limited palettes for each component in the hybrid, or an overall palette to help further unify them.

Integrate typographic forms—single letters, either raw or manipulated; words, as labels or conceptual support; or more extensive texts.

C Combining nonpictorial elements enhances conceptual aspects of the narrative and suggests potential formal relationships to be exaggerated.

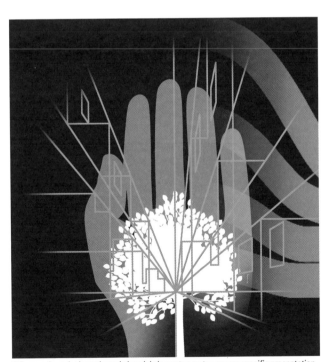

D Purposely reducing selected pictorial elements creates a more specific presentation or "style" and contributes to their formal and conceptual unity.

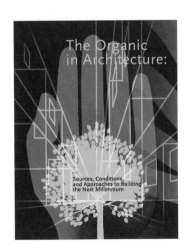

Custom Typeface

This study establishes criteria for unifying a family of characters in consideration of medium, tool, letter structure, stroke/counter rhythm, width, and stylistic detail; it hones sensitivity to positive/negative interplay and form language resolution.

Approach this exercise in either of two ways: to invent a display face for a limited character set (as for a titling element); or to develop a full alphabet for display or text use. Creating a display face is less rigorous a process and open to more radical experimentation. Developing a text face calls for more exacting criteria. You may opt to frame the search—as a house style for a magazine, institution, or a particular client to use as part of an identity; or to convey a certain style that is intended for a certain use or audience.

Begin by selecting four capital characters that comprise a variety of structural formations: orthogonal (vertical/horizontal); diagonal; all-curve; and a hybrid of these (the combination of *E*, *A*, *O*, and *R* is a good mix). As in previous exercises, study structural and stylistic possibilities for the intended typeface: weight, width, serif versus sans-serif style, stroke contrast, slant, and qualities that may be imparted by the tool using many mark-making methods. Through this research, define the attributes that you would like to pursue, comparing the effect of their combination on the four characters you selected.

Among these first four characters, the following should be confirmed before proceeding /**A**/:

The letters must be optically the same height, width, and weight; if there is shading (stroke contrast), the thins and thicks, respectively, should be the same weight.

Crossbar divisions in *A*, *E*, and *R* should appear optically centered top to bottom in their respective letters; this means that their upper and lower counters should appear to be equivalent in volume.

The apex of the *A* must be centered and the side angles appear equivalent; the upper lobe of the *R* must appear balanced and evenly situated above its leg.

Curves in the *O* and *R* must appear similar in radius and transition decisively into straighter forms and into joints.

The outer and inner contours of curves should track each other; expanding outward from each other as they leave a joint or straight stroke, and smoothly coming toward each other as they approach the next juncture.

Then, explore these same characters' lowercase versions, along with additional lowercase characters /**B**/ that comprise structural variations not included in the original character set—for example, if you chose *A*, *E*, *O*, *R* as capitals (meaning you'd be testing a set of lowercase composed mostly of curves), also draw *f*, *g*, *k*, and x to see how the evolving visual language will apply to these varied forms.

A Even for a display face—one not intended for text use, or for limited use for callouts or titling—achieving visual unity depends on creating optical relationships between the parts of different kinds of characters, based on historical precedent. This face exhibits such qualities, even though it strays far from convention and even challenges it.

B The lowercase follow the same logic established in the uppercase. Because most of the lowercase letters are curvilinear in structure, it's important to include angle-based forms during the preliminary study to appreciate their interaction with the visual logic.

Determine an *x*-height for the lowercase; typically this measurement is 75 percent of the cap height, and the aspect ratio of the lowercase is similar to that of the capitals. Draw the lowercase characters to conform to this height, following the models shown. The distance from the mean-line (which defines the height of the lowercase) to the cap-line, which establishes the height of ascenders, should also govern the depths of descenders.

All the visual qualities that are apparent in the capitals must also be apparent in the lowercase—this applies to width, slant, weight, contrast, curve shaping, joint structure, and stylistic details such as the shaping of terminals and serifs. In evolving the typeface, compare your own forms with existing typefaces of various styles (oldstyle, script, italic, transitional, neo-classical, slab serif, and sans serif; as well as display and text faces). Look to the relationships of structure and detail that these models have established to guide you in resolving the attributes of your own typeface. As the characters within the set approach a refined state, test their visual continuity by shrinking them /**c**/ to a typical text size—note how disparities in proportion, shaping, and weight appear extremely exaggerated at a small size. Use this test to help continually refine the characters.

Ideas for Development

Use unexpected tools, or use tools in an unconventional way, to generate the stroke formations of the letters—for example, hardware, natural objects, liquids under the effect of gravity, burning or melting objects, and so on.

Splice or hybridize attributes from alternate weight or width studies, or those created by different media, to discover new forms.

Purposely reverse the typical, historically derived weight-distribution relationships within characters.

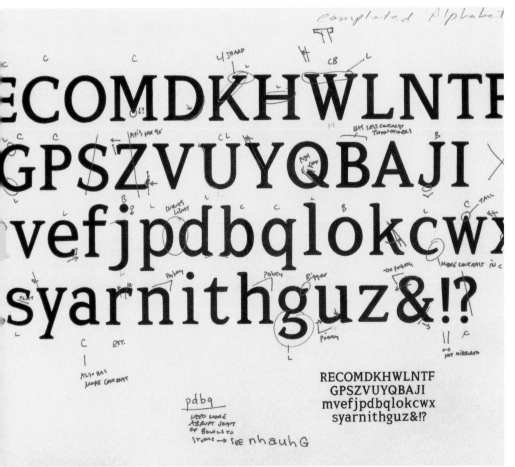

C The extensive notation marked up on this printout attests to the exhaustive commitment required to develop a text typeface intended for extended reading. / Andrew Scheiderich, SUNY Purchase *United States*

Transformational Nonpictorial Narrative

This study integrates skills and understanding gained from previous exercises with nonpictorial drawing; it helps build mastery in developing clear messaging with abstract representation; it further augments sensitivity to, and control over, form language resolution, compositional structure, positive/negative interplay, perceptual space, and visual hierarchy.

Begin this exercise with an intended concept or message to convey; feel free to frame the communication as an independent, hypothetical exploration, or as a practical project—perhaps one on which you are currently working in a professional context. In contrast to subjects you may have explored in previous exercises, the one you choose to pursue here should express a multi-level story; the image should encapsulate a sequence of events or a transformation in condition or state. That is, to tell a complete story without the benefit of pictorial imagery.

To do so, first explore form languages to capture an identifiable essence of the base subject—characterize it through your choice of medium, mark- and gesture- language, and structure /**A**/. Whether this subject is a concrete object, figure or character personality, intangible emotion or conceptual idea, engage all the strategies for nonpictorial representation you have discovered thus far. It is helpful, in preparing for the next stage, to develop multiple options for representing the subject—each different in medium and form language—from which to compare and select attributes that will help you build the story that you wish to tell /**A**/.

During the second stage, explore how to represent the action, temporal sequence, and changes that the subject should be perceived to undergo /**B**/. Look to your experience with nonpictorial action representation; it is possible that you have already encountered a form language relevant to that you're working toward now. If so, evaluate what alterations may be needed to more clearly offer a viable approach for this new narrative. Test these action- or process-based form language strategies on several versions of the subject: Which create the clearest understanding and, further, which offer related (or contrasting) formal qualities in doing so?

A Delving into material from previous exercises could yield a treasure trove of material with which to work when creating a non-pictorial, transformational narrative for the first time: rubbings, concept drawings, and mark-making motifs of the field variety (top); reductive singularities (middle); gestural action drawings (bottom).

Consider the compositional arrangement of the forms that identify the base subject relative to subsequent states. Remember that relative sizes suggest parity, or closer relationship in state or time; size progression and changes in rotation may suggest movement; the directionality of movement (upward, downward, repeating, or cyclical, among others) may alternately suggest growth or degradation; changes in form language between areas will similarly contribute to an understanding of changes in identity, emotion, or time. Direct these compositional attributes to create a clear hierarchy that first focuses attention on the base subject, to provide the viewer with an appreciation of the narrative's beginning point; further direct the viewer's eye through a path, articulated by hierarchical changes in scale, value, and relative activity to guide them through the narrative sequence.

Also explore the role color may play in helping to identify the subject— by adding associated emotional messages—and further, by also helping to distinguish its changed state and transitional states in between /**c**/. Enforce a clear logic in the color palette; fewer hues, whose variations in saturation, temperature, and value are similarly limited and easily identifiable, will simplify the experience and help unify the composition.

B A rough graphite sketch shows a combination of nonpictorial images (top) culled from among those shown in **A,** left. It provides a basis for reconceiving it with variations of different form languages, as well as digital manipulation, (bottom) for greater specificity.

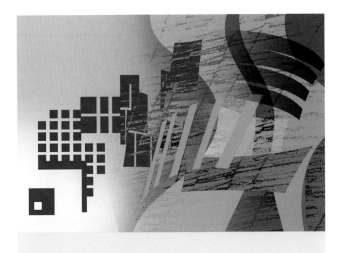

C Following a period of further refinement, color was introduced to support the narrative thorugh it s psychological and emotional associations.

Ideas for Development

Develop a series to support a fictional or journalistic text, in place of pictorial imagery.

Combine the nonpictorial language with drawn typographic forms to support, or possibly evolve or alter, its narrative meaning.

Integrate photographic elements, using the nonpictorial drawing as connective tissue or to create a surreal, yet meaningful, environment for the naturalistic images.

Test digital filters and photographic techniques on selected elements of the drawing for their visual, as well as narrative, effects.

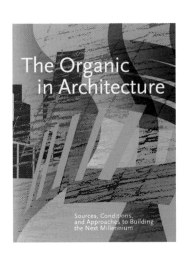

The Organic
in Architecture

Sources, Conditions,
and Approaches to Building
the Next Millennium

Arti-
f/
act
s

This section presents
a showcase of graphic
design projects in
which drawing is an
intrinsic part and
plays a dramatic role.

Designers work with drawing every day and in every medium: in print, interactive, and environmental projects. From integrating it as a method for planning and ideation, exploiting it for unique manipulation of typography or photography, to its implementation as a medium of communication itself—the possibilities for enriching the design process are endless, as is the range of stylistic approach and the potential for robust visual voice.

The work shown here, by no means exhaustive, demonstrates the commanding presence of drawing in projects by students and professional designers and studios from around the world, each as diverse as the methods and visual languages that they explore.

Event Poster/ A massive, figural brush drawing and sharply contrasting red dot capture the power of Sumo with nods to its cultural heritage. Jin Kwang Kim, School of Visual Arts *United States*

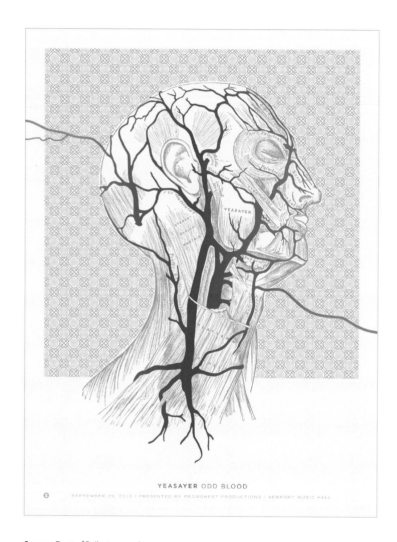

Magazine Cover/ The extreme scale of a reductive translation of pulsing neurons situates the viewer inside the featured article's subject. Hinterland *United States*

Concert Poster/ Delicate engraving supports a network of vivid arteries; against a decorative, Victorian pattern, they evoke rhythm, science, and the surreal. Base Art Co. *United States*

Exhibition Poster/ Lacelike patterns, deftly defining a very intimate anatomy, contrast a sharply drawn icon and sensuous gradation of color that suffuses the poster with a suggestively tactile quality. Yuri Surkov *Russia*

Drawing
/ for Graphic
Design
Artifacts
**Showcase
of Real-World
Projects**

Political Poster / The overwhelming tension of confrontational type forms gives way to delicately scrawled emotional symbols within the figure's relatively calm interior. Chacundum *Brazil*

Condom Packaging/ Gestural marks—in varied palettes that differentiate products—lend discreet elegance while alluding to the effusive joy of sexual relations. BAI.S Design Office *China*

Restaurant Identity/ The flared strokes of a calligraphic logo and translation of roiling flames, applied to banners and an exterior window-wall, characterize this eatery whose name means "on fire." PCD Estudio de Diseño *Argentina*

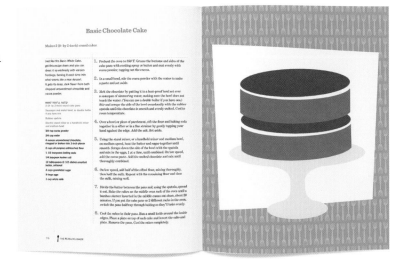

Cookbook/ Flatly cut-out, iconic still lifes that accompany text and recipes minimize intimidation toward baking, supported by a comforting, nostalgic color palette. AdamsMorioka, Inc. *United States*

Chef's Apron/ Flowing, parallel lines become spaghetti as they draw the letters of a logotype and icon of a fork holding pasta on this promotional novelty product. LoSiento *Spain*

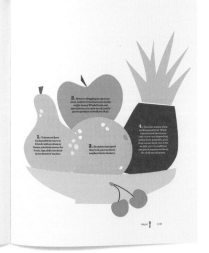

Product Brochure / Friendly, spontaneously sketched line drawings create an accessibly homey, day-to-day context for images of sleekly designed kitchen and dining products.
Sägenvier DesignKommunikation *Austria*

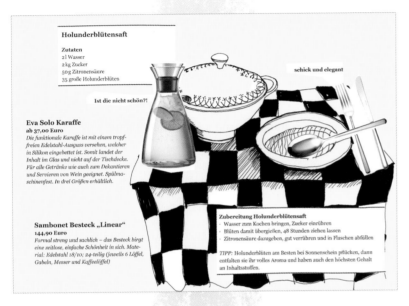

Holunderblütensaft

Zutaten
2 l Wasser
2 kg Zucker
50 g Zitronensäure
35 große Holunderblüten

schick und elegant

Ist die nicht schön?!

Eva Solo Karaffe
ab 37,00 Euro
Die funktionale Karaffe ist mit einem tropffreien Edelstahl-Ausguss versehen, welcher in Silikon eingebettet ist. Somit landet der Inhalt im Glas und nicht auf der Tischdecke. Für alle Getränke wie auch zum Dekantieren und Servieren von Wein geeignet. Spülmaschinenfest. In drei Größen erhältlich.

Sambonet Besteck „Linear"
144,90 Euro
Formal streng und sachlich – das Besteck birgt eine zeitlose, einfache Schönheit in sich. Material: Edelstahl 18/10; 24-teilig (jeweils 6 Löffel, Gabeln, Messer und Kaffeelöffel)

Zubereitung Holunderblütensaft
· Wasser zum Kochen bringen, Zucker einrühren
· Blüten damit übergießen, 48 Stunden ziehen lassen
· Zitronensäure dazugeben, gut verrühren und in Flaschen abfüllen

TIPP: Holunderblüten am Besten bei Sonnenschein pflücken, dann entfalten sie ihr volles Aroma und haben auch den höchsten Gehalt an Inhaltsstoffen.

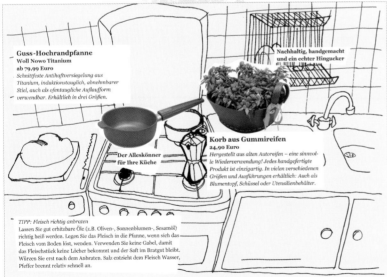

Guss-Hochrandpfanne
Woll Nowo Titanium
ab 79,99 Euro
Schnittfeste Antihaftversiegelung aus Titanium, induktionstauglich, abnehmbarer Stiel, auch als ofentaugliche Auflaufform verwendbar. Erhältlich in drei Größen.

Nachhaltig, handgemacht und ein echter Hingucker

Der Alleskönner für Ihre Küche

Korb aus Gummireifen
24,90 Euro
Hergestellt aus alten Autoreifen – eine sinnvolle Wiederverwendung! Jedes handgefertigte Produkt ist einzigartig. In vielen verschiedenen Größen und Ausführungen erhältlich: Auch als Blumentopf, Schüssel oder Utensilienbehälter.

TIPP: Fleisch richtig anbraten
Lassen Sie gut erhitzbare Öle (z.B. Oliven-, Sonnenblumen-, Sesamöl) richtig heiß werden. Legen Sie das Fleisch in die Pfanne, wenn sich das Fleisch vom Boden löst, wenden. Verwenden Sie keine Gabel, damit das Fleischstück keine Löcher bekommt und der Saft im Bratgut bleibt. Würzen Sie erst nach dem Anbraten. Salz entzieht dem Fleisch Wasser, Pfeffer brennt relativ schnell an.

GRESSO® Chef
COOKLAB

Drawing
/ for Graphic
Design

Artifacts

**Showcase
of Real-World
Projects**

GRESSO®

Branded Collateral / A cluster of carefully reduced culinary icons lends a dynamic, almost clinical, authority to materials for a prestigious training center for catering professionals. Flúor *Portugal*

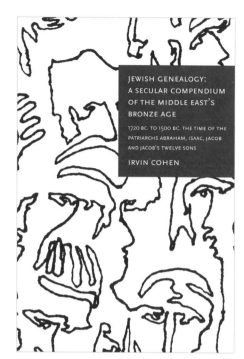

JEWISH GENEALOGY:
A SECULAR COMPENDIUM
OF THE MIDDLE EAST'S
BRONZE AGE

1720 BC. TO 1500 BC. THE TIME OF THE
PATRIARCHS ABRAHAM, ISAAC, JACOB
AND JACOB'S TWELVE SONS

IRVIN COHEN

Book Cover/ Rough, yet fluid, contour drawings allude to the continuity of Jewish history and ancestry, the focus of this publication's study.
Post Typography *United States*

Poster Series (selected)/
Arabic calligraphic forms, scraped with a flat stylus from a prepainted surface, commemorate the Islamic holy month of Ramadan with spiritual messages grounded in tactile physicality.
Mehdi Saeedi Studio *Iran*

Institutional Identity/ The linear translation of religious symbols speaks of the faith's narrative heritage in a contemporary idiom and suggests an ethereal spirituality.
Paone Design Associates
United States

Institutional Identity/ Arching, branchlike structures simultaneously evoke growth, Hebraic characters, and the iconic Menorah in this mark for a long-established synagogue.
Tactical Magic *United States*

Institutional Identity/ A bold, rough mass—housing an equally primal, seemingly unrefined symbol—conveys the powerful, historical imprint of Jewish culture on behalf of a museum.
Studio Apeloig *France*

Poster/ The alternately opaque and transparent, positive and negative, floating meditative figure literally and conceptually advocates for spiritual enlightenment.
Fang Chen *United States*

Book Cover Series/ Austerely delicate geometric line configurations resonate with deep intellectual messages—the Koran's metaphysical focus; the circularity and misdirection of the "Illiad"; and the unachievable aspects of Utopia.
Studio Astrid Stavro *Spain*

Drawing
/ for Graphic
Design

Artifacts

**Showcase
of Real-World
Projects**

Identity/ Custom letters constructed of geometrically intertwined and looping lines suggest the nature of this textile designer and consultant, as well as her vaguely exotic inspirations and fabric designs. Post Typography *United States*

Wine Branding/ Vines and leaves, curling around icons of watering cans, fence posts, and birds form elegant letters for labels that are nonetheless rustic and a little homey. Brandever Strategy, Inc. *Canada*

5ek.hr

5ek.hr

5ek.hr

hrvoje petek
snimanje i dizajn zvuka
i. mažuranića 50, 10340 vrbovec
jmbg: 1912975392107
žr: 2360000-1101960833

Identity System/ In each application (stationery, promotional cards, and website), multicolored, organic shapes animate a different line drawing to unify wine and sound—expertise the client offers for events. Fiktiv *Croatia*

5ek.hr

hrvoje petek
sound & wine design
zagreb bakačeva 5
091 508 7967
hrvoje@5ek.hr
čujemo se...

Environmental Graphic Program /
More than sixty color-coded icons distinguish product categories and establish wayfinding in one of South America's largest supermarket chains.
PCD Estudio de Diseño *Argentina*

Drawing /for Graphic Design

Artifacts

Showcase of Real-World Projects

Restaurant Branding / The letters of the client's eatery, finger painted on plates, become graphic identifiers for a set of menus.
LoSiento *Spain*

Promotional Mailer Series / Collaged letterforms lend pictorial detail and contrast to simple icons of the animals that represent aspects of the Chinese zodiac; the animals come alive as pop-ups in the greetings of the new year, embellished with gold and vivid red ink. Gee+Chung Design *United States*

Theater Poster / The subtly dimensional icon of a postman set in motion with a slight blur and a flurry of letters define a simple structure of diagonals and verticals in tandem with titling and text typography. Studio Apeloig *France*

Environmental Branding / A heritage of Mexican sign and wall painting informs the exterior and interior branding of this eatery, drawing on vibrant, sometimes jarring vernacular color and letter-drawing languages. AdamsMorioka, Inc. *United States*

Logo Proposal / A smart offering for a redesign of the U.S. space program identity juxtapose authoritative, technologically-inspired custom letterforms with the dynamic liftoff of a rocket, accomplished through the deft use of figure/ground reversal. Topos Graphics *United States*

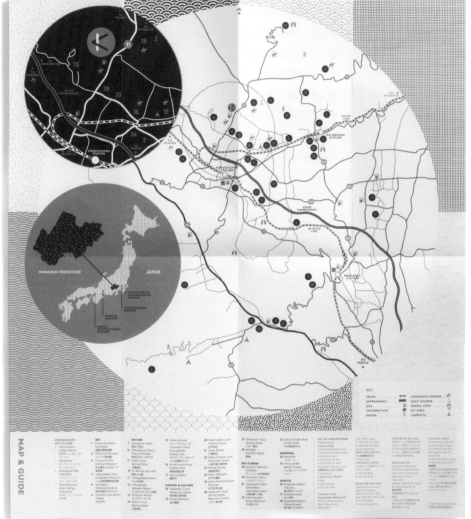

Institutional Brochure / Careful attention to the weights of lines and dots helps distill a complex area map to nearly Zenlike clarity. Smaller, inset maps provide macro- and micro-level orientation, as well as restate the language of the logo. Decorative patterns soften the diagrammatic intensity of the map and add cultural context.
Hinterland *United States*

Music Packaging / This CD's design mixes numerous drawing languages—pen-scrawled lettering, paint drips, cut/paste collage, tape, and altered fonts—for a lively expression of a diverse, kinetic urban narrative.
[ths] Thomas Schostok Design *Germany*

Promotional Ad / Neutral, informational text makes way for a playful and surreal deconstruction of a fish into a type form in this poster for a dance club venue. BAI.S Design Office *China*

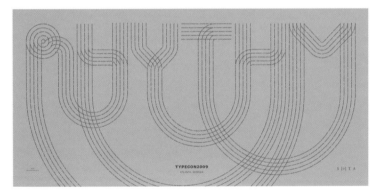

Design Conference Identity / Inventively arranged lines of text form the name of a conference devoted to typography, kinetically expressing the particular thematic focus of that year's meeting. Under Consideration *United States*

Educational Video / A boldly illustrative animation, designed to teach children to count, uses transitions between positive and negative forms in a number to reveal kinetic scenes of animals in their habitats; second in a series of ten. Pettis Design *United States*

Public Awareness Ad / Various icon languages of architectural and environmental subjects are bound into a spherical configuration that conveys the integrated strategy of an eco-conscious urban planning organization.
Post Typography *United States*

Drawing / for Graphic Design

Artifacts

Showcase of Real-World Projects

Environmental Design / Illuminated, glass ovoid forms installed in a grid formation below the ceiling in a corporate environment translates the luminous, gestural rhythm of a school of fish into ever-changing, animated, sculptural drawing. Troika *United Kingdom*

Advocacy Poster / Custom type forms, generated from the shapes of found stones, integrate with the diagram language of topographical notation to raise awareness of an environmental initiative.
Andrew Scheiderich, SUNY Purchase *United States*

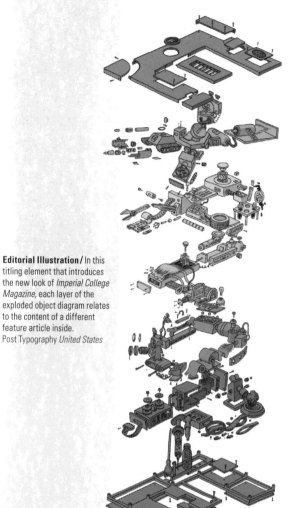

Custom Type Manipulation /
A found typeface acts as a framework for circular elements, carefully scaled and positioned to evoke bubbles filtering up from the deep—a clever narrative about the client organization's oceanic activities.
Isela Archenti, SUNY Purchase
United States

Editorial Illustration / In this titling element that introduces the new look of *Imperial College Magazine*, each layer of the exploded object diagram relates to the content of a different feature article inside.
Post Typography *United States*

Advocacy Poster / The interplay of hand print and animal forms in positive and negative—merged with the French curves used by architects—suggests the mutual influence of human activity and the environment in this poster.
Yuri Surkov *Russia*

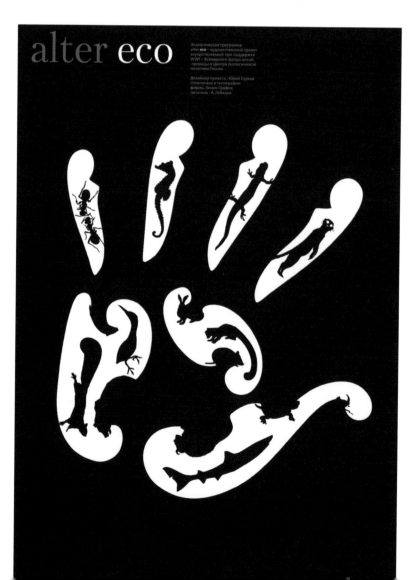

Advocacy Poster / Structural parity between two object forms allows them to merge as a hybrid icon; a dramatic causal relationship results between the two. Half-empty numerals compound, and add urgency to, the disturbing message. Shaung Wan, School of Visual Arts *United States*

Promotional Poster / Wackily distorted flowers, growing from a hybrid garden pot/house, are rendered with rough, scratchy lines and bold color blocking that impart an edgy, childlike energy to entice the public to attend a horticultural event. Modern Dog Design Co. *United States*

Exhibition Poster / The dynamic, ever-changing overall contour of the pomegranate tree, made from Arabic calligraphy and brush-drawn fruit forms, imparts an effusively organic energy to the format space—practically exploding from the tensely arranged trunk of Arabic and Roman typography. Mehdi Saeedi Studio *Iran*

frogzone®
indumentaria casual

Apparel Identity / This punchy, iconic mark for a clothing retailer delivers youthful energy and—by isolating the frog's feet and spots with color—the opportunity to brand in shorthand with only selected elements. PCD Estudio de Diseño *Argentina*

Custom Typeface / Rubbing graphite inward from the contours of freely drawn letters (over crumpled paper) generated the basis of this house face for an environmental organization whose focus is elephants; the translated texture and exaggerated proportions alternately evoke trunks, massive bodies, thin legs, and leathery skin. Rhiann Irvine, SUNY Purchase *United States*

Gallery Bulletin and Poster / A symbiotic language (linear constructs, snippets of neighborhood snapshots, deconstructed letters, and collaged vector silhouettes) captures the interim nature of a gallery's community—based programming after it was forced to move from its original location. Post Tool Design *United States*

Promotional Posters / These posters announce an exhibit about nocturnal animals with engaging, stylized icons. Each presents a full-color image during the day and an alternate, glow-in-the-dark image at night. Shaung Wan, School of Visual Arts *United States*

Magazine Cover/ Rolled architectural plans—themselves drawings—become polluting smokestacks with the introduction of rough scribbles, creating a cause/effect narrative in support of the publication's editorial focus in this issue. D.J. Stout, Pentagram *United States*

AgriculturaBiológica

Institutional Identity/ The prefix "bio" means "organic." Characterized by a gesturally drawn initial B that resolves itself into a refined icon, the mark conveys the primary focus of the client it identifies. Flúor *Portugal*

Logotype/ Balancing exceptionally light, precise letter strokes with the effects of moisture, this designer's identity embodies the Japanese aesthetic of *wabi-sabi*—the embrace of a sublime imperfection and transience. The designer describes the mark as resulting from the tears of joy that result from first meeting a new client. Takuji Omori *Japan*

Advocacy Poster/ The profound impact of industrial disasters resonate from the inarguable simplicity of positive/negative iconography. Martino *Argentina*

Info-Graphic System/ A stylized, reductive leaf form becomes the module for a series of statistical data graphics that depict changes in energy use and environmental impact. KAKO *Brazil*

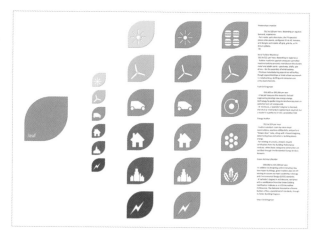

Brochure Design / Stylized graphic translations and icons merge with engravings and symbols in a clustered, deconstructed space to tell the romantic story of an author whose travels influenced his writing about Eastern cultures. Flúor *Portugal*

GALLERY
LITVAK

Institutional Identity / In this mark for a Tel-Aviv contemporary art gallery, regularly punctuating (dotlike) and irregularly vertically thrusting (linear) typographic rhythms distinguish hierarchy and suggest the push and pull of tradition and innovation. Studio Apeloig *France*

Music Packaging / A surreal image built from engraved architectural elements for an album by Finnish band, Disco Ensemble, represents psychic and emotional constructs that the music explores—and its cut-and-paste compositional quality. TSTO *Finland*

Drawing
/ for Graphic
Design

Artifacts

**Showcase
of Real-World
Projects**

Public Installation / An ever-changing, animated typographic composition, drawn across an LED structure along a window wall within a busy transit hub (Heathrow Airport, London), presents statistics and philosophies related to time.
Troika *United Kingdom*

Look deep into nature, and then you will understand everything better.
– Albert Einstein.

Advocacy Poster / Extrapolating gesture, contour, and axis lines from an abstracted calligraphic ideogram, signifying nature, expresses the interconnectedness of the living world as a basis for self-awareness and empowerment.
heSign International GmbH *Germany*

Identity / The custom type forms of this design and new media company's logo refer to Modernist stenciling, engaging the client's brand in a dialogue with a previous industrial revolution.
Post Typography *United States*

CRAFTWORK

Institutional Identity/ Icons of Spain's Argentina's Catholic and agricultural heritage—the bull and the cow—welcome visitors to the cultural center they brand with charming expressions and softened contours. Martino *Argentina*

Public Installation/ This design of a public space transforms drawn linear figures into dimensional icons that express the movement of Spanish cowboys going about their day's work. Javirroyo *Spain*

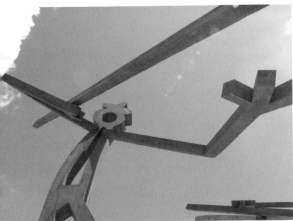

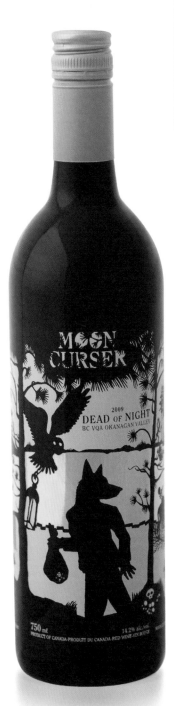

POSTER FOR JAPAN

Humanitarian Aid Poster/ A clever hybrid of Japan's rising sun and seismic graph line offer an immediate, experiential sense of a recent earthquake's impact on the island country. Studio Astrid Stavro *Spain*

Wine Branding/ Gothic storybook style illustrations turn an anecdote—nineteenth-century gold smugglers crossing the Canada/U.S. border (the vineyard's location) under cover of night, only to be caught in the moonlight—into an engaging, nearly mythical, brand narrative. Brandever Strategy, Inc. *Canada*

Drawing
/ for Graphic
Design

Artifacts

**Showcase
of Real-World
Projects**

Promotional Poster/ The rustic, hand-hewn edges of distorted type forms and the surrounding landscape in this poster, along with the low horizon that enhances its spatial vastness, all emphasize the natural setting of the festival. Jud Haynes *Canada*

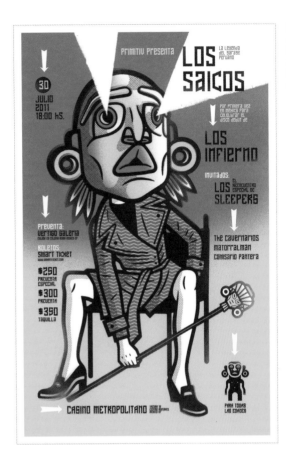

Promotional Poster/ A cheeky, stylized update of classical Mayan iconography lend a fun, but historically grounded context to a Mexican performance-based casino event. Jorge Alderete *Mexico*

Branded Restaurant Menus/ A primary floral motif—itself a dimensional, yet reductive, translation—presents a bold contrast to a linear type lockup; varied patterns differentiate the menus and introduce rhythm, movement, and depth. Base Art Co. *United States*

Product Design Awards Identity/
A simple, unifying logo—a triangle made from triangles, echoing the Greek letter Delta, is deconstructed and remade as various products; color creates a perception of 3-D form among 2-D elements.
Estudio Diego Feijóo *Spain*

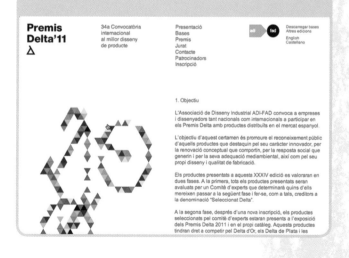

Concert Poster/ Against the bold backdrop of historical painting's reduced iconography, brushed letters impart a dynamic, contemporary flair to this dynamically rhythmic image.
Lauren Chan, School of Visual Arts
United States

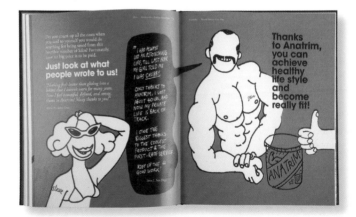

Drawing
/ for Graphic
Design

Artifacts

**Showcase
of Real-World
Projects**

Product Showroom Environment /
A mural of icons, swirling organic
line gestures, and bold, high-contrast
serif type form a backdrop for a
line of lighting fixtures, providing
them an aesthetic context in situ
and a connection to daily life.
LoSiento *Spain*

Branded Institutional Poster /
A fine arts museum's logotype—
custom-drawn geometric sans serif
letters merged into a seemingly
ancient, textured surface—first
defines this poster's spatial structure and then a dense collage of
pictorial elements and text. Color,
as well as spatial position, turns the
logo into both a protective edifice
and a window to some mystery
within. Yuri Surkov *Russia*

Paper Promotion Catalogue /
Titled *Spam Jam*, this celebration
of email spam (with statistics,
visualizations of actual spam
messages, and musings about the
future) shows off paper stock offer-
ings with surreal illustrations that
recall circus sideshow posters and
counterculture comics; the majority
of the display type is drawn by hand
as well. Brukêta & Zinić *Croatia*

Environmental Design/ Applied with paint, vinyls, and as backlit cut-outs, hand-drawn typography and illustrations envelop patrons of the Wonka Bar in a captivating visual fantasy. Chacundum *Brazil*

Identity/ Planar interpretations of the letters' stroke formation in this mark for an interior design consultancy give a subtle nod to the business's name; color application creates the perception of 3-D space. AdamsMorioka,Inc. *United States*

Custom Typeface/ Developed in three weights, this typeface was inspired by the Japanese tradition of giving a *Senzaburu*— 1,000 origami-folded cranes held together by string. Topos Graphics *United States*

Technology Conference Collateral / In the poster, catalogue, and other applications for an event, geometric, linear constructs and patterns vibrate together with geometric text fields, diagrams, notations, and map elements in a complex visualization of the digital realm. Bizu Design *Brazil*

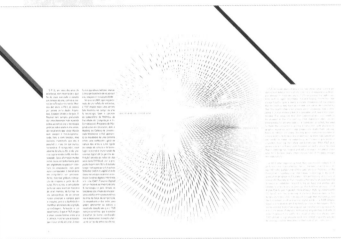

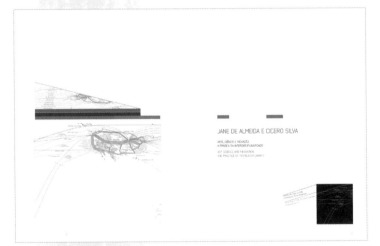

Promotional Poster / Fanciful, swirling, intricate doodle-like line forms, representing creative possibility, attest to the potential of a newly acquired, high-end device in this announcement for a local printer. 344 Design, LLC *United States*

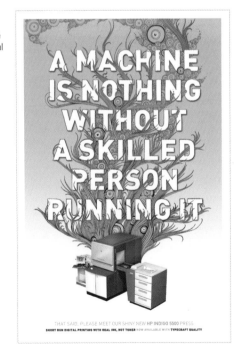

Event Branding / The architectural, deconstructed letterforms of a custom typeface, mingled with intricately collaged and redrawn illustrations and luminous organic shapes, create a visual framework for photography and brand a Finnish fashion event. TSTO *Finland*

Exhibition Poster / Squiggling, free-form lines and stylized quills link writing and illustration to convey the subject of a juried exhibit of picture books; grid-based structure and linear details in the accompanying typography allude to notebooks and provide a contrasting geometry to the imagery's organicism. Type.Page [Park Woohyuk] *Korea*

Theater Poster / A strangely proportioned and obsessively detailed pencil drawing suggest complex psychological narratives while representing the play title's metaphor, Ivory-Billed Woodpecker. TSTO *Finland*

Motion Design / An experimental typographic animation blends font styles, nonpictorial forms, and pop-cultural iconography in a short film about Japanese export culture, part of a five-minute subprogram shown on Japanese television.
Strange Attractors *The Netherlands*

Cover Design System / Dramatically enlarged, tightly cropped ornamental patterns distinguish a series of essays, each metaphorically representing a given publication's content.
Studio Astrid Stavro *Spain*

Mario Vargas Llosa
Sueño y realidad de América Latina

ARCADIA

Wolf Lepenies
Melancolía y utopía

ARCADIA

Rob Riemen
Nobleza de espíritu
Tres ensayos sobre una idea olvidada
Prefacio de George Steiner

ARCADIA

Ilana Shmueli
Fragmentos de una época
Una carta
Prólogo de Rob Riemen

ARCADIA

Juan Luis Arsuaga
Selección inconsciente
La clave para comprender a Darwin

ARCADIA

Ramin Jahanbegloo
Elogio de la diversidad
Prólogo de Juan Goytisolo

ARCADIA

Drawing / for Graphic Design

Artifacts

Showcase of Real-World Projects

Apparel Advertising / Influenced by graffiti, gaming imagery, and street culture, an explosion of illustrative type forms, sporting goods, and organic shapes customizes photography expressing the brand and associating it with a specific lifestyle. Alex Trochut *Spain*

Hotel Branding / Casually elegant, stylized illustrations of a concierge, bell hops, and porters add high-brow, friendly chic to a hotel's identity program, anchored by a custom, brush-drawn logotype. TAXI Canada, Ltd. *Canada*

Online Branding / The precisely ordered, geometric custom forms' strokes of the logotype—together with its pattern of decorative scrollwork—bring the heritage of industrial-age apothecaries to bear in a website for organic fragrance products. Topos Graphics *United States*

Please respect my privacy.

New York is a city of dreams. And dreams are best left undisturbed.

Think of this as your VIP card to New York City.

Meri J. Greene
Marketing Manager

CARLTON

88 Madison Avenue
New York, NY 10016

Direct: 212.502.6100
Reservations: 1.800.601.8500

carltonhotelny.com
mgreene@carltonhotelny.com

Preferred Hotels & Resorts

ONE LIFE. HOLMES PLACE LIVE IT WELL.

.210
.177

.65

Environmental Design / This collage of vector-drawn trees, birds, and animals at differing scales and in neutral colors, transforms the walls of a health club into a contemplative, empowering environment for its members. Jewboy Corp. *Israel*

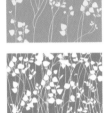

Hotel Branding / Stylized ink drawings accompany philosophical musings in a promotional booklet for a "hotel that whispers, advises, and guides" its visitors. Their quirky, personal gestures ground the metaphysical experience.
LoSiento *Spain*

Hotel Branding (Guest Amenities) / For a restored nineteenth-century luxury hotel on the Italian Riviera the designers developed a family of patterns evoking the property's impressive gardens; floral translations keep the language from being overly sweet.

Identity / This calligraphic update of an existing pharmaceutical company's logo humanizes the organization and links its products to an ancient heritage of shamanism and healing arts.
PCD Estudio de Diseño *Argentina*

AAQTIC

Psychotherapy Website/
A rhythmically shifting pattern of lines—in a different palette upon each reload of this site's landing page—slowly deconstruct a philosophical headline to convey the client's systemic approach to consultation.
Topos Graphics *United States*

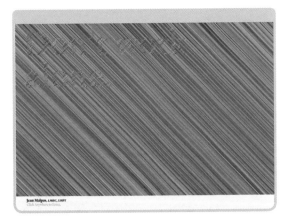

Humanitarian Aid Poster/
Outstretched arms, frustratingly bound together by the crossbar of the gigantic letter H they form, signify the country Haiti and the desperate need of its people following a recent earthquake.
Un Mundo Féliz *Spain*

Advocacy Poster/ The clever redrawing of a cigarette's curling wisp of smoke as a snake delivers an urgent, sinister—and universally understandable—message for contemplation. Milani Design *Italy*

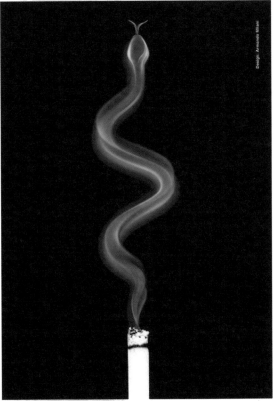

Health Industry Advocacy Campaign / A series of postcards and flyers juxtaposes bold, silhouetted figures and scenes and the iconic speech bubble—representing advocacy—to raise awareness about a code of anti-tobacco initiatives among health professionals. Fabrica *Italy*

Humanitarian Aid Poster / The brutally figured, anonymous crowd of hands becomes a specific people when dramatically altered by a rip that reads as a crack, as though jarred by the movement of an earthquake. Scott Laserow *United States*

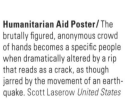

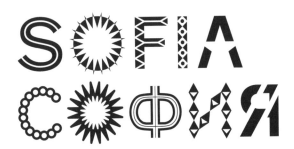

Promotional Identity/ The rendering of a city's name in Roman and Cyrillic characters—unified by a geometric matrix—underscores its heritage and diversity, positioning it for designation as Europe's "Capital of Culture" in 2019. Shapes from within the type generate a festive pattern language that integrates the colored blocks which announce the city's candidacy. Büro Uebele Visuelle Kommunikation *Germany*

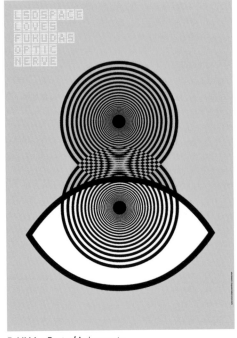

Exhibition Poster/ An homage to an important Japanese designer, produced for a retrospective of his work, trades on his characteristic merging of pictorial and abstract visualization. LSDspace *Spain*

T-Shirt Design/ A graphic tee for skaters merges letterform, skateboard, and stairway bannister rail—a favorite public feature on which to skate—in a sharp-edged, luminous, and geometric language that conveys velocity. Alex Trochut *Spain*

Music Branding/ Used to characterize a CD titled Luxury and associated paraphernalia, this wordmark of the band's name—a composiiton of anxiously compressed letters drawn from concentric repetitions of their respective forms—suggests a culture of compulsion. Post Typography *United States*

Theater Poster/ A boldly geometric, reductive icon of an eye is transformed into an open womb, simultaneously representing origin and vision to communicate the subject of a play, *Birth of the Green Movement.* TSTO *Finland*

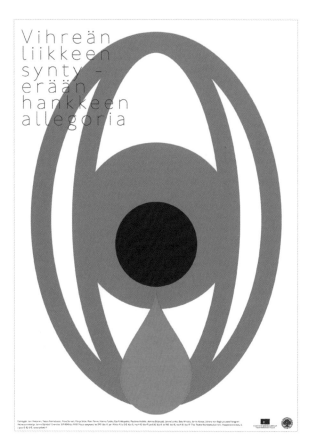

Vihreän liikkeen synty – erään hankkeen allegoria

Promotional Campaign/ One of a series of posters for a shoe company, flatly and drolly depicting a boring conformist to routine (the "everyday circus"); after a short time, the base posters were covered with banners encouraging the audience to refute boredom with style. Fiktiv *Croatia*

Identity/ The back of a New York City theater group's business card carries a logotype (produced with stencil and spray paint) whose counterforms and rough exterior contour create a narrative of images suggested by the group's name. Steff Geissbühler and Max Millermaier, C+G Partners, LLC *United States*

Identity/ Angled line forms that suggest folded cards integrate the initials of the client's company, which specializes in stationery created from children's artwork used for school fundraising. STIM Visual Communication *United States*

KidsArt

STATIONERY

JIM CARRY

JIM CARRY
KATE WINSLET

Film Branding/ Hand-drawn typography and tenuous, fading illustrations help depict the story of a film about a man who is systematically being wiped from his former lover's memory; the language was applied to DVD packaging, interactive menu screens, and the film's title sequence. Youngmi Jung, School of Visual Arts *United States*

KATE WINSLET
KIRSTEN DUNST

Haunted Attraction Logo/ The specific approach to this logo lends whimsy to the macabre (a scary, fun-house event based on local, morbid folklore and held underground) by merging comic book art and Victorian identity design; the intricately detailed and colored emblem was designed with respect to its use on T-shirts and novelty items. Tactical Magic *United States*

ASSOCIATE PRODUCERS
LINDA FIELDS HILL

CASTING BY
JEANNE MCCARTHY

DIRECTOR OF PHOTOGRAPHY
ELLEN KURAS

MUSIC BY
JON BRION

EDITOR
VALDIS OSKARSDOTTIR

ETERNAL SUNSHINE OF THE SPOTLESS MIND

You can erase someone from your mind.
Getting them out of your heart is another story.

directed by Michel Gondry
Jim Carrey / Kate Winslet / Kirsten Dunst
United States / March 19, 2004

PLAY MOVIE

SCENES
LANGUAGES
BONUS MATERIAL

A conversation with Jim Carry
"Light &day" music video
A look inside Eternal Sunshine of the Spotless Mind
Feature commentary with Michel Gondry
Deleted scenes
Interview of Kate Winslet

Institutional Poster/ A three-dimensional "cityscape" of extruded geometric shapes and art-related icons inventively organize a group of descriptive photographic images to attract prospective students. Post Typography *United States*

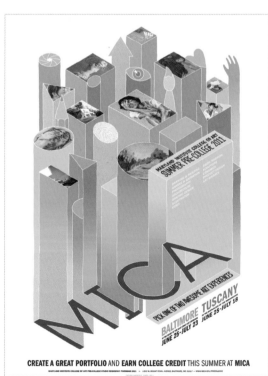

Promotional Calendar / Languid line drawings of nude models responding with their bodies to music during studio sessions became the basis of a calendar for Qichyuan Record Company in Guangzhou, China. The delicate tracery of the figures is punctuated by the fluid, dotlike rhythms of the days of the month.
Fang Chen *United States*

Holiday Promotional Coasters / The client's initials, set as type, combine with line drawings of holiday symbols suggested by their rearrangement; the letters take on imaginative new forms, evoking the venture capital firm's innovative approaches to investing.
Gee+Chung Design *United States*

Institutional Poster / The boldly geometric stylization of a tree bearing a diversity of both flowers and fruit captures the theme of a series of performances and presentations at a university.
AdamsMorioka, Inc. *United States*

Drawing
/ for Graphic
Design

Artifacts

**Showcase
of Real-World
Projects**

Branded Animation/ The common cliché of the lightbulb representing creativity is reinvented through a sequence of clever transformations in this online animation for an advertising agency. Steff Geissbühler and Max Millermaier, C+G Partners, LLC *United States*

Theater Poster/ Ripped paper and rough gestures—for icons and titling type—combine shapes and textures in a subtle nod to 1950s advertising languages while lending an edgy, youthful quality to the promotion of a theater school's performance. Laurent Pinabel *Canada*

Bank Identity Program/
Extrapolating from their high Modern, black-and-white line-formed logo, the designers of this bank's collateral kept the palette monochromatic, emphasizing pattern and typographic experimentation for brochures, checkbook cases, and promotional marks.
Topos Graphics *United States*

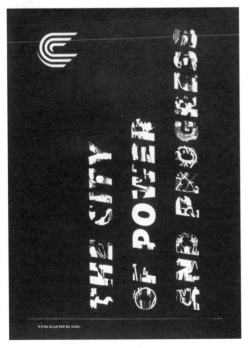

Exhiobition Poster/ Stripped down, geometric, custom Arabic forms—rhythmically shifted across a grid and set aglow with digital filter—capture the essence of the subject in this announcement for an Islamic-focused photography biennial. Mehdi Saeedi Studio *Iran*

Identity/ A decorative configuration of a scrolled S and italic lowercase F creates a dynamic, but friendly, mark for a professional photographer. Gee+Chung Design *United States*

Institutional Brochure Cover/
UCLA's Extended Campus catalogue covers feature commissioned images every semester; this edition integrates the designer's signature, surreal illustrative doodles, monsters, and graphical forms with images of school supplies and other student-related paraphernalia in a large-scale, symbolic letterform. 344 Design, LLC *United States*

Promotional Calendar/ Varied, loose freehand drawing techniques of unimaginable hair styles arouse a sense of styling fun for customers who buy the hair care products this calendar promotes. Design Tôge *Japan*

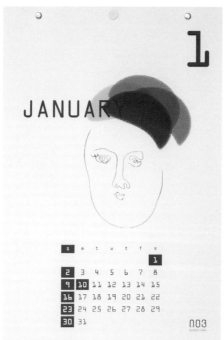

Concert Poster/ Classical music—often perceived as stodgy—benefits from a funky, youth-oriented update that mixes boldly stylized iconography from the classical context and street culture. Shaung Wan, School of Visual Arts *United States*

Festival Poster/ In a quirky, counterintuitive approach, the designers of this poster imaginatively captured its subject with the storyboard of an animated film they also produced for the festival. The frames form a grid that defines the shaping, proportions, and positions of typographic material. Disturbance *South Africa*

Calendar Design/ Against a backdrop of colorful washes that change each month in relation to the seasons, a variety of calligraphic quotations situates the viewer in a philosophical experience of time. Mauro Melis *Italy*

Drawing / for Graphic Design

Artifacts

Showcase of Real-World Projects

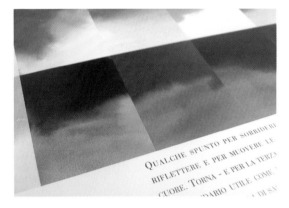

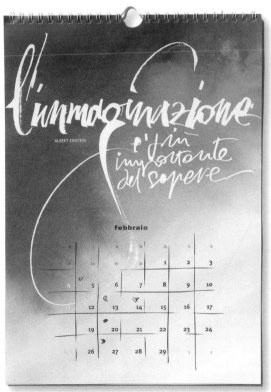

Index

Ack/
-now
ledg—
/men/
.ts}

**Directory
of Contributors**

>>

Once again, as with each book I write, I am indebted not only to the designers around the world who graciously contribute examples of their work, but to the development team at Rockport. Their time and effort in coordinating copy editing, researching paper stocks, reviewing and helping me improve the book's design—never mind their (almost) limitless patience with my sometimes exasperating work process—are invaluable and deeply appreciated. I would also like to acknowledge the critical input of colleagues Steff Geissbuhler, Christine Hiebert, Gregory Paone, and Chris Zelinsky, whose insights, through conversation and contributions of work, have helped me clarify my own thinking and, hopefully, made this book a valuable resource for designers. To my partner Sean, as well as to my parents and students: thank you for your inspiration, encouragement, and the world you make around me.